Sketching & Painting

a step by step introduction

Sketching & Painting

a step by step introduction

F.C. Johnston

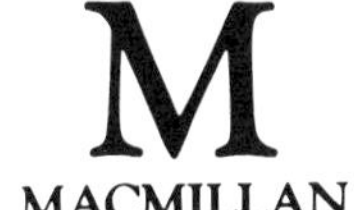

MACMILLAN

To all leisure-hour artists and especially to those whom it has been my pleasure to meet

ISBN 0 333 32981 3

First published 1976 by
MACMILLAN LONDON LIMITED
London and Basingstoke
Reprinted 1979

First published 1982 by
PAPERMAC
A division of Macmillan Publishers Limited
London and Basingstoke
Reprinted 1982, 1984 (twice)

Associated companies in Auckland, Delhi, Dublin, Gaborone, Hamburg, Harare, Hong Kong, Johannesburg, Kuala Lumpur, Lagos, Manzini, Melbourne, Mexico City, Nairobi, New York, Singapore and Tokyo

Printed in Hong Kong

British Library Cataloguing in Publication Data
Johnston, Frederick Charles
Sketching and painting; a step by step introduction.
ISBN 0 333 32981 3 (Papermac)
1. Title
751.4 ND 1342
Landscape painting – technique
Landscape drawing – technique

Contents

Preface

Most people have an instinctive appreciation of the true qualities of painting and many are tempted to take up the brush and try their hand. Unfortunately, without patient and sympathetic tuition, these first efforts are usually rather disappointing. Frustration sets in, followed by disenchantment. What has happened is that a keenly developed aesthetic sense is seeking expression through eyes not yet fully aware, hands not yet skilled, and with materials not yet fully understood.

This book seeks to prevent any such frustrations. It is the result of many happy hours spent with leisure-hour painters whose sincerity and enthusiasm demanded a method of instruction capable of being explained in simple terms and broken down into easily understood but progressive stages. Over the years such a course has been built up and developed, and my gratitude goes to all those whose suggestions helped its progress. This book is meant for the real beginner who is eager to start but a little apprehensive about the first steps; it also contains much of the essential groundwork which so often escapes those who are more advanced.

Perhaps, too, it will stimulate a greater awareness of the beauty all around us and will eventually lead to the development of an original and personal style. Thus by a happy blend of your efforts and my suggestions, I hope you will discover the delights of a rewarding pastime which provides a wide outlet for the full flow of talent and self-expression.

Frederick C. Johnston

Part I
Preparation for Painting

1. *The First Essential: The Artist's Eye*

Most newcomers to painting make the mistake of putting the cart before the horse. In all sincerity they feel that if they can master all the problems of handling their materials all will be well. This is not strictly true. Of course there are certain basic skills which must be mastered and these will be dealt with in due course, but at the outset there are other essential considerations which have first priority. Much more important than manipulation is the appreciation and understanding of how an artist considers his subject; how he simplifies it and how he translates it into terms suitable to the possibilities of his chosen medium.

In the early stages the problem is not so much how to get the paint on, but rather how *dark and light* to make the colours and *where* to place them so that what was originally a perfectly flat surface can be made to assume an appearance of recession, thus giving the various masses in the picture not only shape, but also volume. They should in fact assume a third dimension—depth.

It is the ability to get depth, light, air and space into a painting that is most important, and the artist must always study his scene with this in mind. He must look at it in such a way that this effect can, at the outset, be expressed in the most simple terms. He must develop what is known as the artist's eye. This really means the ability to look at a subject and decide exactly what are the basic ingredients which make it so attractive. It soon becomes obvious that this has little to do with minute details—how many bricks in a wall or how many leaves on a bush—but has a very great deal to do with the pattern created by the arrangement of the various light, dark and medium-toned areas. If these are incorrectly stated in a subsequent painting, either in their shape or in their degree of lightness or darkness, no amount of laboured detail or intricate technique will ever put the work right.

Another essential thing to bear in mind is that a truly successful painting has about it an aura of complete sincerity and honesty. It makes no pretence to be anything other than what it is—a painting. It does not, and should not, look like a very good coloured photograph. One merely has to consider a thick and creamy mound of oil paint or, on the other hand, a liquid and transparent pool of water-colour to realize that it would indeed be working against the nature of such materials to try and produce with them the same result as with a lens and a sheet of sensitized film. The photographer, too, can be an artist, but he would surely never falsify his results by trying to include brushmarks!

It is a good idea to make a sketch first, and although this may be quite simple, it is in the preliminary work that the 'story' of the scene can be captured in clear and simple terms. Having established this, one must always be on guard to ensure that nothing is done to destroy or confuse its essential quality. Irrelevant detail or false colour and untrue shapes will only detract from the simple and delightful original conception.

To help you to understand the way in which an artist looks and translates, I would like you to study the illustrations in *Figure 1*. These show the stages of a preliminary sketch made on the spot for a painting which I did later. Although I have attempted to show the sketch in three stages, it was of course a continuous process. I was in the village of Canwick. Below me lay the city of Lincoln. A rough pasture land fringed with trees descended into the valley, and through a break in these could be seen the high ground on which the cathedral is built. The buildings around the cathedral were lost in the haze of distance and could be seen only vaguely, clustering around the huge structure. The sketches were made

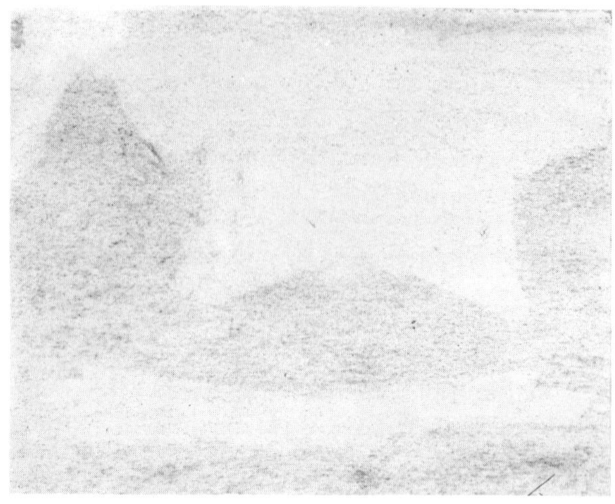

(*a*) *Look first for the 'anatomy' of the scene, showing the basic structure of the arrangement*

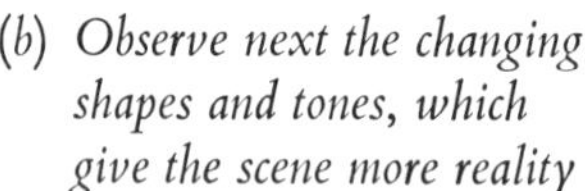

(*b*) *Observe next the changing shapes and tones, which give the scene more reality*

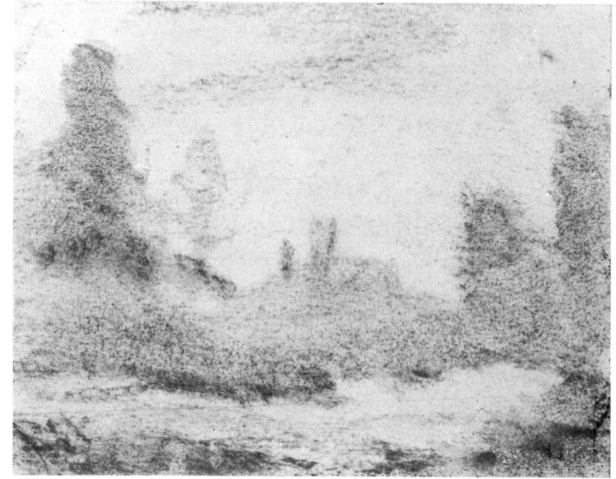

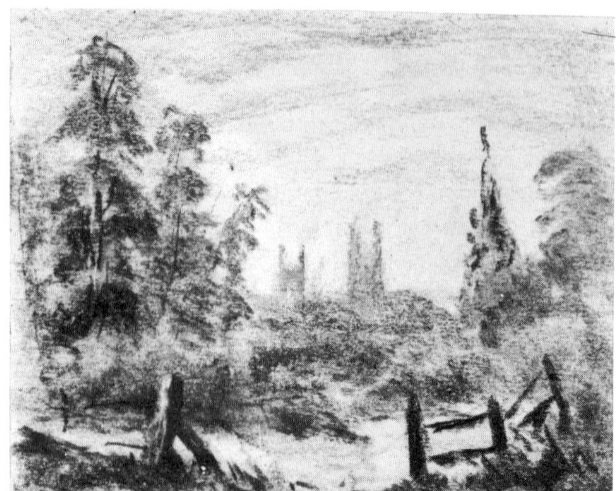

(*c*) *When fuller details are added they do not destroy the basic pattern of shapes. The contrasting areas of light and dark are still clearly seen*

Figure 1

with a small stick of charcoal and a piece of special rubber. The method will be explained more fully later, but at the moment I merely want you to look at the sketches with an artist's eye.

In (a) you see an arrangement of the main masses of the picture with an indication of how the light areas fit into the composition. Further observation (b) shows the appreciation of the changing shapes and the inclusion of a few darks which gives the scene a sense of recession and distance. As further details (c) are observed they are carefully kept not too dominant so that the basic 'anatomy' of the scene is retained.

Although this illustration was made to help you to understand how an artist looks at a scene it is worth noting that the completed sketch looks very much like a reproduction of a painted picture. It was in fact produced mainly by applying, smudging and erasing a film of charcoal. From this we can gather that charcoal sketching is a most suitable prelude to painting. Not only will it make us see our subjects in all their variations from light to dark —this is what an artist means by tone—but because it is used in masses rather than in outline, it will help us enormously when later we start using paint. For these very good reasons, and because such a method makes us search for real essentials, the artist-to-be is asked to make his first journey into the realm of landscape painting armed with an inexpensive but powerful little instrument—a humble stick of charcoal.

The materials needed are easily obtainable from your local art stockist, and are by no means heavy on the pocket.

We shall require:

1. Box of charcoal (willow)
2. Plastic rubber (sometimes known as putty rubber, or kneaded rubber)
3. Bottle of fixative
4. Spray diffuser
5. Cartridge paper (students' quality)
6. Drawing board

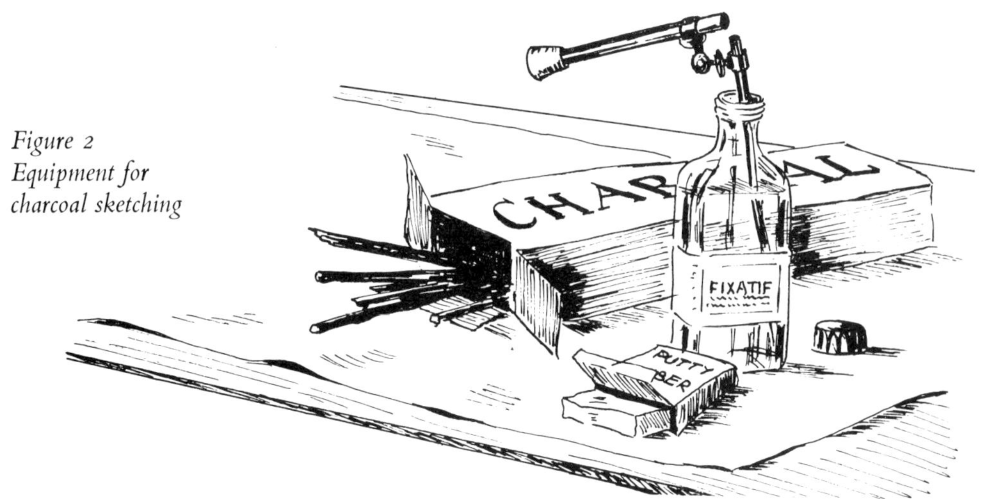

Figure 2
Equipment for charcoal sketching

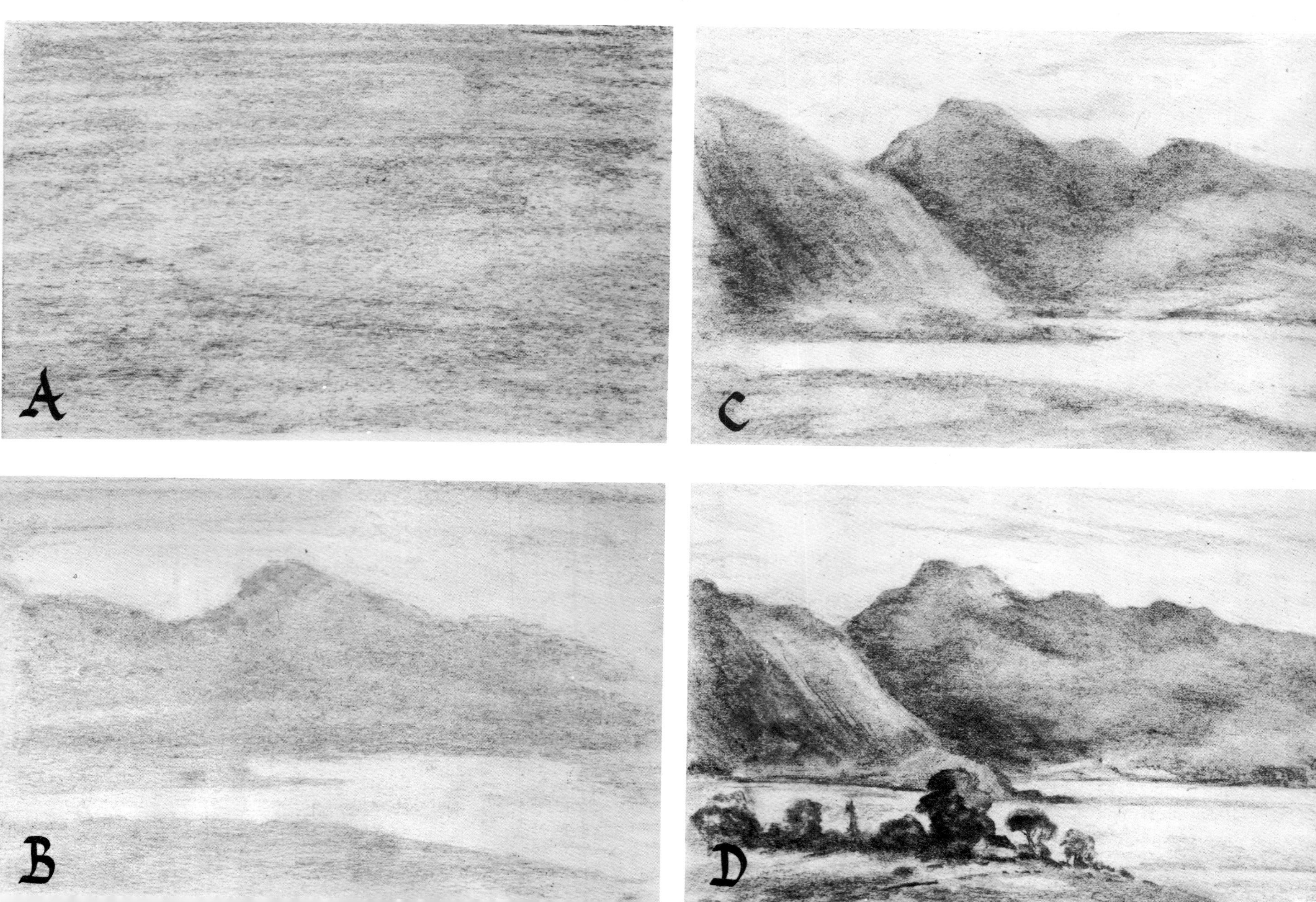
A
C
B
D

Cartridge paper is usually sold in sheets $23\frac{1}{4}$ in. × 33 in. (591 × 838 mm) and students' quality is better because it is very slightly rough and the charcoal therefore has a better grip. A whole sheet is normally enough for four studies. Similar paper can also be bought in books, blocks and pads of various sizes. The drawing board need only be a sheet of $\frac{1}{4}$ in. plywood, a piece about 18 in. × 14 in. being a suitable size. Charcoal is usually made from vine or willow, and the willow type is quite suitable. The plastic rubber is sold in a packet and used in small pieces. The fixative is really a very weak varnish and is applied to the finished sketch to prevent smudging. It is sprayed on with the diffuser. To do this, place the longer arm in the bottle, move the arms to form a right angle, and blow hard down the shorter arm. Fixative is also available in aerosol containers for those who may be a little short of breath.

With these materials we are going to try a simple exercise which will not only help us to 'read' a picture in elementary terms, but which will also help us to give the impression that some parts go back, whilst others come forward. 'Aerial perspective' is a term often used for this latter effect, but as I feel there is a possibility here of another interpretation, I always use the simpler term recession.

First take your stick of charcoal and, holding it fairly flat, make a few bold strokes on an odd piece of paper. This will give you a flat tapering edge which is much wider than the diameter of the stick. With this wide edge make broad strokes right across a piece of paper measuring about 10 in. × 7 in. Endeavour to maintain the same pressure and keep the strokes broad and even. If the charcoal should prove to be at all scratchy, break a piece off, re-fashion the end and continue with broad strokes as in *Figure 3A*.

Now rub in the charcoal very gently with a finger-tip until you have produced a film of grey all over the paper. A piece of cotton wool can be used if preferred, but remember it must be used gently. You will notice that the slight texture of the paper has given this film a fur-like look which should not be destroyed by over-vigorous rubbing. This texture should be preserved, for it is an essential quality of the paper and can be used to advantage. Remember never to fight your materials: like a good craftsman, know your tools and their scope and limitations. Never try to make them perform something they are not meant to do. Thus even at this early stage we are learning two important lessons: to achieve a sensitive touch, and always to have a sympathy for whatever tools or materials we may be using.

Take a piece of putty rubber about the size of a cherry and mould it in the hand until it is quite pliable. It can then be used round and whole to lift out large areas, or made tapered or flat to lift out small areas or fine lines. With it, lift out the areas similar to those I have lightened in *B*. Notice that there is a little more light behind the hills than at the top of the paper. This immediately gives a dome-like appearance to the sky and makes it appear to

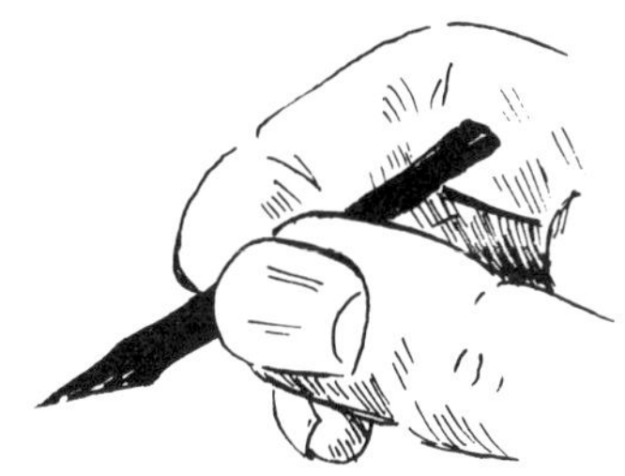

Figure 4

be coming overhead towards the top of the sketch. After each stroke with the rubber remould it, and this will cleanse it ready for the next one. Already you will see we have established the essential ingredients of our sketch—a level area, broken by the water of a lake, which suddenly rises to mountains in the distance. In *C* the charcoal has been applied and gently rubbed to make some parts of the mountains appear to overlap and stand in front of the others. Occasionally the rubber has been used to lift part of the original charcoal film to heighten this effect. Notice how a little light has been introduced into the foreground, and be careful not to get anything too dark too soon. The very dense letter *C* will show how very strong a real black can be. To bring such a strong tone into the far distant hills, for example, would strike a very false note.

The finished sketch is shown in *D*. We have assumed the source of light to be from the right and above, and have therefore carefully kept the light playing on this side. The left-hand side is in shadow. By strengthening the shadowy areas into which light cannot penetrate, and by lightening the various sunlit areas, we have developed the sketch. The main addition is the line of trees along the water's edge. Notice how they dip and disappear down the slope. Take care when making the trees dark not to make them uniformly so. Rather, make them patchy, to help to suggest dense and fluffy foliage. A few minor corrections such as the hinted path and the streaks in the water, and a little personal attention to a few details to preserve the unity of the scene, make our sketch complete.

Do not try to copy this exercise stroke for stroke. Make a few experiments to get the feel of things, and keep your sketch personal and individual. The main thing is to make sure you capture the spirit of the scene and that you avoid getting lights, darks and middle greys in the wrong places.

The next exercise involves the understanding of a phenomenon which must be clearly fixed in our minds if we are to make any real progress. We must always remember that the effect of the atmosphere is to place a 'mist' between us and the things we see. Therefore the greater the distance between ourselves and a given object, the greater the amount of 'mist' our eyes have to penetrate. This makes things in the distance quieter in tone and very much less sharply defined than those which are near to us. The nearest things have very clearly defined highlights and shadows, but the further away we look the more the atmosphere comes into play, and the overall effect is one of a gradual merging of lights and darks until the very far distance appears as one general tone with the difference between dark and light areas almost indiscernible.

This impression can be compared to looking through a series of gauze or muslin curtains such as those used by stage designers. The curtain is placed between the main characters and the backcloth, which now looks far away. Suddenly on go the lights, the curtain is raised and immediately the market place looks quite near. In painting, this curtain should never be lifted, for the veil of atmosphere is always present to some degree, and must be suggested if we wish to create an impression of depth, space and distance.

Now, working with exactly the same method as was used in the previous exercise, try the little sketch shown in *Figure 5*. It is a view of a Hertfordshire meadow quite close to my home. The day was slightly misty and there were no distinct highlights. This emphasized the softening effect of the atmosphere. As you can see, there is no real detail and even the distant church is merely a suggestion. What is so very important is that each clump of trees recedes in succession, one behind another. Not always does nature present a subject which illustrates the point so clearly, but the slight mistiness of the day and the lack of strong sunlight both helped to form this perfect example.

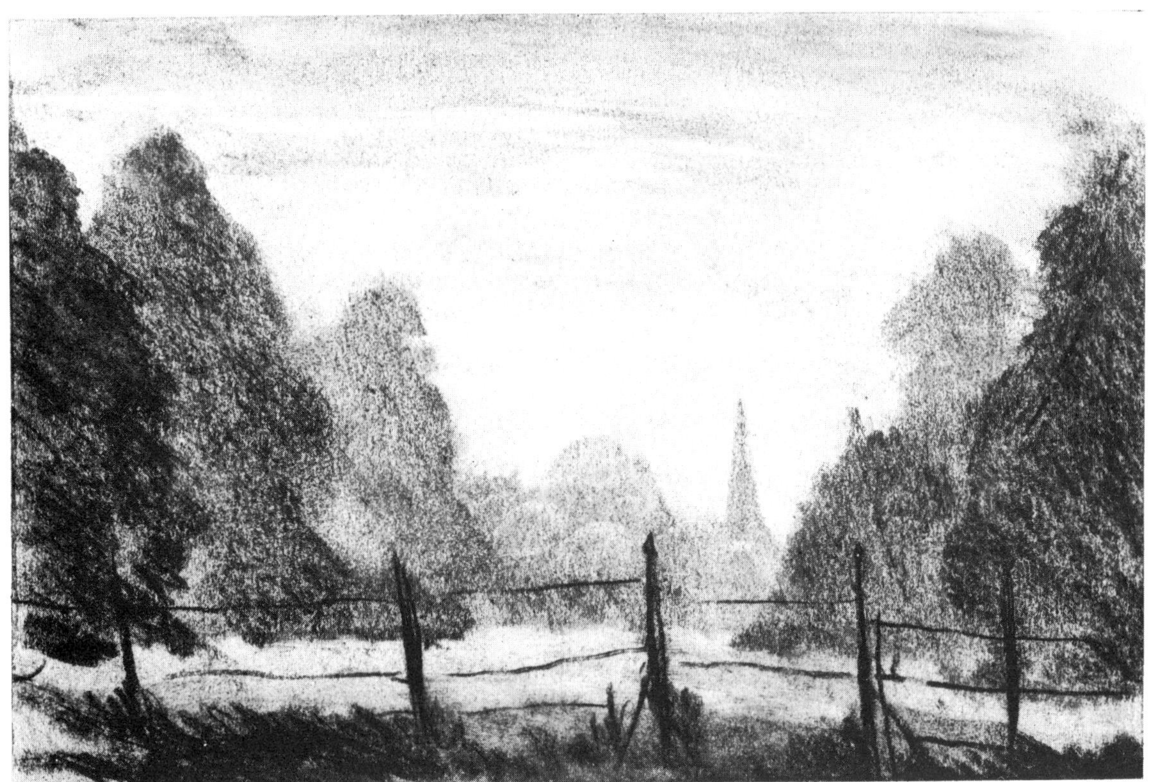

Figure 5. Charcoal sketch showing the effect of distance on tone values

ATMOSPHERE

which has the effect of weakening the tones of distant objects

	FOREGROUND	MIDDLE DISTANCE	BACKGROUND
Drawing	Nearer objects are largest	Similar objects appear smaller	Similar objects are smallest
Painting	Lightest lights & Darkest darks	Lights not so light Darks not so dark	Lights and darks merge

Figure 6. Diagram to explain the effects of recession

If you have managed to copy my sketch by the charcoal method already described, you will realize how this suggestion of depth and recession was achieved. It was done by making quite sure that the tone of similar objects (in this case rows of trees) was made a little darker as the distance between ourselves and each object decreased. In other words, the nearer the object, the deeper the tone. This can be observed even in the ground and the sky, and by making full use of this knowledge we can create, on a perfectly flat surface, the illusion that the ground is level and gradually gets nearer until it is under our feet, and that the sky is like a huge dome which sweeps on over our heads. Whatever kind of day it is, we can immediately see the gradual deepening of the tones of the sky as it passes overhead.

'But', you might say, 'what would have happened if the scene had been sunlit, with strong highlights?' The principle would still have held good. Just as the darks get darker as the objects get closer, so do lights appear to be lighter. Thus both the lights *and* the darks on a row of white cottages would appear very much more pronounced on the nearest building than on one a little further down the lane. This is explained even more clearly in *Figure 6*, which represents a cross-section of our view across the meadow, but please remember it is only a diagram. Interesting as these exercises may be, they are still largely theoretical. Soon we shall put them to the test with our newly chosen medium—first with one or two trial sketches at home, and later out of doors. Nevertheless, please fix the theory firmly in mind, for it is no slick gimmick to help you gain a quick and cheap effect; it is a sincere piece of observation which must be understood, and applied, if you are to succeed with your painting. Often when I am out with a sketching party I hear a plea for help, and nearly always the cause of distress is the ignoring of this elementary fact. The student has been loading his work with more and more paint, cramming the sketch with detail and becoming increasingly despondent. The 'salvage operation' means a few minutes' work in merging and softening the distance and heightening the contrast of the nearer areas. A fuller understanding of the effect which distance has on the tones would have prevented a great deal of frustration, and the elusive quality of the scene would have been captured.

To train you to record and observe this quality there is nothing better than lots of practice in charcoal drawing. It will help you to develop an artist's eye, and everything will seem new and exciting. Instead of merely looking on, you will be truly *seeing*, and already you will be well on the way to being an artist.

2. The Next Step: Working out of Doors

Most landscape painters will tell you that whenever possible it is best to work direct from nature. In this country it is sometimes a little difficult, but the problems are well worth coping with. Our English climate gives us a light that is soft and pleasant, and the changes from one mood of weather to another are, once you are prepared to accept them, a constant source of beauty and delight.

Apart from the mackintosh and the extra sweater, a further piece of equipment that will be needed is a good lightweight stool. Take care when buying it, for an uncomfortable seat will cause cramp and a certain lack of dignity when eventually you try to stand up. Get one which has a reasonably large seat, has the absolute minimum of gadgets, and is not too low. You can now buy a good seat, made from an alloy, which is very strong and comfortable and is so light in weight that it can be carried on the little finger.

Another very useful item is a home-made viewfinder (*Figure 7*). This is merely a piece of card or plywood with a rectangular aperture cut in it, of the same proportions as the paper on which you work. It can be used rather like the press-photographer's viewfinder, and the solid margin will help you to isolate your subject as you look through the hole. By moving it close to your eye more can be seen; by moving it away less of the scene comes into view. Try it out first in the least likely places, and you will be surprised at the pictures you will discover, merely because the margin divorces your subject from all the confusing material that surrounds it. With this little aid I have often found subjects in the most surprising places: the heap of rubbish at the back of a farm, or the pattern of a few chimneys.

Now let us go into the country. At first we shall feel that there is so much beauty that we shall never be able to sort it all out. Therefore a little forethought will help: we must decide not to go for the vast panorama, but to look for things a little closer, and sometimes only a part of things. This is where our home-made viewfinder will prove its worth, for now we shall not stagger on looking for the perfect subject; we might never have found it and might have had to return home with all our high hopes sadly shattered. Rather let us look at various parts of each scene by shifting and moving our viewfinder, and before long we shall see something and say to ourselves, 'Yes, I think I can manage that.'

Let us imagine that the photograph reproduced in *Figure 8* is a view of the general scene,

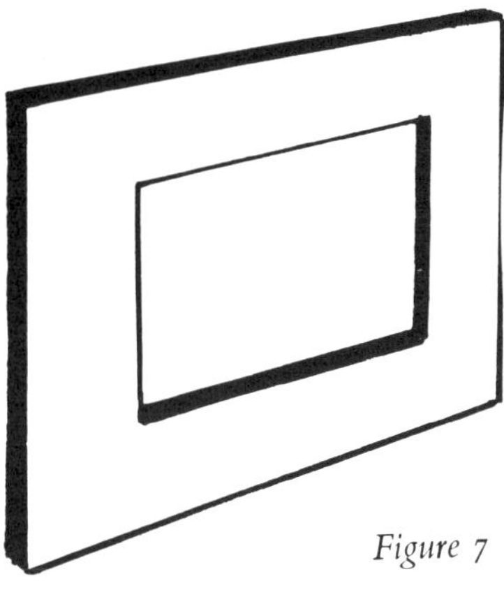

Figure 7

Figure 8

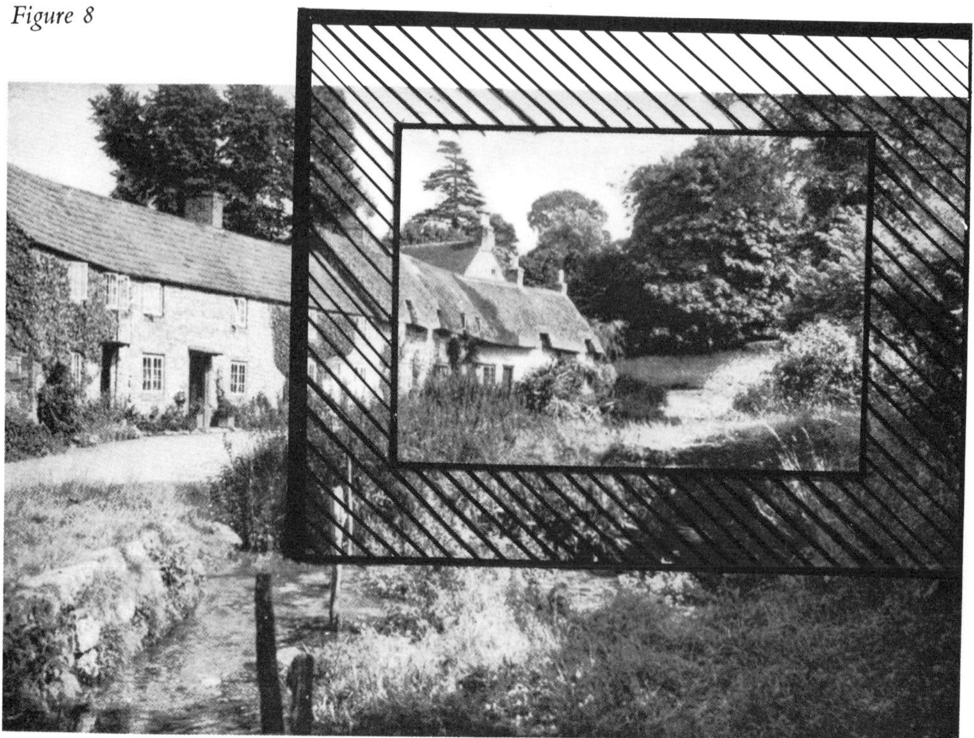

and inside the black line is the part which, by the use of the viewfinder, has been selected as a suitable subject. This, then, is how I suggest you should proceed. First sit down comfortably for a few quiet thoughts on how to tackle the job in hand. Look at the scene not as so many leaves, so many walls and windows, and so many blades of grass, but rather in a general way, accepting *all* the scene *all* the time. By doing this you will very quickly see that you cannot accept the broad conception and at the same time itemize the scene with a lot of finicky detail. The picture will gradually appear as a series of shapes of light, dark and intermediate tones. The ability to look at a subject in this broad way is very, very important. Often it is difficult, particularly if your temperament, or training in another craft or skill, has made your eye very susceptible to fine detail. Practice in this kind of observation is needed to understand the 'story' behind the picture, and this must be understood before any attempt at detail is made in the sketch. If you have not grasped the 'story' which is always one of the patterns made by the play of light, no amount of detail will help you. In this case, it is largely one of two flashes of light, one on the cottages and the other across the grassland with an additional light area in the sky (*Figure 9*). This is really most essential and the newcomer to painting must learn that the influence of light is of far greater importance than the introduction of slick pieces of detail which would probably merely destroy the effect of the lighting.

The next stage in the development of our study would be to compare what had been done so far with the actual scene, and to assess what was next in importance to help with the general interpretation. In this case it would be to give a feeling of flatness to the distant meadow, and also to show that the distant trees recede one behind another. Thus we would darken the base of the trees where they and the meadow meet, and put a subtle light on the

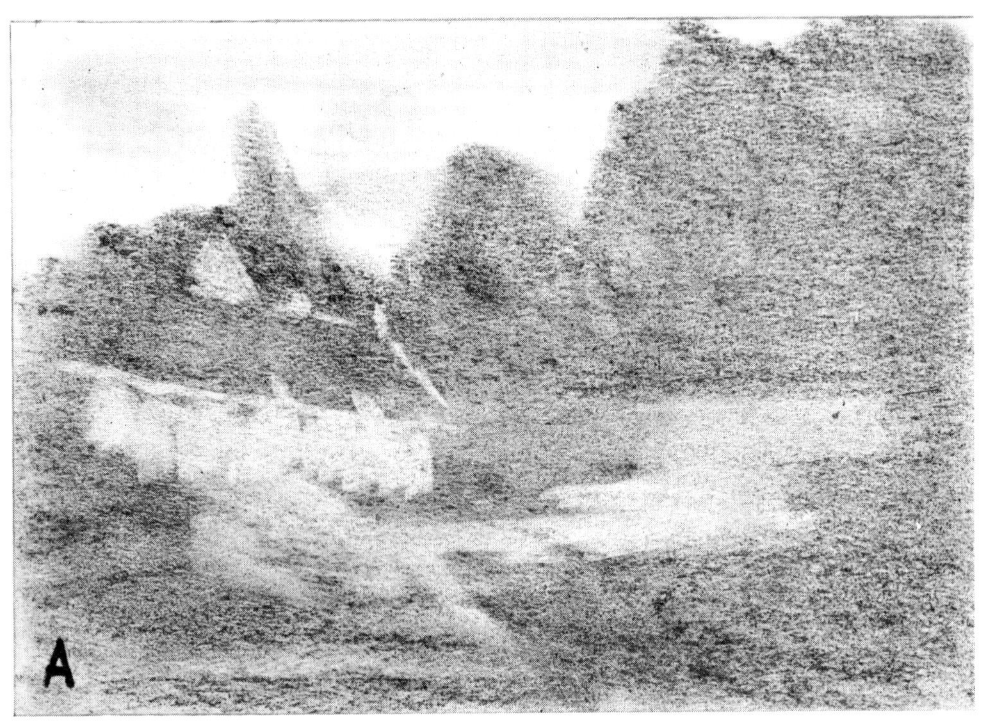

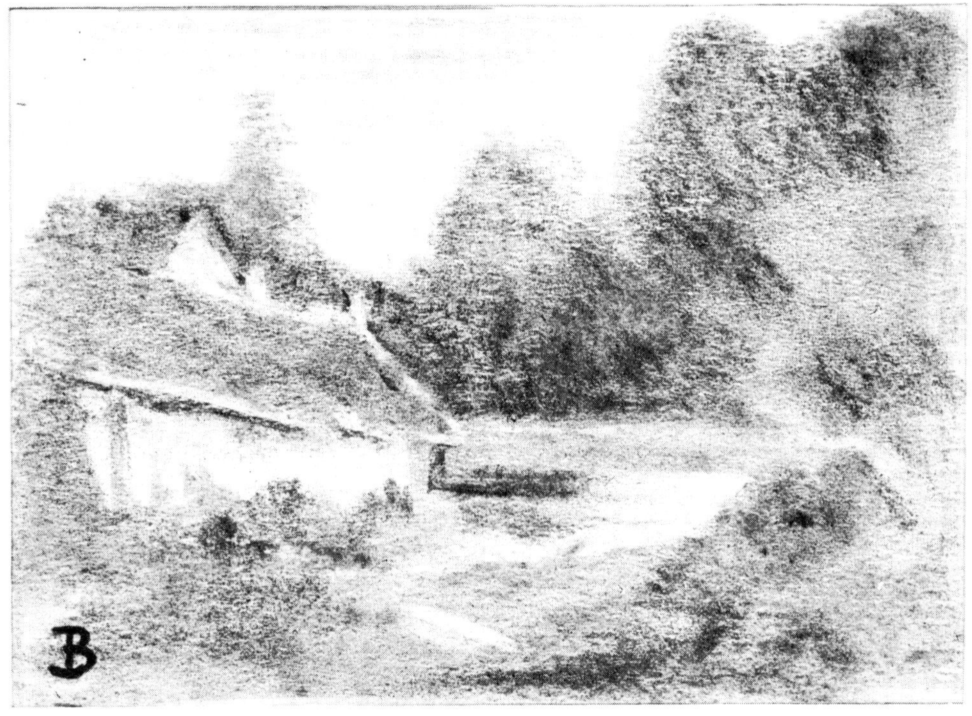

Figure 9. Making a charcoal sketch from the actual scene

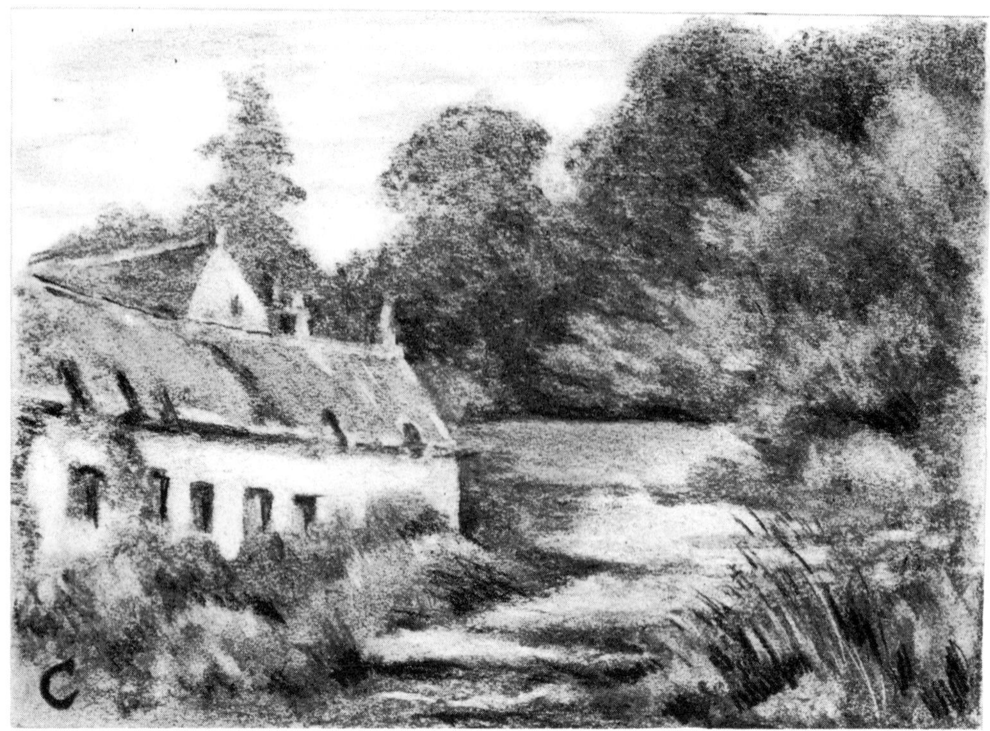

Figure 9 (cont.)

meadow at the same point (see *Figure 9B*). A few darker areas would then be put in to take the distant trees back a little. At this stage, too, we would insert a few of the more important dark passages in the eaves of the roof and in the foreground.

From what has been done so far, the beginner will see that painting is no hit-or-miss affair, where one pours one's material all over the paper with reckless abandon and little thought. The scene must be gradually built up from an understanding of essentials. The 'slosh and throw' method so often recommended is not truly helpful, and is liable to wreck any genuine progress.

Bearing this in mind, our sketch is now ready for its final touches. These we will put in as shown in *Figure 9C*. First, a subtle and gentle suggestion of foliage is made in the distant trees; not too crisp, for that would bring them too near. Next, let us put sufficient detail in our buildings, to give them a semblance of reality. This can be achieved by the inclusion of the extra shadow under the eaves and the dark rectangles to suggest doors and windows. If by now some of our lighter areas have become smudged, or need further attention, we can rectify this as we proceed. Some of the foreground detail now needs attention, and the tall grasses on the right can be drawn in with the fine edge of the charcoal and a thinly shaped piece of rubber. The whole scene can then be studied and the final touches of light and dark included. It is only in this final stage that real drawing is used, and the inexperienced artist may find difficulty here because of a lack of drawing ability. This is quite understandable, and it may mean the need for extra drawing practice, but if the beginner can *see* mistakes and limitations at this point, he is obviously well on the way to becoming an artist.

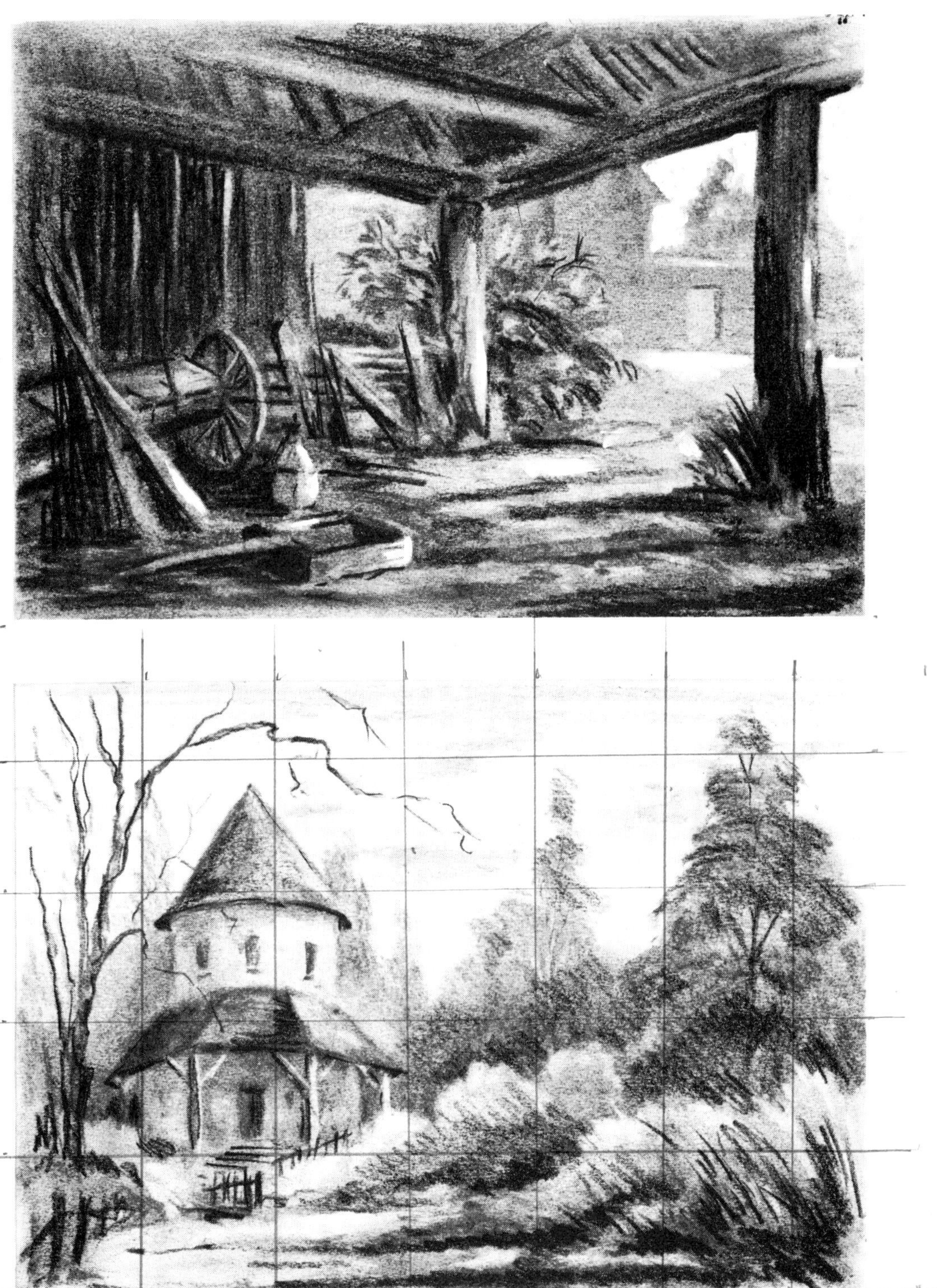

Figure 10. Studies in charcoal

Do not let your lack of experience worry you too much, for improvement will come. The main thing in the early stages is not to be too ambitious. Carefully choose subjects that do not present too many difficulties at once. Your viewfinder will help you with this. Always remember the materials with which you work, and consider how with them you can transfer your subject to paper. Consider its natural look; consider the obvious limitations of your medium. A good charcoal study should *look* like a charcoal study, and any attempt to make it look like a pencil drawing or an etching is asking both the material and yourself to achieve the impossible.

A question that is often asked is whether it is permissible to work from photographs. The answer needs some qualifying. If the questioner means to use a photograph merely as a short cut, allowing him to be permanently a fireside artist, the answer is a definite and resounding 'No!' If, on the other hand, a photograph is to be used mainly as a general reference, which means that something similar has been seen, and has been studied and thought about, then it could prove quite useful. If it is used, you must be extremely careful not to try for an exact copy. Your photograph is merely for reference, and your final piece of work should be an *interpretation*, not a copy. Furthermore, it must be sympathetic to the materials used, and have your own personal stamp on it. If all this is borne in mind, then *use* your photograph. But remember, it is very much a second-best, and the finest place to work is always out of doors, in front of your subject.

Even when working on the spot the artist must be careful not to copy too much. That very fine artist, Edward Swann, once remarked: '. . . never reduce the magnificent to a diagram.' The personal approach, allied to a sympathetic and thoughtful use of the materials, is so much more important than the minute rendering of detail. If the house you are painting has the feeling of shape; if you could walk into it and feel its protective shelter; if you can suggest the subtle mellowing effect of the weather—then you will have a building which will do far more for your picture than if you merely counted bricks. So off you go: good luck to you in your efforts—and may the weather be kind.

3. *The Selection and Arrangement of Subjects*

If a housewife brings home a bunch of flowers to decorate the home, she will be lucky indeed if she finds that, by merely unwrapping them and sticking them in a vase, an arrangement has been created which is exactly what she wants. It is much more likely that the group will require a little lift here, a twist or two there, to make it a piece of decoration which will give her satisfaction. Note that she first *selected* the variety of blooms which met with her approval and then *arranged* them into a satisfactory group.

We should do well to follow her method in preparing for our next effort: first deciding what to include in it and then seeking a pleasing arrangement. It is these two things which an artist considers when he speaks of 'composition' in painting.

Selecting a subject is by no means as simple as it may sound, and on many occasions amateur artists have told me how difficult they have found this, particularly when they are in an area where everything is paintable and the subjects are numerous.

How, then, can elimination be made and a decision arrived at when we are seeking a subject for painting? There are two things to avoid. One is the wide open landscape consisting of simply land and sky. Unless there are some definite forms, such as trees, buildings, hedges, walls, fences, etc., which will give you a sense of scale, such scenes are much too difficult for a beginner. True, they offer few problems of drawing, but the painting requires tremendous experience. The other danger is choosing a subject which is beyond your powers of draughtsmanship. Do not try to paint what you know you cannot draw, for painting is really but another form of drawing, and such an attempt will surely lead to disaster.

Another factor which must obviously influence the choice of subject is the kind of materials that are being used. Each of these artist's materials has its own qualities, potentialities and limitations and these must obviously be taken into account when a subject is under consideration. You must think not only of the scene in front of you, but how it can be expressed in terms of your chosen medium. If it cries out for the subtle, translucent and liquid treatment of water-colours and this is what you have with you, go ahead. If, however, the subject is obviously more suited to the broad opaque treatment of oils or acrylics, or if it needs the fine line work of a pen-and-wash drawing, it is best to choose again—unless you can think of some clever personal interpretation which is in more complete sympathy with your materials. In other words, if, when you first see a worthy subject, you are almost forced to remark, 'Now that's a good subject for the materials I'm carrying,' then count your blessings and set up your easel. It matters not what the subject is, trees, boats, buildings, factories, quarries, mountains, or even a well-arranged heap of rubbish, so long as the setting and the lighting make it suitable for your particular medium at that particular time.

No one can ever say exactly what the components of a picture should be, since so much depends on personal taste and interpretation, but it is hoped the foregoing advice has narrowed the choice a little. Let me assume that you have by now seen something which appeals to you, and that you are trying to decide if it is a possible subject. Were you to ask me, I would suggest you looked at it not just as a group of things, but rather as a pattern —a pattern of light and shade and a pattern of contrasting shapes. Then we would look for something else: we would look to see if things overlapped one another without becoming unrecognizable or uninteresting. This would lead us from one part of the group to another

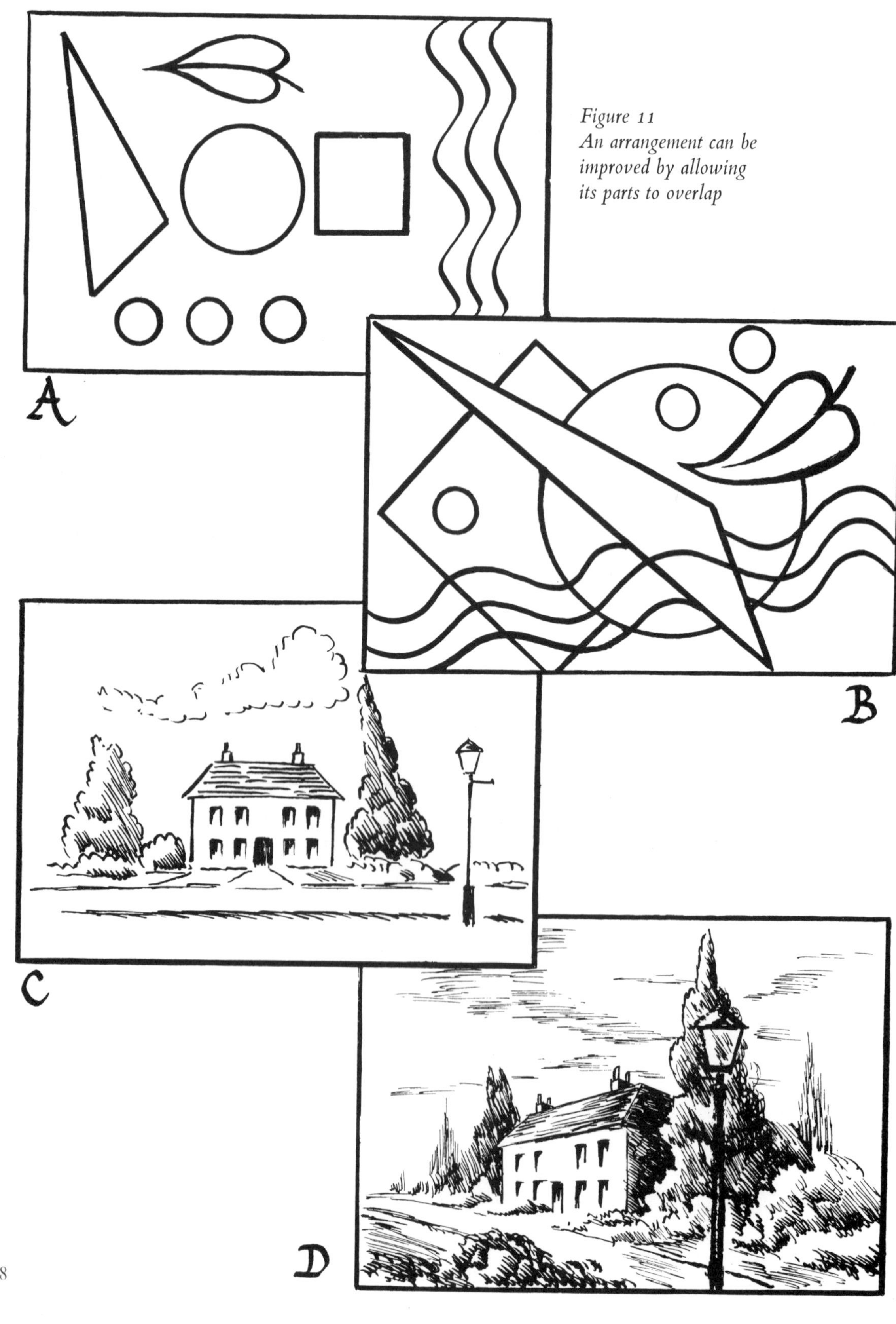

Figure 11
An arrangement can be improved by allowing its parts to overlap

and give the linkage which makes for unity.

The diagrams in *Figure 11* will probably help to explain this. In *A* we have various shapes which, although quite interesting and different, are each separate, like small islands on a sea of paper. This tends to make the whole thing a little jumpy and disconnected. In *B* we have managed to say a lot more than in *A*, whilst still keeping to the same basic shapes. It is most interesting and therefore a better design. All this is quite simple, but is so often forgotten when out of doors. In *C* and *D* the same principles have been applied to an outdoor scene. The frontal view of *C* keeps everything rather distinct and separate, and one's eye is inclined to sweep across the paper hoping to find greater interest somewhere else. The sketch *D* is the same scene from a different viewpoint, and the theory of overlapping has been put to use. I am sure you will agree that the house looks very inviting as it settles itself down behind the trees. The lamp-post, too, by being in front and therefore larger, helps to give a feeling of recession.

The humble viewfinder which was described earlier comes into constant use, because it helps to divorce the subject being considered from outside influences which would otherwise intrude into the scene and distract our eyes from it. As you move around to view the subject from different angles you are really doing what our housewife did with her flowers: you are altering the arrangement. Often it is a delightful surprise to see how different the same scene can be when seen from a changed viewpoint.

Another essential to composition is knowing where to place the main features. Nearly always it is best to avoid having our main centre of interest in the very middle of the paper. This *seems* to be the most obvious place, but to choose it will generally make all the rest of the picture look uninteresting. In *Figure 12* you will see that I have ruled up the paper as if to play noughts and crosses. You may remember that it is often a good plan to start this game off with a cross in the centre, but I hope that the cross in this case will indicate that it is wrong in the vast majority of pictures. The same is true of putting a vertical or horizontal feature halfway across or halfway up the paper. Usually it will simply cut the work in two.

Our paper ruled into thirds (both vertically and horizontally) will serve to remind us of a very important aspect of composition. If the main features fall near one of the verticals and one of the horizontals you will find the arrangement is nearly always one that gives pleasure. This point of intersection can be called the centre of interest, and it will of course come a little to one side or other of our previously noted danger spot. This is not an exact rule, because happily there are no hard and fast rules in painting and we all find that we are always learning a little more. It is rather in the nature of an aid, to help us to arrange a picture that will satisfy. You may be interested to know that it is an approximation to the 'Golden Rule' or 'Golden Mean', a mathematical formula similar to our 'thirds' which has been applied by mathematicians to many of the paintings of the old masters, and has proved to be surprisingly accurate. However, I am quite sure these artists never worked out their masterpieces with a slide rule: their successes were created merely by a feeling that what they had done looked 'right'.

With the knowledge of these aids to composition we should now be well-armed to find countless subjects. In fact subjects can be found everywhere, and you will join company with Constable, that wonderful landscape painter, who, when asked by a lady if he did not consider the subject he was painting to be rather ugly, replied, 'Madam, nothing is ever ugly.'

It has already been stated how extremely useful is our viewfinder, but equally important is the small sketch which enables us to see how our chosen scene looks on paper. Always

The use of "Thirds"

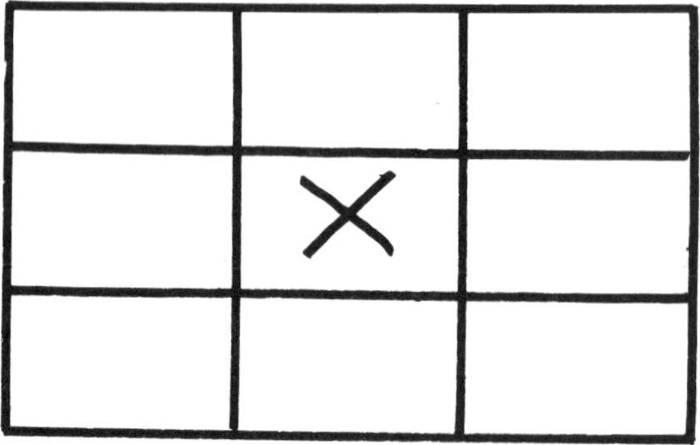

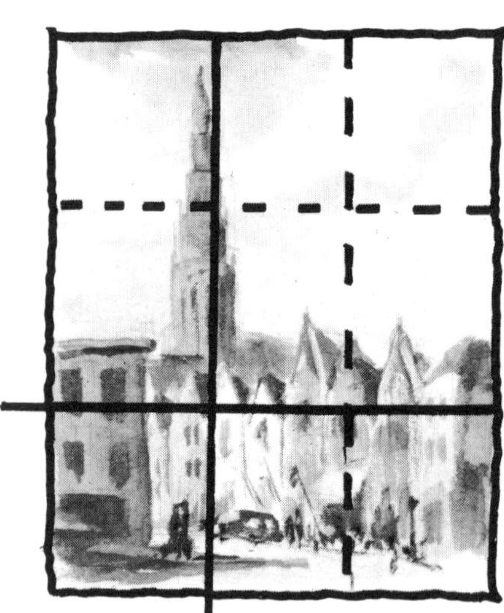

X marks the danger spot in picture composition. Dividing lines help because......

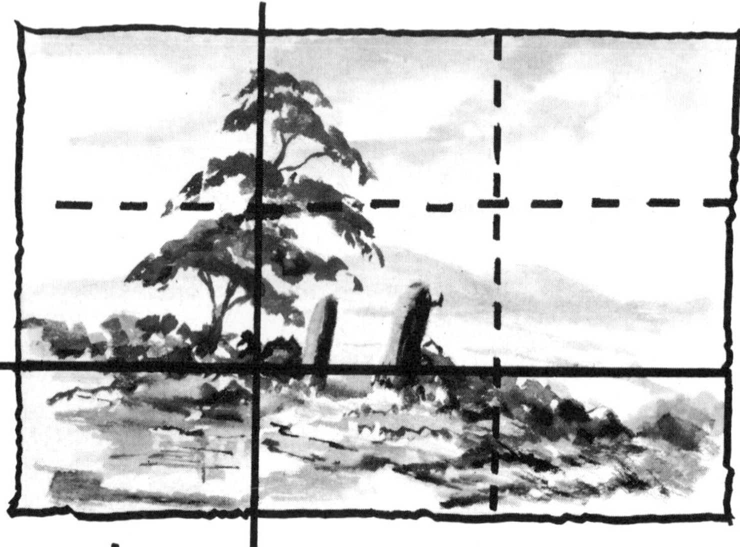

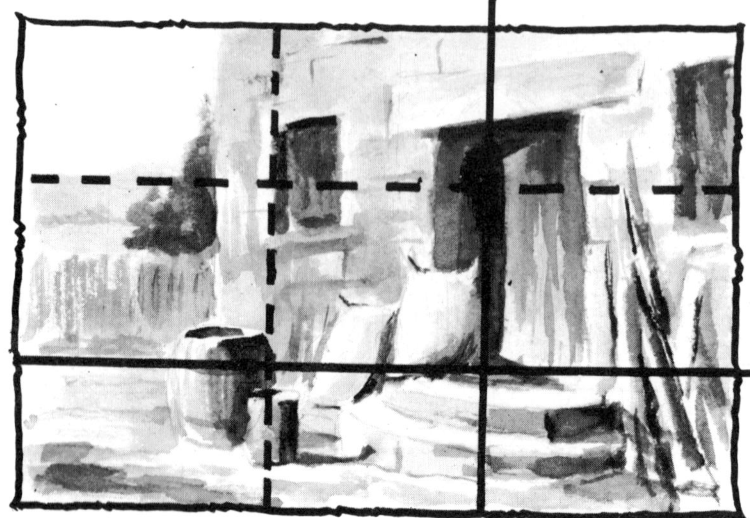

... one of the verticals and one of the horizontals usually cuts through the main features

Figure 12

make plenty of sketches, and by this I mean serious little notes of shape, form and colour. Only when experience enables you to see the picture in your mind's eye will it be safe to dispense with a preliminary sketch.

Another problem which often puzzles the newcomer to painting is the difficulty of transferring the approved small sketch on to a bigger piece of paper. The sheet suddenly seems frighteningly large and empty, and we are filled with all kinds of doubts. If the enlargement is done hurriedly we often get our proportions wrong, and find that all sorts of extra details have crept in around the subject—details which were not in our original sketch. *Figure 13* explains a very simple method of enlarging, by once more dividing both our small sketch and the larger sheet of paper into thirds. By observing where the lines of the small sketch cross, follow, and wander away from the lines of the 'thirds', it is possible to make the same strokes in corresponding places on the bigger paper. The two sketches will thus be in proportion to each other. The only point to watch is that both sheets must be similar in shape: obviously one cannot change a square into an oblong and still have an accurate enlargement.

Perspective! The very word seems to frighten the would-be artist. This is a great pity, for it is a fascinating subject and one which should not be shirked, for in one form or another it comes into every painting. In this book my aim is to give a few hints which should have proved helpful in the past and which will, I hope, remove some fears and lead you on in search of further knowledge.

To encourage you, perhaps I can be forgiven for including a little personal story. My wife was also, at one time, a little scared of any subject which contained a fair amount of

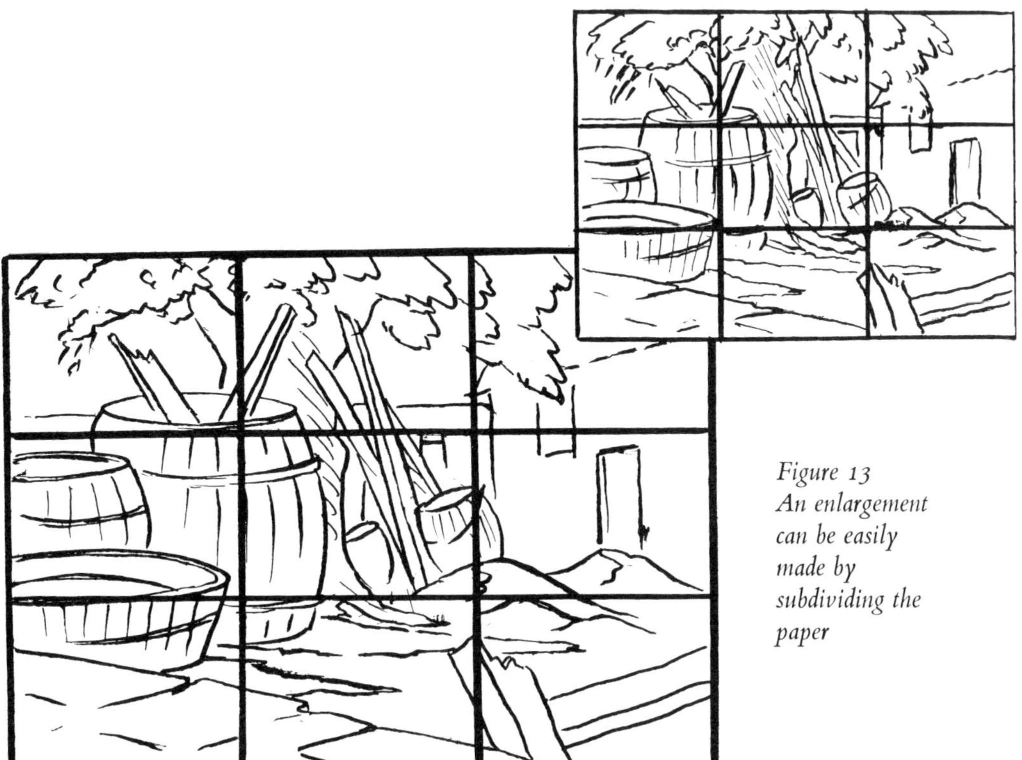

Figure 13
An enlargement can be easily made by subdividing the paper

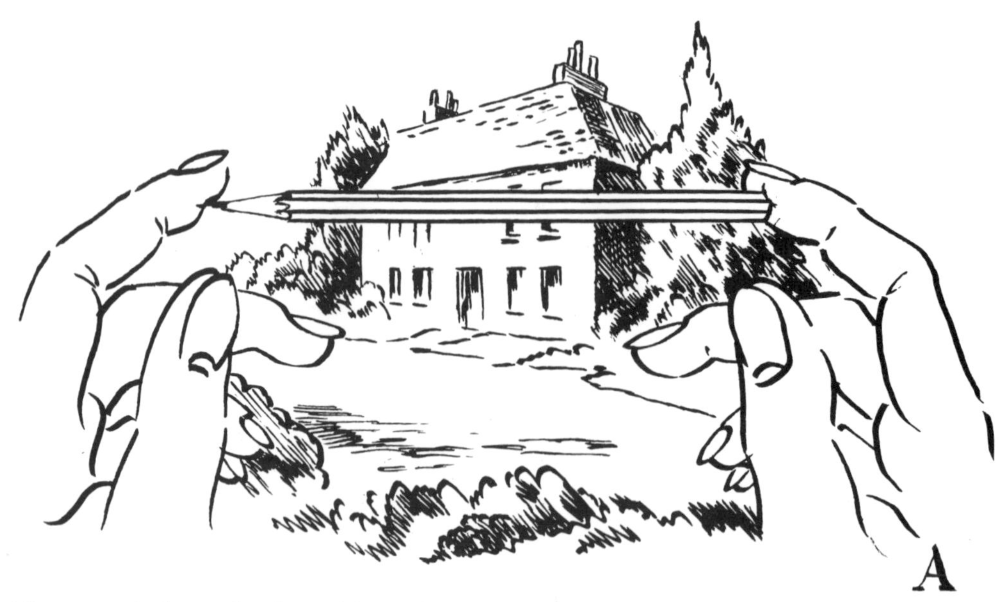

Figure 14. Angles can be observed by holding a pencil horizontally between the fingertips

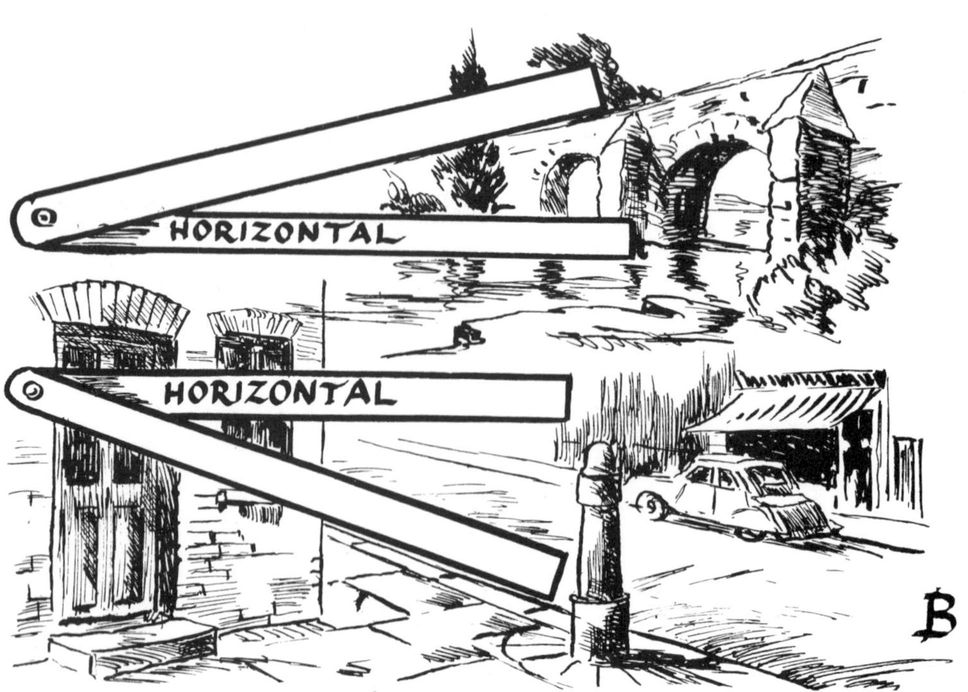

Figure 15. Two strips of card with a firm but movable joint help to transfer difficult angles from scene to paper

perspective drawing. She accepted only minor challenges in this direction, until one holiday when we were painting in Oxford. Suddenly all the preparation in previous work bore fruit, and she found great satisfaction in painting scenes which took in parts of the architectural splendour of this delightful city. Now she loves the subject which once scared her.

The basic fact of perspective is that what we know are parallel lines on, let us say, a building, appear to be at an angle or a slope when viewed from any position other than one directly facing it. This can be seen by looking again at the building in *Figure 11*. In *C* all the lines across the house are horizontal, whereas in *D* they appear to converge as the further parts of the building recede. It is essential, when making a drawing of this sort, to get at least two of these angles down accurately. The rest will follow. I usually endeavour to establish one line at the base and one near the top, as these show the greatest difference in direction. Although it sounds foolish, many of us find difficulty in deciding exactly which way a certain feature tips, and we find ourselves wondering which end of it goes up and which goes down. A simple method of finding out is to hold a fairly long pencil between the finger-tips of each hand. If it is kept at arm's length, and perfectly level, it can be brought up slowly until it appears to touch some important corner—say the line of the roof in *Figure 14*.

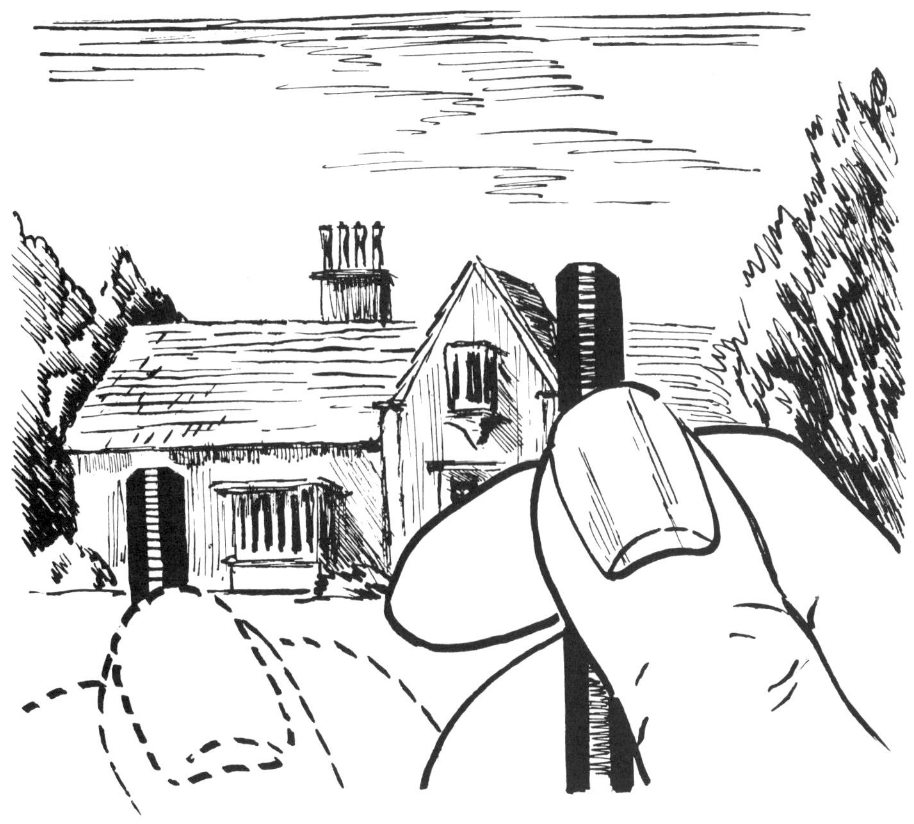

Figure 16. A sliding gauge made with thumb and pencil is a simple method of deducing relative angle sizes

An extension of such a seeing-aid is a gadget which can be made quite simply with two strips of fairly stiff card joined by a paper-fastener. You then have two long arms which swivel open like the blades of scissors, with the joint stiff enough for the arms to stay fixed in any position. *Figure 15* shows it in use. One arm is marked 'horizontal' and must always be in that position. The other is moved until it appears to run along the feature to be drawn. Make quite sure the device is held 'square' to the body, and you will then have the correct angle, which can be very easily compared with your drawing.

It has been established that similar objects appear to decrease in size as they recede into the distance. To help to compare the different sizes of various objects, a very simple sliding scale can be improvised by moving the thumb-tip along a pencil. This can be held at any angle and the comparative sizes can be studied by noting the distance between the thumb-tip and the end of the pencil, as shown in *Figure 16*. Be absolutely certain when using it to keep the arm fully outstretched, as otherwise the comparison is untrue. Keep a good straight arm and the scale of things will be recorded with ease and accuracy.

With these few hints your composition should progress quite satisfactorily, but such aids are only a small part of a most interesting study. As you improve you will want to know more, and then it will be time to delve a little more deeply.

Part II
Painting in Water-colour

1. *Introducing Water-colour*

Painting in water-colours is by no means easy, for a mastery of the techniques of this medium calls for a combination of skill, knowledge, patience and even courage. Water-colour has fascinating qualities; the almost transparent films of colour bring an enchanting luminosity and the watery nature of the paint allows it to blend and merge in a most exciting manner. These characteristics make it particularly suitable for the translation of the gentle, and let us face it, watery, British landscape.

I feel that it would be too much at this stage to attempt a full-scale water-colour so let us take the first steps by progressing from what we have already discovered and understood in our previous outdoor studies with charcoal.

The picture reproduced in *Figure 17* depicts a scene in the old town of Hastings, Sussex, and shows the large wooden sheds in which the fishermen dry their nets. The unusual shapes of these buildings, their interesting silhouette, and the contrasting modern lamp standard, made it an irresistible scene to record. The method used was this: a charcoal drawing was made and thoroughly 'fixed', and water-colour paint was then floated over the whole thing in thin watery films of colour. These are called 'washes', and the complete process is known as 'charcoal-and-wash' painting. If desired, the order can be reversed by applying the colour first; but we will use the original method, as it is so obviously a good follow-on from our earlier work.

Paints are the next thing to consider, and although it is possible to buy various kinds of water-colour boxes already filled, I suggest you obtain an empty one and fill it yourself with pans of colour. The box I recommend is the type illustrated in *Figure 18*. This has a ring on the underside for your thumb, which will hold the box steady as you work, and has adequate wells (or depressions) in which the paint can be mixed. I suggest the following list of colours, for it has been for many years my basic palette and I have added to it only as general experience or some special circumstance has suggested. From it an adequate range of colours can be obtained.

Two yellows — Cadmium Yellow, Yellow Ochre
Two reds — Alizarin Crimson, Cadmium Red
One blue — Ultramarine Blue
One brown — Burnt Umber
One green — Viridian
One grey — Payne's Grey

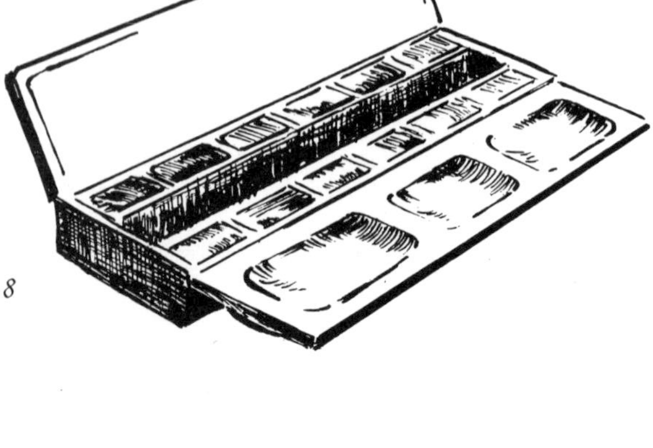

Figure 18

Here I feel I must insert a note of explanation. Nearly every professional artist I know has very definite ideas on what colours to use, and what to avoid. That, of course, is inevitable: otherwise we should find nothing delightfully personal about them or their work. The right choice is always one that is reached by experience, and by trial and error. I have suggested to you the foregoing palette because it is reasonably safe; and it is also one to which you can add as your study of this fascinating business of painting progresses. When buying your paints try if possible to purchase 'artist's' quality rather than student's; the extra expense will prove well worth it.

The same applies to brushes. You will need two, a No. 10 and a No. 7. Buy sables, if you can possibly afford them, for although expensive they are by far the best, and have a very long life. I have in my box a sable brush which is a great favourite, and is now nearly ten years old. Ox-ear hair brushes, which are not so pliable or hardwearing as sable, could be a first substitute. If some of this sounds a trifle expensive, remember that your materials are important and that in the long view good ones are usually cheaper . . . and there is always that very broad hint which can be dropped a few weeks before a birthday or Christmas!

The last requirement is a container for your water. I use a polythene cup, but any container which has a wide neck will do. A narrow vessel is unsatisfactory, as it will not allow sufficient space for the brush to be swirled around; and it is absolutely essential that you wash the brush after each application of colour. When working out of doors a flat bottle for your supply of water must be carried. Again, it is possible to get nice flat polythene ones, but usually students think up their own original ideas. A friend of mine hangs a rubber ball with a large hole in it from his paint-box, and for his reserve supply of water he carries a flat hot-water bottle. So far, in spite of many comments, he refuses to change, as he insists it is the easiest way of carrying this most necessary of materials.

Before getting down to work with our charcoal-and-wash study, one extra bit of preparation is needed. It concerns the paper. As you know, if water is dropped on to paper it will, unless the paper is very stout, make it wrinkle and buckle. This has to be avoided, as otherwise our paint would run into little pools and rivers and completely destroy the effect we desire. To overcome the difficulty we stretch and secure the paper to the board, and this is done as follows:

First sponge the paper on both sides so that it is uniformly wet. Now place it in the centre of your board and as flat as you can. Sponge off any surplus water and then with a strip of 1 in. gummed paper (not Sellotape) stick down one of the long edges, keeping half the width of the gummed paper on the drawing-board and the other half on the cartridge paper. Again smooth your paper and secure next the other long edge and finally the two short ones. Do not be worried if there are bumps and wrinkles in your paper, for as it dries out it will shrink back to its original size, and because the edges are gummed to your board it will become more and more taut and, finally, extremely smooth and flat. One word of warning: when putting on the gummed strips make sure they adhere by carefully nursing the paper with your thumb in a series of gentle pressures, not by running gaily from one end to the other, for such casual treatment will probably pleat your paper at one corner and cause a most annoying wrinkle on an otherwise perfectly flat sheet. Only if the paper is very stout and heavy can it be safely used unstretched without fear of buckling. Cartridge paper is not usually made in this weight.

Now for the charcoal-and-wash drawing. On the newly stretched paper make your charcoal study according to the method previously explained. The only point worth remembering is that we shall endeavour to use a slightly lighter touch. The darks will still be dark but not truly the blackest of black, the reason for this being that when colour is placed over them we want it to show, and not be dulled by too much charcoal underneath. So perhaps we could say that although all parts of our charcoal drawing are in complete harmony it is 'painted' in a slightly higher key. Fix it and make sure it does not smudge. If it does, give it an extra spraying with the fixative.

Before we tint over the charcoal sketch it will be wiser if we curb our enthusiasm for the moment and indulge in a little experiment or two which will familiarise us with the contents of our new colour-box. All we need are a few odd pieces of paper, our paint-box, some water, and the large brush. Dip the brush into the water and transfer a little pool of liquid into one of the depressions in the lid of the paint-box. Then gently agitate the colour you have chosen until the brush is well loaded with paint. Mix this thoroughly into the pool of water, making quite sure the brush is free from any tiny patches of undiluted paint. We now have a supply of wet colour into which we can dip. Have your paper at a slight slant—a book under the drawing-board will do—so that you are working on a slightly inclined panel similar to an old-fashioned desk-top. Boldly, and with a fully-charged brush, put a firm horizontal stroke across the top of the paper. Try not to be timid, and endeavour to use most of the length of the hairs of the brush. The resulting brush stroke should be an even band of colour some $\frac{3}{8}$in. wide. You will notice that the colour tends to collect in a thin watery line at the base of this stroke, but this is immediately absorbed as you make the second stroke—again with a fully-charged brush. To remove this wetness at the end of the area to be painted, wipe the brush until it is almost dry, and a further gentle stroke will lift the wetness.

This is known as 'laying down a wash' and is an absolutely indispensable technique for water-colour painting. Practise it on several sheets of paper until you have the feel of it, and do use plenty of water.

Back then to our charcoal sketch, over which we are going to lay these washes of colour. Our task is reasonably simple, as we only have to use a general colour—the lights and darks are already in place. There is no definite rule where to begin, but I usually start at the top and work down. This does not mean that we cannot return to a previously painted passage if we feel it needs further attention, but I must stress that it is generally better to work directly and freely and to resist strongly the temptation to 'touch up' parts that have already been painted. Various thoughts will come to you as you work; at times you will wait for an area to dry before proceeding with the one next to it; at other times you will happily let one colour flood into and blend with another. It is by these experiences that our knowledge increases, and with a charcoal-and-wash drawing we can take a few liberties because we know we have a good tone drawing underneath to hold the whole thing together. In my sketch of Hastings (*Figure 17*, page 64) you will notice that there is a blending of wet paint on the sunny side of the old buildings, where yellow ochre and green have merged. A similar effect has been used in the ground colours where the shadows and the sunlit shingle meet. I have also made use of the blending of *damp* colours, which is very helpful, for although it retains the correct shape of things it prevents the rather stark appearance of a hard, brittle edge. It helps to keep a feeling of softness and of delicate lighting which is true to the effect of atmosphere on objects out of doors. This can be seen where the rooftops meet the hillside, and also in parts of the reflections.

What I am trying to convey is the wonderful quality of water-colour paints. They are soft and flowing; they merge and blend; they can be both firm and delicate, strong and gentle: contrasting qualities which should be made use of. I am sure you will agree that it is quite wrong to confine them into stiff, hard patches of brittle, half-dry colour. Give them scope and freedom, particularly in these charcoal-and-wash drawings, and you will create pictures of distinction and beauty.

Artists, like everyone else, speak little of their failures. If, whilst on this path towards landscape painting, you occasionally lose your way and turn out work that is dirty and muddy, do not despair, for you will be in quite good company. Failures happen to us all, but if you can come back smiling, even if a little grimly, you will find the mistakes getting less and less and your knowledge and ability growing step by step. Remember not to tackle too much too soon. Look for subjects you feel you can manage, and content yourself at this stage with 'studies' rather than 'pictures'. You will find, of course, that a really good study *is* a picture.

Finally, although I have used the charcoal-and-wash method as a stepping-stone, do not put it to one side as being merely a stunt for beginners. It just so happens that I consider its use to be progressive; but it is also a well-established method of painting (see page 65) and one which can be most expressive and profound. Long after you have read this chapter I hope you will use it again and again.

At this stage you will find your critical powers developing, and you will be dissatisfied with certain passages in your work. Do not despair, as this is a very good sign of real progress. A small sketch-book into which you can enter lots of reference drawings is the answer, and by continual practice you will find that you are, by your own efforts, solving the problems that these difficult passages presented.

2. *Monochrome Painting*

Having now had some experience of our paints by practice washes and by floating such washes over a charcoal drawing, the next step is to work with the pigment only. This means that the paint must be mixed and applied at varying degrees of strength to give reality to the light and dark areas of our work. Remember the terms 'weak' and 'strong', for you will often hear them. In water-colour a weak colour is one where so much water is introduced that the colour is considerably reduced. On the other hand a strong colour is one where plenty of paint is added, and although the mixture is still very fluid the colour content is considerably higher. Let us suppose we are painting in one colour only—that is, in monochrome—and that we are using a very dark brown. By adding water we can weaken this colour considerably, and we might be tempted to say it was now a light colour. Actually the *colour* has not been changed, but only its *strength*. We can have light colours such as yellow and dark colours such as Prussian Blue, yet both light and dark colours can be painted at varying degrees of strength.

As we are now working with paint only, this is the time to find out more about paper. Previously we have used cartridge paper, but there are many other kinds and what you must now purchase is a heavier-type paper, specially made for the water-colourist. There are many trade names, but be particularly careful to insist on 'water-colour paper', not cartridge. I regret to say that many shop assistants are themselves not sure, so be careful. The proper water-colour paper is made in three surface finishes. The first is one that is left with its natural texture, which is slightly coarse and has a certain roughness. It is not pressed or rolled after it has been made and is therefore listed in the artist's catalogues as 'NOT'. This is the most popular. The other surfaces are 'H.P.' which means 'hot-pressed' and in consequence has a fairly smooth surface; and 'Rough', which is a very coarse grain.

The thickness of paper is indicated by stating its weight. There are two methods of doing this. One is by stating the weight, in grams, of a *single* sheet measuring one square metre; the other is by giving the weight in pounds of a complete ream of 500 sheets. Thus a sheet of '160 g.s.m. (72 lb) NOT' would be a fairly light paper with a moderately coarse surface. As a very rough and ready guide, by doubling the pounds per ream number, one will have the approximate figure for grams per square metre. For example, 300 lb per ream equals 600 g.s.m. Paper up to 250 g.s.m. (120 lb) needs stretching, but beyond this point one can paint direct. All water-colour papers can be purchased in blocks and pads of various sizes or by the sheet which usually measures 22 in. × 30 in. (560mm × 762mm). This is known as an Imperial Sheet. In some instances the paper is a little larger, 23¼ in. × 33 in. (591mm × 838mm) and such a size is known as an A1 Sheet.

Having obtained a few pieces of water-colour paper (a block of 90 lb or 190 g.s.m. NOT about 9 in. × 7 in. would be fine), the next step is to practise graduated washes of colour. This means starting at the top of the paper with a colour at full strength and bringing it down slowly to its palest tint. The idea is that as you proceed down the paper, remembering to have the drawing-board tilted, the brush is replenished with less and less colour but more and more water, until at the last stage the brush is being dipped only into the water.

Ultramarine is an excellent colour to begin with, for the result of a graduated wash in this colour will be a perfect example of painting a clear blue sky. There will be a strong blue at the top, representing the sky overhead, and the colour will decrease in strength just as a sky does in nature, until at the horizon there is only the slightest suggestion of colour. Thus you will have painted a truly dome-like sky. Should this surprise you, look out of the window on a good clear day and this dome-like quality will be easily observed.

After becoming proficient in laying down these graduated washes, a few experiments would be a good idea. Try, for instance, putting in a faint range of hills about halfway down the paper. Apply it first on an initial wash that is still a little damp, then on another wash that has thoroughly dried. You will have two distinct effects, which can be added to your store of experience and used later. After painting the hills, try reversing the graduated wash so that the colour gets stronger and stronger as you come down. You will now have the effect of land coming to your feet. A further experiment would be a slightly uneven stroke to suggest the broken nature of the ground. Do not attempt to scrub backwards and forwards, but float the colour across the paper in one direction, and never go up and down with the strokes—a common bad habit at this stage.

The next stage is to put the knowledge gained to the test out of doors. As we are going to paint in monochrome, the first thing to bear in mind is that the colour used must be one that has a sufficient range to give us all the tones we require. Payne's Grey would be admirable. Make sure that you have an adequate supply before setting out, and check the rest of your painting and personal equipment too. Many an artist has felt very sheepish to find, when he unpacked his bag, that a most essential item had been forgotten.

Let us imagine that we are in the Lake District and that we see the scene reproduced in

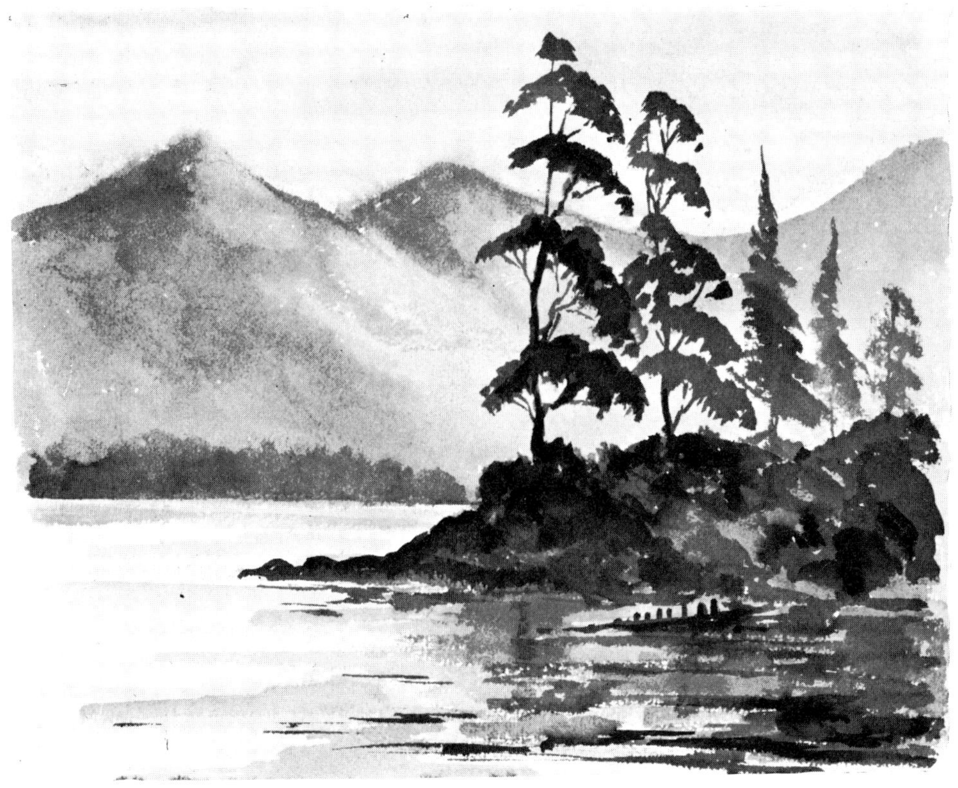

Figure 19. A study in monochrome

Figure 19. Our first thought, having decided on the viewpoint, would be as to how we are going to tackle the painting, and I would suggest that we sit down quietly and think out the problems. We must decide how much of this delightful scene can be included, how much will be firmly stated and what will be hinted at in a subtle way. Can we paint every twig? What would be the best way to suggest those mountains? These and other questions must be asked and answered before the actual painting begins, because once we start we want the whole thing to proceed with a swing and a flourish, and with no timid hesitation.

First, we shall probably have to pencil in very lightly the shapes of the various masses on a quarter-Imperial sheet. Accuracy should be aimed at, but not detailed drawing, because as we paint we also draw. The brush not only puts on the paint, but is also a very sensitive drawing instrument, and can often suggest with a delicate flick what would be almost impossible with a pencil.

Now for the painting. The colour should be mixed, ready to be strengthened or weakened, and with a well-loaded brush the sky should be quickly painted in. In this picture I would recommend that the sky in the first instance be brought right down over the area occupied by the mountains, making sure that the colour is very weak behind the trees to give the effect of a haze. The mountains should be painted before this first wash is quite dry, giving them the impression of going up and over. Whilst still wet, the lighter side of the nearest mountain could be lifted out with a well-squeezed brush and the dark areas be painted into the wet paint. Already we shall have observed that it is important to assess how wet or how damp to have the painting before adding the next passage. The distant belt of trees should also be introduced whilst the painting is still wet.

Even at this early stage it will be apparent that by using our paints in this sympathetic way we are getting a better effect than if we tried to introduce any details of individual rocks or trees. We have established distance.

Next come the gentle tones of the water and at the same time the weakest passages in the rocks. These should be followed by other passages of stronger tones, which can be dropped into wet colour, taking care at this stage not to suggest the outcrop of rocks or anything that has a firmer edge. These ought to come when the work is a little drier, but the soft ripples in the water could be carefully brushed in while we are waiting.

Lastly would come the strong areas, which are carefully painted after considering how wet or dry should be the surface which receives them. Such items as the trees and the breakwater should be painted on a surface which is reasonably dry, and possibly with these it would be wise to use the smaller brush. Notice the slight weakening of tone as the trees recede.

A last look around the painting for any final touches (but take care—no fidgeting) and the work is complete—your first monochrome painting. Date it for further reference, as it will be a valuable guide to your progress. Do plenty of these sketches: they are useful practice. You will be in very good company, for most artists do the same. Not only do these monochromes help them to establish the correct tonal qualities of a scene, but they can, if done well, be truly delightful paintings.

3. *The First All-Colour Painting*

The enjoyment and appreciation of colour is universal, and plays a far greater role in our daily life than is often realized. Colour can excite or soothe, and even lift us to heights of real emotion. It is no accident that the strong dominance of red is used to signify danger; it is a colour which immediately catches the eye and creates an attitude of alertness. Strong and vivid colours fill us with excitement and gaiety, whilst quiet and gentle ones suggest restfulness and calm. In the hands of a competent artist colour is indeed a great vehicle for expression, and can go far beyond the mere recording of the scene before him. He can, for instance, be like the stage designer who, without altering the scene, creates a variety of interpretations by the careful choice of coloured lighting.

There can be no doubt that in painting, colour can be deeply expressive, and can be the added ingredient which gives full flavour to our work. But it can be a dangerous ingredient —one that will, if not controlled, completely spoil that flavour. Crudity can so easily appear if colour is used without a true understanding of all the other fundamentals that go into picture-making. I often tell my students not to be over-zealous in using too much brilliant and strong colouring at the expense of all else, for fear they may make their work look overdressed. That is why I ask you to enter the world of colour with caution and to remember that, although colour can give added charm to our work, unless we have an understanding of tones as outlined in the previous chapters it can easily destroy the balance and harmony in what would otherwise be a thoughtful piece of painting.

We must not forget that lighting and atmosphere will have their effect on colour and that such effects are only noticed after keen and careful observation. We have learnt from our charcoal studies the effect of the film of atmosphere between ourselves and distant objects. Try to imagine for a moment a painting in which this has been ignored. It shows a scene in which exactly the same green at the same strength of colour has been used for a tree in the foreground as for another some distance away. The far one is drawn smaller to show the distance, but its colour is such that it wants to join up with its much closer partner.

To introduce you gently, our first colour work will be limited to a range of three colours only. In this way it is hoped that the usual difficulties confronting the newcomer to painting will be overcome. The colours we shall use are:

Cadmium Yellow
Ultramarine Blue
Burnt Umber

As Burnt Umber is a rather reddish-brown it will be seen that we are, in effect, working with a slight variation on the three primary colours—red, blue, yellow.

For a first exercise, make a graduated wash on a small piece of paper, starting with Ultramarine. Gradually weaken this and bring it down a little below halfway and then, while it is slightly damp, introduce a fairly weak yellow. Gradually increase the strength of the yellow, and merge a brown into it while it is still wet. From such a simple exercise you will create an impression of both the land and the sky receding into the picture. You will also have shown another very important feature of landscape painting, and that is that distant colours always appear a little bluer than they really are. Trial and error is the next step and I would suggest many of these little simple washes, which can have various details introduced to add interest. Only by handling and by constant use can you come to grips with the material being used. Try mixing colours and dropping them into damp colour which has already been applied, and study the effect.

It will soon become apparent that quite a range of colours can be obtained, and it is suggested that a simple colour chart as shown in *Figure 20*, page 66, should be made and kept for reference. This can be done by painting patches of the three colours side by side to show their appearance when pure. The second row shows yellow blended with brown, which gives a pleasant sunny mixture. Remember that this mixture can have a balance tipping towards either brown or yellow, giving quite a range, and that such colours can be considerably weakened by the addition of water. Next to this mixture carry out the same idea, but mix yellow with blue. From this you will obtain a variety of greens, from a very yellow-green to a deep blue-green. Immediately ideas of differing greens in the landscape come to mind. In the third row brown is mixed with blue, and from such mixture we can get a variety of browns, purples, greys and blues. Now we can take the experiment a little further by trying out various combinations of all three. In the first of this threesome mix-up, I have put in a little more yellow, in the second a little more blue, and in the third a little more brown. Naturally the exercise could be taken even further, and additional experiments are always profitable, but already we have a considerable selection of colours with which to venture forth.

So much for theorising. The real job now is to get down to the pleasant business of putting our knowledge to the test. Take out your equipment and let us search for a simple tree study such as the one illustrated in *Figure 21*, page 67. After a careful look at the subject we must think how to suggest it with the materials we have to hand. A quick glance at the third illustration should be enough to show that our materials are unsuited to a detailed or spotty effect. Such treatment only tends to agitate and worry the eye, and the soft dignity of the tree is lost. Obviously the sponge-like look of the foliage is better suggested by a watery application of the paint with only a few drier touches here and there.

In order to obtain such a watery look the first thing to do, after lightly pencilling in the shapes, is to prepare a good supply of two or three greens—otherwise one stage of the painting might dry before the next colour was ready. As the painting proceeds, these colours can be added to and altered. For this study a yellow-green, a brown-green and a blue-green should be mixed and ready in the wells of the paint-box. Observing that the light is from the left we will very simply suggest the background, making quite sure it is weak enough in colour not to jump forward and being careful not to let it run over any area which needs to be very light. Taking a good brushful of our yellow-green, paint the lighter areas of *one* of the clumps of foliage and while it is still wet drop in the darker side. Should it run in too much, a dry brush will lift it and tell us just what degree of dampness will give the desired effect. Branches can be suggested quite early and thus we shall work down our paper quite quickly, letting the paint run and blend as much as we can without destroying the effect we are after.

Having got the paper covered, we can now quickly view the work as a whole, and decide when and where to place any additional strokes which need to be added when the work is a little drier—such as the extra dark area on the bank, the dark patches in the water, and the mere suggestion of modelling in the tree. A few dry strokes in the branches, and you will have your sketch.

You will, I am sure, have found not only that we have been using all our previous knowledge of tone and colour mixing, but that timing is most important. The time factor in water-colour painting is both its charm and its difficulty. Not only must we know what to do and how to do it, but when. Should the paper be wet, damp or dry? This is a question that must be constantly in our mind. For your guidance may I say that the wet or damp effect usually looks best, but naturally it must be controlled. A further tip is that a gradual blending rather than a complete merging occurs on damp paper, and this dampness can be estimated by waiting for the shine of the water to disappear.

Now a word about tone and colour. Often the transfer from monochrome to colour causes some confusion, and our artistic vocabulary also becomes confused, making communication difficult. Tones tend to merge as the scene recedes, but because colours register different tones, it is quite possible for a distant object to be lower in tone than a near one of a different colour. For example, a yew tree in the distance could, because of its strong colour, be lower in tone than a privet hedge in the foreground. A look at the chart in *Figure 22*, page 68, will explain this. The areas marked are approximately the same tone value (that is, they would, in a black and white photograph register the same tone of grey), but they are obviously of a different *strength* of colour. On the other hand we could easily speak of two colours being of the same strength but of a different tone value.

4. *Colours at Our Command*

Tone is more important than colour! This well-known statement often causes confusion, but as I consider it to be utterly true and most important to the understanding of this difficult business of painting, it must be fully appreciated. When dealing with our simple three-colour palette of yellow, blue and brown, it was found that these colours each had a different tone value when painted at full strength, and that such values could be altered by the inclusion of more water. We found, too, that perfectly adequate interpretations of a subject could be made with only one colour, as in the monochrome sketches, and that even with only three colours, quite profound and expressive work could be done, which lost little of its appeal through the limitation of colour. Any success that was gained was achieved not by the use of bright and varied colour, but by the understanding of tone. Franz Hals, whose work is so sparkling and alive, painted many of his most famous portraits with the use of only four colours!

Colour, therefore, is the *extra* jewel which can give an added sparkle and quality to our work, but like all forms of decoration it must be respected and understood and never over-done. In painting it must be used in conjunction with and after consideration of things like shape, form, tone and composition. Imagine a beautiful woman in a well-cut gown who is so bedecked with buttons, bows, posies, clips, clasps, jabots, brooches, bangles and beads, that the beauty of the gown is obscured. All those extra decorations not only hide the thing of real beauty, but are so confusing that whatever attraction each piece may have is lost in the conflict for our attention. The lady is overdressed. So it is with colour. It can be a great aid to our paintings, by giving them extra richness and quality, but it must be used with discretion and as part of a whole.

Having, I hope, made my point, let us see what subtle delights the use of extra colours can offer. You will remember that in Part II, Chapter 1, I gave a list of colours which were recommended as being adequate for most purposes. For easy reference, this list is repeated here:

Two yellows	—	Cadmium Yellow, Yellow Ochre
Two reds	—	Cadmium Red, Alizarin Crimson
One brown	—	Burnt Umber
One blue	—	Ultramarine
One green	—	Viridian
One grey	—	Payne's Grey

Newcomers to painting often express surprise at the small number of colours recommended. If you also are surprised, and perhaps a little doubtful, let me reassure you that for the vast majority of our paintings these colours will, with a little mixing, give us everything we need. May I beg you not to succumb to the persuasion of some keen salesman and arrive home with one of those enormous boxes filled with dozens of colours. The largest box ever made would never be adequate, as it stood, for every occasion. What is more, it would spoil your enjoyment by taking from you the fun and excitement of discovering new and unusual mixtures. Worse still, it would rob your work of its individuality by always trying to force you to accept the 'ready-made' answer to any colour problem, and this in turn would discourage the absorbing and instructive habit of truly searching for colour. These huge boxes are also too cumbersome to carry and too heavy to hold.

It would now be useful to conduct an experiment in the mixing and blending of colours. From it can be found what happens when any two colours are mixed together. By painting each part in a very moist and fluid way a variety of effects can be observed, many of them creating exciting and subtle colours. Use only seven of our eight colours: exclude Payne's Grey, as we are going to deal with that separately. It is seriously recommended that you make a chart and carry it in your sketch-bag, where it will be at hand to give help and reference when working out of doors. All you need is a sheet of quarter-Imperial paper (15 in. × 11 in.), ruled out to give seven horizontal rows. In the top row place a dab of each of our seven colours, starting with Cadmium Yellow. In the second row, Cadmium Yellow is mixed with the remaining colours in the top row in turn. The third row is the turn of Yellow Ochre, and so on in decreasing steps down the page. To show best the blending effect have two arms of colour, say Cadmium Yellow and Burnt Umber, meeting to form a V shape.

When painting a picture, the colours are usually mixed in the depressions of the palette attached to the paint-box, but in this experiment, as you want to observe the mixture made by varying proportions of two colours, allow the paints to run freely together whilst on the paper, and whilst both are quite wet. It is the freely mixing quality you want to observe. Thus the two colours merge and blend where the two arms of the V meet. Then, to see the effect of a weaker mixture, water is added and the V is 'washed' down to make a Y. This gives some surprisingly pleasant results. The delightful variation of colours of great subtlety that comes from the mixing of Crimson with Viridian is a fine example—and just look at the variety of greens that can be made.

Examine carefully the areas where two colours meet, for if you have kept the work clean and rather wet, it is here that small blurred patches of about four differing mixtures will be seen. Thus in each of the twenty-one mixtures there will be at least four variations, which gives us a selection of more than eighty-four colours, plus our original seven. This is a considerable range. If you made a success of the chart try making another, only this time use mixtures of three colours. You will then find you have the beginnings of a palette of infinite scope and variety.

Until you are fairly experienced I would not advise mixing more than three colours. The important thing is to experiment by trial and error, remembering that the man who never made a mistake never made anything. By experience you will remember the mixtures more easily, and (what is equally important) you will get a sureness and speed which is a great asset. It is most disappointing to find that, having taken so long to get the desired mixture, the part of your painting which you hoped to catch while still damp has dried, and what was to have been a pleasant feathery edge has become a hard and brittle line.

Experiment like mad. You will find all sorts of surprises, delights—and sometimes disappointments. As you progress, try mixing colours in the orthodox way in the palette, adding a little colour at a time. Some mixtures will be wonderful and then, with the merest touch of something already used, the mixture becomes a hippopotamus special—mud! Try it again, altering the proportions of the mixture. You may still have a greyish hue, but this time it is one with a gentle hint of colour, and you have found something that had previously been elusive.

Greys are truly worthy of an independent mention. To the artist greys are very subtle for they have all been influenced, however slightly, by the inclusion of colour. If this is puzzling, perhaps I can explain in a way that often presents itself when working with students out of doors. If one of them states that a certain area, let us say a stone wall, is grey, I usually accept the remark but immediately follow it with a question something like this: 'Yes, I know it is grey; but supposing in some magical way I could remove all the black-and-white greyness. What colour would it be then?' This immediately makes him or her search for the colour content, no matter how elusive or fleeting it may be, and leads to the more neutral passages of the work remaining subdued but having much greater interest. Moreover, the colour within these areas is almost invariably of the same family as the main parts of the picture, and by absorbing some of this over-all colouring the completed work has a much greater feeling of cohesion and unity.

We have already used greys with a hint of colour, for it was found that a tinted grey could be made from such mixtures as blue-brown or green-crimson and one or two others. In later work on trees we will find that grey-greens are essential to give a feeling of volume and rotundity. There are, however, many objects which have a natural greyness before the atmosphere begins its tricks. Such things as various kinds of stonework and some varieties of bricks, old and weather-beaten timber, concrete and galvanized iron are just a few examples. In coping with such things it might cause almost insurmountable problems if we had continually to keep mixing a basic grey to which colour had to be added. Because of this, Payne's Grey has been recommended as a useful colour to include in your paint-box. Now at last it will be put to use. We shall not use it 'neat' for it is so strong that this can only be done, with great restraint, for a few incidentals. We shall, however, use it as a basis for making these subtle and delightful slightly-coloured greys which are so typical of the landscape and which will grace our work with a dignity and restraint that cannot be obtained by using only bright and vibrant colours. The chart in *Figure 38*, page 73, explains how to obtain some of these colours using oil paints but the principle is the same for water-colour.

5. *Trees, Foliage and Grass*

Trees are among the most beautiful of all living things and it is not surprising that they have for so long been the source of inspiration to writers, poets, musicians—and artists—offering, as they do, enormous scope and a great challenge to all who desire to express their many beauties. Their importance in the landscape cannot be over-emphasized, for they are probably the loveliest feature in any composition. Gentle, soft and feathery shapes provide delicate and decorative silhouettes; trunks and branches provide a crisp contrast to the rhythmic curves of the masses of foliage, presenting us with a scene so gracious that it pleads to be painted.

The best policy is a step-by-step advance, for it would be foolish if we rushed for our colour box without first having some understanding of how to proceed and what to look for. The actual business of putting paint to paper is not very difficult; it is the problem of what to include and what to discard that causes the artist to ponder. Too often the beginner who rushes at the subject in a burst of enthusiasm finds that the painting gets out of control, and the result is bitterly disappointing. So beware of over-enthusiasm and make haste slowly.

Were I your artist-tutor on a painting holiday, I would at this stage take you and the rest of the party for a ramble. No equipment would be carried, as our intention would be merely to 'read' the landscape story. In other words, we would set out to translate subjects into simple terms, so that our mind was clear before the actual painting was begun. This is our thinking time, during which we are making observations and deciding how the various problems which confront us can be simplified and unified in order to translate the subject into the terms of water-colour painting. This is very important. A famous artist was once asked, in my hearing, how long it took him to complete a particular painting. His reply was: 'About three hours' work and twenty-five years' thought.' He was, apart from being a little facetious, trying to force home the necessity of adequate preparation and observation.

On our walk the first thing to observe would be the silhouette of a tree (or trees) as a mass. Always try to see things not as an outline but as a mass of fairly solid tone. This has been done in the sketch in *Figure 23(a)*. Having such an image in mind will immediately create an impression of solidity and will tend to bring the tree away from its background. Shape alone, however helpful it may be, will not give sufficient information for us to begin painting. The great temptation now is to look for all kinds of unnecessary detail. It is a temptation which must be sternly resisted, as what we need are essentials. There would be little point in counting all the leaves and painting them, if we found that we still had not managed to capture the protective and embracing rotundity of the tree. Rather than search for insignificant tiny items, let us now look within the solid masses for the large clusters of foliage which go to make up the whole area. Think of these clusters as green sponges on stalks, like those effective little trees that can be seen in an architect's model, for that is exactly how they are made. Each cluster will have its own ration of light and shade, and each has the ability to cast a shadow which may affect adjacent foliage. This image is illustrated in *Figure 23(b)*.

From these two images the tree can now be visualised as if painted—*Figure 23(c)*. Notice how the edges have been blended to have a softening effect, and that the various tones range from white to a very low tone indeed. The outside edge of the main shape has also been 'chattered' to suggest leafiness. This is very important, for no tree has a silhouette so smooth that it appears to be a cut-out shape. Such an appearance is exactly what we wish to avoid, as most trees blend into their setting and seldom appear stark and brittle.

All that has been written so far about trees is equally true in relation to other types of foliage and grass. When dealing with grass, first establish the main area and then break that area down into the shapes made by the most important clumps. Each of these will have its own light and shade, and the result will prove far more satisfactory than trying to make hundreds of strokes to represent the countless blades. If the latter method is used, even the most painstaking work merely looks like a flat wall decorated with lots of little strokes.

By now we probably have a fair idea of what to put into our tree study. I would suggest making a few monochrome studies, as I have done in *Figure 23(d)*. First comes the pencil sketch, which serves to indicate the position of our tree and also reminds us of the placing of the smaller areas and the various accents which we have decided are important. At this stage there is always a temptation to over-draw, but hold on to the visualised interpretation as illustrated and only draw what is essential to your desired result. Do not misunderstand me: preliminary drawing is absolutely essential and some mere nebulous scribble simply will not do; on the other hand, resist the temptation to put in a lot of niggling detail which, at best, will only confuse. Having made your pencil 'indication', now paint it in, trying to work with a fully-loaded brush of the right tone. Endeavour to estimate when to put one tone on to another. If the work is too wet it will run, but with a little practice you will soon get the feel of things and know when to work with the paper wet and when to wait until it is merely damp. Occasionally a few crisp touches can be made when the work is dry, but have care: this is the point when so often we get carried away, and freshness is lost at the expense of over-decoration of detail.

Assuming that this preparatory work has been done diligently—and, I trust, with great enjoyment and satisfaction—now is the time to enter the luscious land of colour. At first glance all the trees, grass and foliage seem overpoweringly green, but here again our little ramble of observation has helped. If we were truly looking we would have noticed a tremendous variety of greens. Some were warm greens, some cold; some were purple greens, some grey. An oak tree in summer is a grand example, for its greens range from almost yellow ochre to a rich deep purple-green. A further example is the rose bush with leaves which sometimes make one wonder whether they should be described as red or green. With beginners, a very common fault in tree painting is the use of only a light and a dark green. The introduction of grey-greens and purple-greens is imperative if the tree is to display depth and substance.

To help you, make a chart for the making of greens which still uses our basic palette of seven colours. Mix some Viridian with each of the other colours, and then add a little of each mixture to each of the rest of the colours. In this way a series of greens is made (each containing three colours), all of which can be varied by slight alterations in the proportions of the included colours. I do strongly advise you to make such a chart and to study the results at first hand. To read and understand the theory is not enough; practice and experience are also needed. When the chart is complete, use the surplus colour around the paint-box for a little 'quickie'; you will notice once again that the cold colours 'go back' and the warm colours 'come forward'. If you put down something quite casually, keeping this in mind, you will be surprised how such a quick impression will 'hold together', and it is very good practice. The chart in the oils section, *Figure 39*, page 74 will help.

In the tree study in *Figure 24*, page 69, I have made use of many of these greens, and three stages have been shown in an attempt to simplify the procedure. In Stage I the sky was

Figure 23

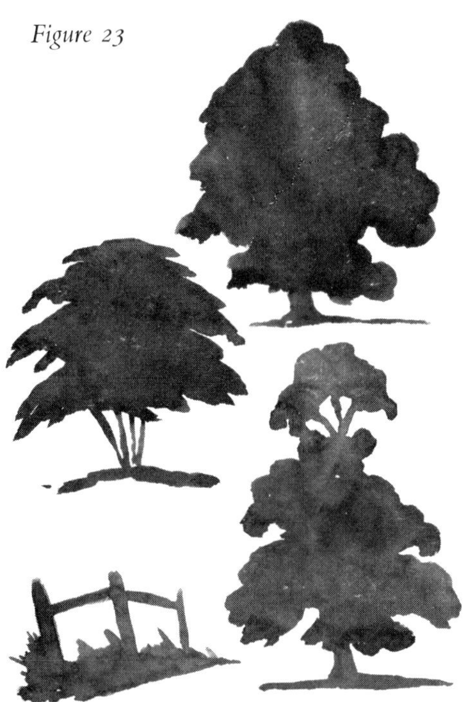

a. *When observing trees, look for the general silhouette rather than for a lot of detail*

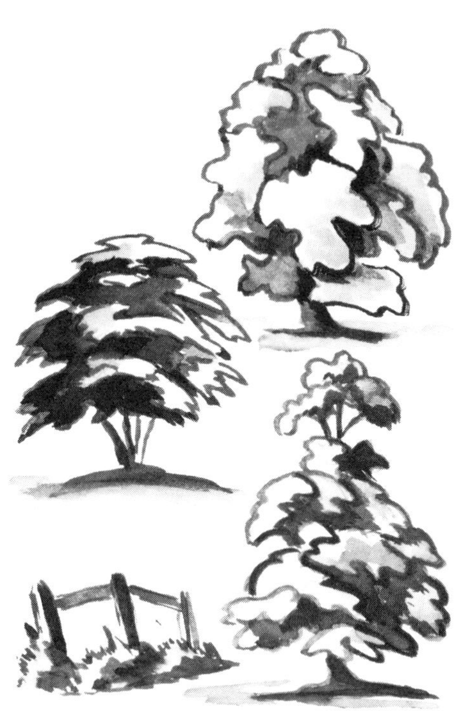

b. *Within the silhouette look for the main shapes of the largest masses of foliage*

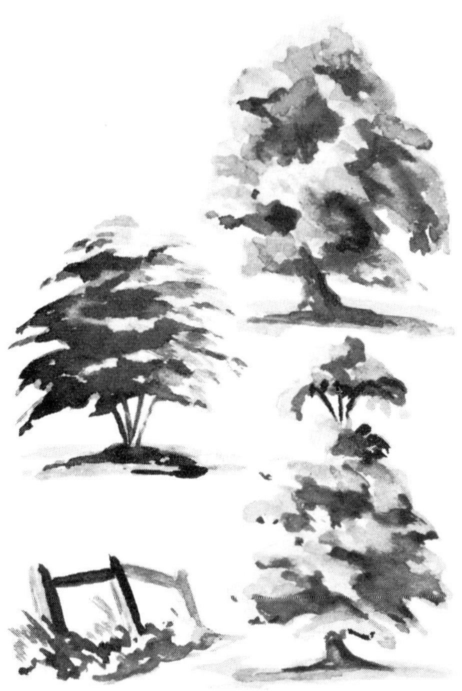

c. *Keen observation of shape and general masses will translate the scene into terms such as this*

d. *Before painting, keep the drawing to a minimum, as further drawing is done with a brush*

painted first. I started with a thin wash of Yellow Ochre, and before it was quite dry a mixture of Ultramarine and a little Cadmium Red was added, dragging the brush to give a broken texture. This was changed for a very weak Cadmium Red as it descended to the horizon. Before the background was absolutely dry the tree shape was washed in with a mixture of Yellow Ochre, Viridian and the merest touch of Cadmium Red. The trunk is weak Cadmium Red and the background trees are Ultramarine with a tiny spot of Umber.

Stage II, which was commenced before the previous work was quite dry, shows the definition of some of the main masses by the use of Viridian-Ochre-Crimson, taking care with the proportions to ensure the correct colour and tone. A little of the same mixture was used for the foreground and the cast shadows.

Stage III shows the inclusion of the deepest tones, which were made with Viridian-Ochre-Umber and Viridian-Umber-blue. The path and the trunk were a blend of Umber-Cadmium Red, and the final accents were extra darks made with Ultramarine-Umber. Occasionally a little Ochre, Umber or purple was dropped in whilst other colours were still wet. Throughout, the brush was held very lightly so that it dragged and danced across the paper to give the work a lively and atmospheric texture.

This is the method I normally adopt, but it is by no means the only one. There are dozens of ways of scoring a goal other than the delicate fleet-footed cross-shot; there are many ways in painting. This method which I offer is one which will assist the progressing painter to attain a reasonable measure of success. With practice comes confidence and a certainty of touch which allows for countless personal interpretations.

6. *Look Over My Shoulder*

In this chapter you are invited to do what the heading suggests, and look on whilst I am painting. In this way I hope to anticipate your questions and many of the problems concerning the handling of water-colour will be solved. Furthermore, such a demonstration will serve to show how the many skills and techniques can be kept together as a team working on the various parts of the picture, without losing the essential feeling for unity and harmony. Not only must each part be well done, but all parts must live happily together.

The chosen scene is shown as a finished painting in *Figure 25*, the original work measuring 14 in. × 10 in. It shows a typical piece of Derbyshire in one of the many delightful villages that can be found a few miles from Buxton. This is a rewarding area in which to work. Mountain and hill arise to cast their shadow over rich and fertile valleys, punctuated with charming little groups such as this, which are far removed from the bleakness and industrialisation which are so often associated with the Midlands. Bleakness and industrialisation can be found here too, but these also can produce the most interesting subjects.

However, we must return to our village. It is in a limestone area, and this material is widely used in rural architecture. After years of absorbing and repelling the elements it takes on a great richness which naturally blends well with the surrounding countryside. Occasionally other materials are used, but again time and weather have their softening effect, and eventually the artist is presented with an almost 'ready-made' picture.

Like all good things, the group illustrated was not easily found and was eventually discovered whilst looking around the local churchyard. A peep over the low wall, and there was this obscure back lane—almost as I have shown it. As far as I can remember, the only alteration made was to move the big tree a little to the right, as in its original position it almost appeared to grow out of the chimney. Also, moving it to the right prevented a rather unpleasant gap appearing between itself and the large building.

I settled down comfortably with all my materials to hand and carefully considered the scene. The day was a little gusty, with broken cloud, so I waited until a shaft of sunlight heightened the scene, making everything much more interesting. I quickly made a mental note of the nicely-shaped shadows and proceeded with my preliminary pencil sketch, which is shown in *Figure 26*. This was made after first getting the whole group to sit comfortably in the picture area as seen through my viewfinder. An ordinary HB pencil was used with quite a light touch so that the lines could, if necessary, be erased when the painting was completed. As you can see, sufficient drawing was included to help in establishing the important shapes, and such detail as needed careful painting was also put in. On the other hand the pencil work is not so detailed that it would not allow scope for additional and expressive drawing to be completed later with the brush.

Then I began to paint, starting with the sky. This is my usual approach, for if the sky can be correctly established there is immediately a point of comparison for every other part of the picture. Great care is essential here, for since you are working on a surface of glaring untouched white there is a tendency to under-estimate the amount of colour needed. It is most disappointing to paint a good sky and to find later that, in comparison with the rest of the work, it appears weak and insipid.

In this picture I noticed an ochre glow over quite a lot of the scene, and so a little Ochre, very weak, was dragged into the lighter areas of the sky and washed off at the edges, and

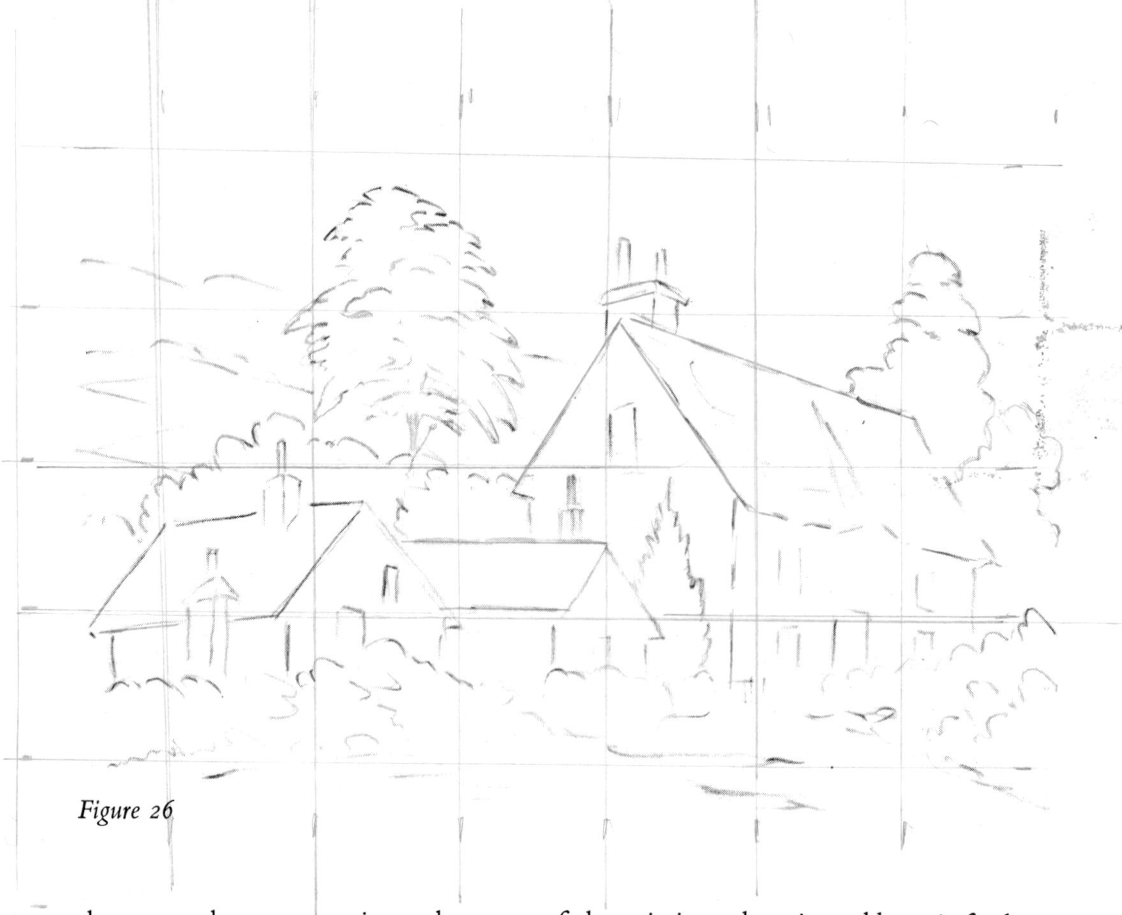

Figure 26

the same colour was put into other parts of the painting where it could await further attention. Before this Ochre wash had dried, the sky was worked on with a mixture of Ultramarine-Viridian, drawing in the cloud formation with a sideways dragging stroke which left tiny areas of the paper untouched. This mixture was weakened as it got to the horizon to keep the dome-like quality. Again before the area was dry, a little Cadmium Red was added to the mixture and this was touched into the central area.

A little clean water was the next thing, as I wanted to include the fresh and very light passages that occurred. The roofs were painted in very light tones of blue, red and purple, as a foundation for extra applications of colour. The grassy banks were blocked in with a mixture of Ochre plus a very little Viridian, and this also served as an underpaint. Thus the work, although still very damp, was gradually taking shape and the glare of the white paper was being overcome. As previously stated, this dampness, although difficult to control, is essential, as it keeps edges soft and prevents a hard and brittle look from creeping into the scene. An example of such a soft edge is where the hills meet the sky, giving the impression that the range of hills has solidity, and not only goes up but also goes over and down. The completion of this stage is shown in *Figure 27*, page 71.

Progress was, of course, continuous, but for the convenience of demonstrating I have shown a further stage in *Figure 28*. My next step was to paint in the background of trees in the manner explained in Chapter 5, that is, by working from a general colour and gradually dropping in darker colours. These trees were painted *into* a sky which was barely dry, using mainly an Ochre-Viridian and Umber-Viridian mixture with either a little blue or a little red added to give greyness or warmth. Notice how the trees tend to darken as they go down behind the buildings. Whilst the greens were in use, the small tree was added and some of the darker parts of the grass banks were dropped in.

By now, the light colours previously painted on the buildings were practically dry. This was the time to paint the darker walls with a mixture of Umber-Ultramarine. As soon as it was applied a little was lifted with an almost dry brush, thus giving the effect of one colour glowing through another. The same technique was used, with subtle variations of colour, on the other buildings with a little extra colour occasionally dropped in. Thus it can be seen that in this second stage the plan was gradually to establish some of the darker areas. Extra colour was applied to the roof to suggest tiling; a shadow with a water-softened edge was placed under the eaves; the dark general tone of the garden was inserted, and the chimneys painted. All this enhanced the form of the various items and increased the effect of the lighting.

Lastly came the extra touches which gave the work its finished appearance. These can be seen by again referring to *Figure 25*. This is always the dangerous stage, for it is now that we are tempted to include lots of detail. To put in too much would destroy the beautiful broad simplicity that is the charm of a good water-colour, and would make the eye flicker and fidget instead of encouraging it to rest calmly within the picture. Therefore, with care and restraint, the windows were suggested with various blue-greys and purple-greys. An extra tile-edge or two was painted, a branch was hinted at here and there, in went the little gate and, lastly, the lovely rich foreground shadows. To ensure a soft edge to the latter, the area of the path was treated with clean water, and the dark colours were applied before it was quite dry. The colours used for this shadow were mixtures of Payne's Grey/crimson with additions of blue or brown. Then, with great deliberation, the painting was carefully put aside to dry. Any more work, and it would have been spoiled.

Water-colour painting is by no means easy, but it is a most joyous and satisfying method of working, capable of effects ranging from the delicate and misty, to the bold and vibrant. I trust I have not only transferred some of my enthusiasm for the medium, but have also paved the way for you to make a smooth and trouble-free start. Very soon your efforts should merit the gentle flattery of a good frame, and advice on this is given in a later chapter.

Part III
Painting in Oils

1. *Oil Paintings: The Things We Need*

With the knowledge gained from Part I of this book we should be well prepared for a smooth transition to the use of oil colours. Obviously some quite new techniques and skills are to be mastered and the new materials of oils must be used with an understanding of both their scope and their limitations, but you will be heartened to know that the actual application of the paint is not really all that difficult. It comes down to an intelligent handling of a rather creamy and opaque paint and a knowledge of what tools to have and how to use them.

As we progress, the skills and techniques will follow naturally but at the outset let us make sure we have all the necessary equipment. We already possess what is needed for our charcoal drawings, but we now need additional materials as illustrated in *Figure 29*. Firstly an easel (*A*). Later on, when we are working out of doors, a proper folding easel will be absolutely essential, but at this stage, when we are practising at home, the improvised table model which I have illustrated will prove quite adequate and will also avoid too much early expense. It is made from the corrugated cardboard from which large cartons are constructed; no doubt your grocer will give you one. When making the easel be sure to have the ribs pointing in the direction I have indicated and it will be quite rigid. Fix it to the table by placing drawing pins in the two flat flanges. If the table has a fine surface, one can easily attach little rubber suction pads which will grip quite firmly. This type of table easel is surprisingly efficient.

Next we need something on which to paint (*B*). Later I shall be telling you more about these 'supports' as they are called, but the one I recommend for general use is a specially made material known as Oil Painting Paper. This has been treated to give a non-absorbent surface which is also rough enough to grip the paint—both essential qualities for oil painting. Be careful when making this purchase, as there are many so-called oil-sketching papers which are useless because they have no 'bite', and the paint tends to slide off instead of

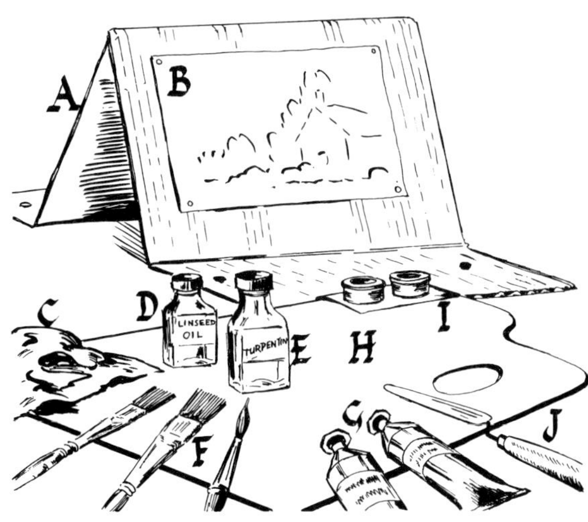

A. *Simple easel made from cardboard carton*
B. *Oil painting paper*
C. *Pieces of rag*
D. *Small bottle of linseed oil*
E. *Bottle of turpentine*
F. *Brushes*
G. *Tubes of paint—students' quality*
H. *Palette—bought or made from hardboard*
I. *Dippers to contain linseed or turpentine*
J. *Painting (or palette) knife*

Figure 29. Equipment for the early stages

forming a pleasing opaque stroke. If in doubt, a good test is to pinch the paper firmly between fore-finger and thumb, making a stroking movement. A good surface will grip, and prevent this movement; a poor one will allow slipping. Oil Painting paper is sold in sheets $20\frac{1}{2}$ in. × $30\frac{1}{2}$ in. and in blocks of various sizes. It is also available already mounted on cardboard and in the more popular sizes. For most of our work the large sheets are advisable and on these you will see the maker's stamp on the *wrong* side. Before cutting a large sheet into smaller pieces, make a few broad pencil strokes across this side in order to identify it.

Pieces of rag (*C*) are essential items of an artist's kit, as oil painting can easily become a rather messy business unless one is constantly wiping and cleaning. A few small squares of newspaper are also very handy, and I know many artists who use cheap paper napkins. These are soft, absorbent and ideal for our purpose. Do not forget to spread large sheets of newspaper over the table. This will be appreciated by whoever is responsible for keeping the house tidy.

One of the small bottles (*D* and *E*) contains linseed oil, the other turpentine. These can be purchased from your artists' colourman, but the turpentine bottle can subsequently be refilled from a larger one from the local hardware store. Turpentine is occasionally used to make the paint very thin, but it is more generally employed for cleaning purposes. A mixture of linseed oil and turpentine serves as a medium or conveyor when you wish the paint to be a little more slippery than as it comes from the tube. A word of warning here, which will be enlarged upon later: do not paint thinly *all* the time. Used properly, oil and turpentine are a great help, but a most common fault with the leisure-hour painter is that he uses them far too much and in consequence his work is too thin to have the truly desirable texture.

Brushes (*F*) are most important: the type I advise is a flat hog-hair, and you can buy these with either long or short hairs. (I generally use the longer haired type.) Size 6 is a good all-purpose size (about $\frac{3}{8}$ in. wide), and I suggest you start with half a dozen of as good a quality as you can afford. Do not get *very* cheap ones, as this will prove a false economy—splayed and curling hairs can cause tremendous frustration. You will also need a water-colour

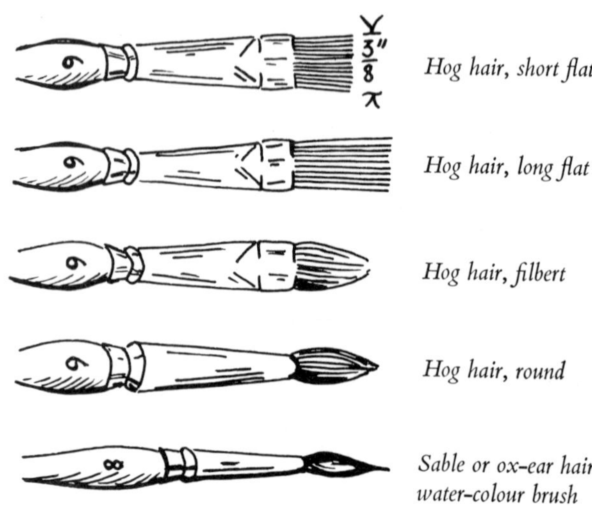

Figure 30. Types of brushes

brush for occasional fine work. As you proceed you may wish to try brushes of other shapes, as shown in *Figure 30*, but my personal preference is for the flat type, which encourages the bold, vigorous approach which I feel is the very essence of good oil painting. Treat your brushes kindly, always remembering that they are really an extension of your own hand. Wipe them constantly whilst work is in progress, and do this carefully by doubling the rag or newspaper over the end of the hairs, squeezing them between finger and thumb, and withdrawing the brush firmly in a manner which automatically re-fashions the shape of the hairs. Brushes must be cleaned thoroughly at the end of each day. The best way is to wipe off the surplus paint and then wash them in soap and lukewarm water. Do this by rubbing soap into the hairs, agitating them in the palm of the hand and reshaping them between finger and thumb. Then rinse. The brushmakers tell me that the liquid brush cleanser used by decorators is a good substitute for soap, and is in no way harmful. Store brushes in a jar with the hairs uppermost, and if they are not to be used for some time, fix their shape with a little petroleum jelly.

When buying your tubes of paint (G), buy a fairly large size—say No. 8, which is about 4 in. long. There are two reasons for this advice; one is that it is much more economical and the other is that it will discourage you from putting out such tiny little mounds of paint that you will be unable to obtain the rich opaque and textured look that your work should have. As the oil painter has to make all his very light colours himself, the tube of white paint should be much larger—say No. 20, which is about 5 in. long and a good deal fatter. Caps of tubes which stubbornly refuse to budge can easily be loosened if held in the flame of a match for a few seconds. Alternatively, apply friction by rubbing them along a taut string. As these caps can easily get lost it is wise to have with you a few spares salvaged from old tubes. Getting a tube home without a top can be a messy operation.

I suggest the following list of colours, which for many years has been my basic palette, and I have added to it only as general experience or some special circumstance has suggested. From it a more than adequate range of colours can be obtained.

Two yellows	—	Cadmium Yellow, Yellow Ochre
Two reds	—	Alizarin Crimson, Cadmium Red
One blue	—	French Ultramarine
One green	—	Viridian
One brown	—	Burnt Umber
One grey	—	Payne's Grey
One white	—	Titanium White

Don't be surprised at the small number of colours as they will be quite ample for all your needs. As you progress you may wish to make certain changes, for colour, quite rightly, is a very personal thing. But do not make changes until you have a good grasp of things, and only then do so for very good reasons. Often one colour can be changed unwisely and the balance of the whole range is upset.

I am often asked about the different kinds of white paint. Zinc White is not much used because its covering power is not very good. Flake White, an old favourite, is a lead-based paint of good opacity, but it is a little sticky and stiff in handling. Titanium White has a fine creamy texture, mixes easily and has great density and covering power. When purchasing your paints you will notice that there are the two qualities—artists' and students'—and until you are working with a high degree of performance in mind, the students' quality will prove quite adequate.

The palette or board (*H*) on which colours are mixed can be bought ready-made, and is of thin close-grained wood—usually mahogany. This can be fairly expensive, and hardboard is equally efficient—particularly if the smooth side is saturated with linseed oil before using. Hardboard is not difficult to cut, but if you cannot manage it yourself, I am sure a handyman will oblige. Remember that the palette is held in the left hand and that the thumb points *outwards*.

The dippers (*I*) can be single or double. I use the double type, keeping turpentine in one container and a mixture of equal proportions of linseed oil and turpentine in the other. Not a great deal is needed at any one sitting: a depth of $\frac{1}{4}$ in. is ample.

Now the painting knife (*J*). This is trowel-shaped, which helps to keep the fingers out of the way. There are various types of blade, but the kind shown, with a blade about two inches long, should be quite suitable. There is another type of knife which has the blade in a direct line with the handle. This is the palette knife, and its purpose is to facilitate mixing, scraping and cleaning.

These, then, complete the basic materials needed for our preliminary work at home. Later, when preparing to work out of doors, a few further items will be suggested. You will notice that I have not recommended a large self-contained box, for I feel that it is better at this stage to build up slowly. It is all too easy to carry a lot of things which will not be used—and oil paints can soon feel very heavy.

Even the most skilled and talented person finds it very much more difficult to work with materials which are of poor quality and therefore so much less responsive to a deft and delicate touch. So please, when you start building your kit do not make do and improvise with all manner of left-overs and hand-outs. Only accept or purchase such things as will do the job properly. Thus armed, your progress as a painter should be relatively free of frustration.

2. *Getting the Feel of Things: Monochrome Painting*

The actual process of putting paint on canvas is deeply satisfying, and gives great pleasure. The equipment itself has a purposeful look whilst the pigments are rich and colourful and cry out to be used. The creamy nature of the paint tells us that it will stay where it is placed, but can then be brushed, mixed and spread at the whim of the artist. All this is true, but there are hidden snags, and many of these desirable qualities can be the very ones which cause muddy colours and general despair. To save you from such despondency, the aim of this chapter is to explain some of the uses of your newly-acquired materials.

We shall go through a few very necessary warming-up exercises to learn about the behaviour and potentialities of oil paints, and we shall also produce a simple monochrome painting similar to the one shown in *Figure 31*. In this way we shall gain a certain facility in the handling of our tools and at the same time discover the most satisfying and satisfactory method of applying the paint. Thus we may hope to avoid the pitfalls and the attendant despondency.

The very first requirement is to be relaxed and comfortable, with all your materials close at hand. It is most frustrating to find that, just as things are going along smoothly, a break has to be made in the rhythm to get an extra tube of paint or find a missing brush. Spread out the newspaper, arrange the table easel, and on it pin a piece of Oil Painting paper about 10 in. × 15 in. Have all the other materials a little to the right.

Take up the palette and clip on the dippers. Place about $\frac{1}{4}$ in. of turpentine in one container and the same amount of a 50–50 mixture of linseed oil and turpentine (hereafter called the medium) in the other. On to the palette, near the edge furthest from you and when holding it, squeeze out a supply of Payne's Grey about 1 in. long. Some distance from this put out two separate piles of Titanium White, making these also about 1 in. in length. Never put the supply of paint near the middle of the palette, as this area should be kept clear for mixing purposes. Now hold the palette in the left hand with the thumb through the hole, so that most of the under side rests on the forearm.

Another very good hint is to cover your thumb with a hood or rag before putting it through the aperture in the palette. This gives a nicely protected thumb with which to wipe and squeeze the brushes if they become overloaded with paint. Between the fingers of the left hand push three No. 6 brushes with the hairs pointing upwards and fanwise (*Figure 32*).

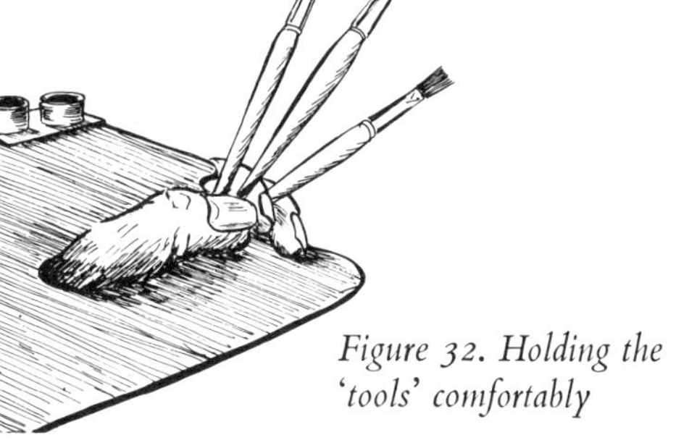

Figure 32. Holding the 'tools' comfortably

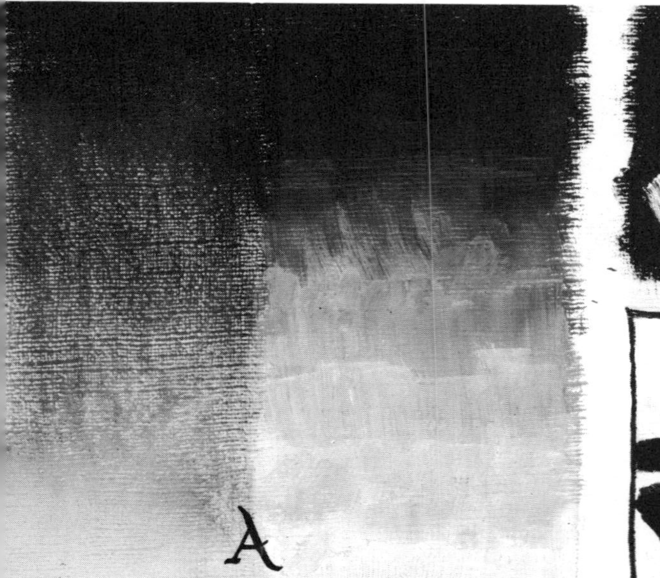

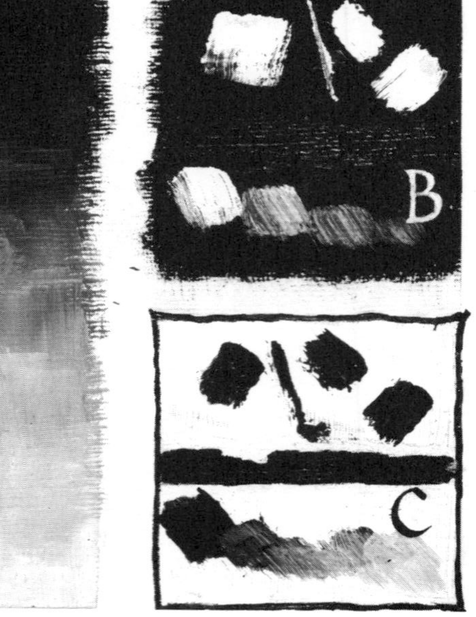

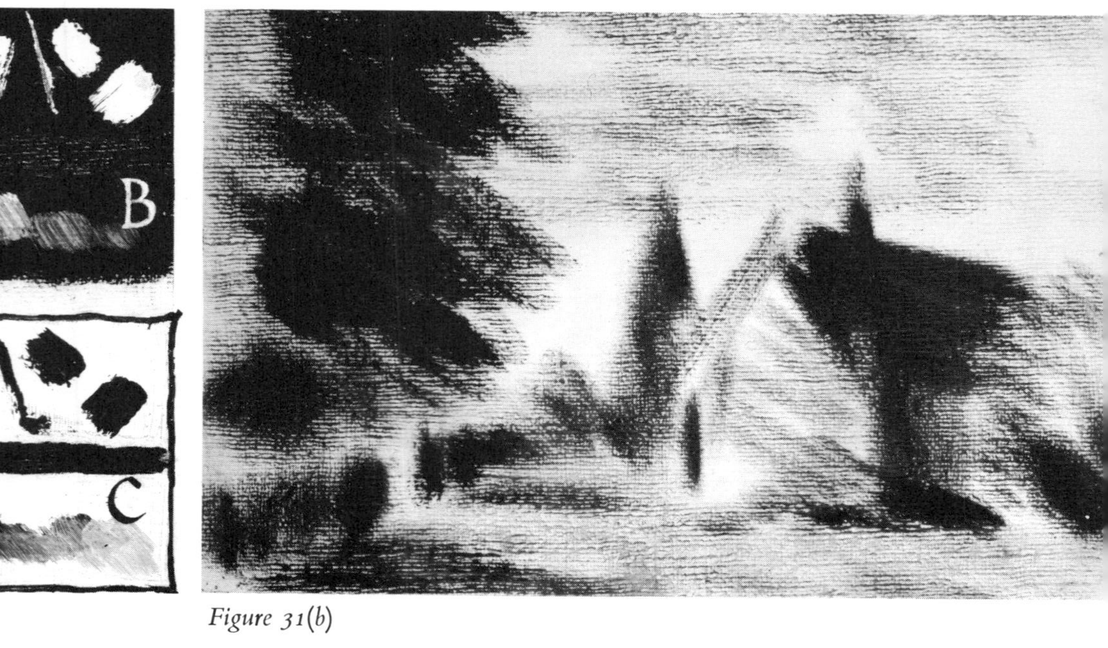

Figure 33

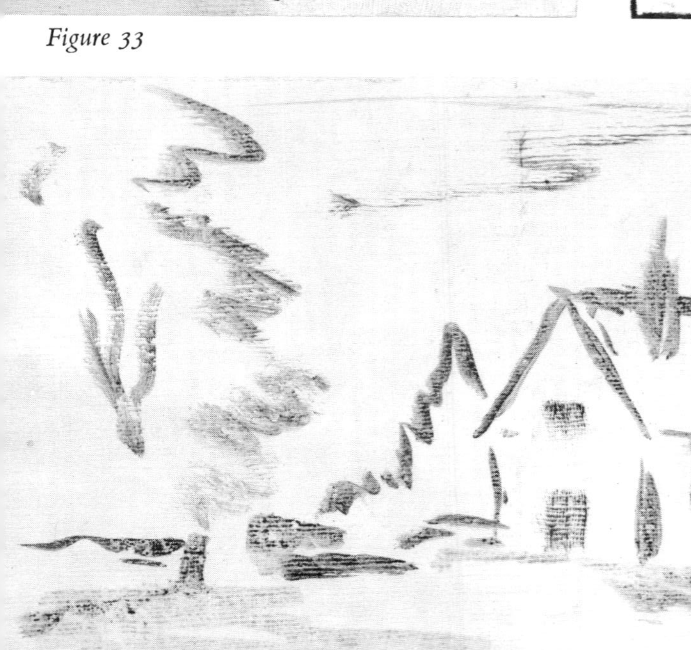

Figure 31(b)

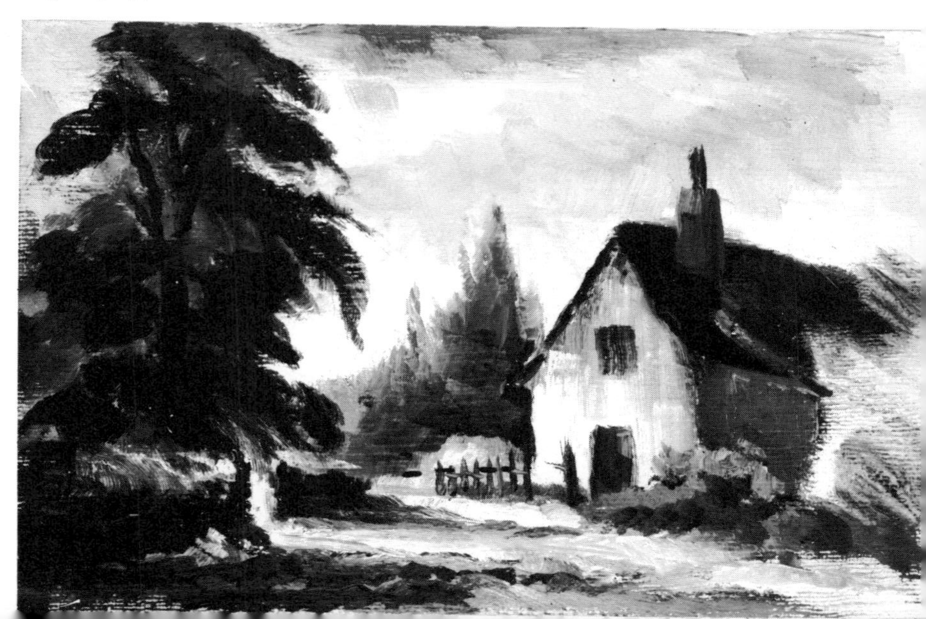

Now take the first brush and hold it near the middle, at the point where it will balance. You will probably find that you are still holding it in a conventional pen-grip, and whilst this is by no means wrong it is not the only way. Try holding it in the same place, but with the thumb on top, almost as if it were a conductor's baton. If you make a few strokes in the air you will soon find that the second grip will give you much more freedom of movement, and it will be most useful for broad strokes.

Rule out on your painting paper areas similar to those shown in *Figure 33*. Our purpose now is to find the difference in appearance and quality between oil paint which is applied thinly and that which is a little thicker and more opaque. Even in the photographic reproduction the right-hand portion of *A* looks much richer than the area on the left, and would be much more desirable in a finished painting.

This ability to paint first thinly and later more thickly is essential for the oil painter, and we are going to practise it. Allocate part of your paper for this purpose and take up a No. 6 brush. Dip it in the medium and *wipe it quite firmly* under your protected left thumb. Then drag down a little Payne's Grey to the centre of the palette and brush the colour this way and that until it looks evenly spread. At this stage only enough colour to stain the brush is needed. Make a stroke across the top of the paper, ensuring that it is in no way fluid or runny. Then, with a scrubbing action, endeavour to make the paper quite dark towards the top and, by lessening the pressure, gradually lighter towards the bottom. This is using the paint exactly as we used the charcoal—producing lighter areas by allowing the paper to show through. Because the paint is so thin and has little medium in it, this first coat will soon be dry to the touch, and in a few minutes we can proceed with the next step, which is to paint over it more thickly and opaquely.

Using the same brush, bring down a small quantity of the Payne's Grey; not too much at a time, for it is wise not to load the brush so that paint gets beyond the metal ferrule. Again spread it in a small area on the palette, and with a shovelling action pick some up and start to cover half the underpainted area. Keep the paint fairly thick so that the brush-marks show a little and the covering quality is dense and opaque. If the paint is too thick to manage, use a *little* of the medium from the dipper, but only if absolutely necessary. I estimate that you will require three or four brushfuls of paint to cover the darkest area at the top. With a fresh brush, mix up a supply of Titanium White. *Wipe the brush*, lift up a little Payne's Grey, and mix it into the white by brushing it gently on the palette until you have a colour which is just a little lighter. Again lift it with a shovelling action and apply it to the area already painted, remembering to paint fairly thickly. With gentle strokes merge together the line where the two repainted areas meet, until it is difficult to say exactly where the join is. Take a little more white and repeat the process, and so on until a little more than halfway down. Remember that brushstrokes can, *and should*, be in many directions. Complete the last part with a clean brush, not forgetting to wipe after each mixing.

The significance of this exercise is that, by painting very thinly first, not only does one know where to make changes in the second coat, but the actual painting surface has been improved, and of course two coats are better than one. In some respects oil painting is rather similar to household painting. In both, the surface must be good and well primed (in our case the paper makers have done this), then comes the undercoat, and finally the finishing paint. The main difference is in the application, as the artist seldom uses the long strokes of the decorator. The reason is simple: the decorator concentrates on retaining a smooth flatness, whilst the artist endeavours to make a flat area recede into many planes, and to help in obtaining this effect he usually paints in short, irregular strokes in all directions.

In *B* can be seen the result of painting an extra stroke on top of paint which is both wet and fairly thick. In the top area the surface was painted quite thickly with black paint. Then, with a well-loaded *clean* brush, a stroke was made with white paint. As you can see, it is quite dense and clean. However, for the next stroke I was most careful to wipe the brush because I had noticed that in making this clear white mark I had lifted a little of the black paint and transferred it to the clean white brush. A firm wipe, and it was clean again and ready for the next stroke—and so on. From this exercise you will learn that in order to paint clean fresh colours on top of paint that is still wet one must always wipe the brush after each application.

In the lower part of *B* the first stroke was made with a clean brush, but subsequent marks were made with the same brush without wiping or taking up any extra paint. Here we can see the gradual blending of one application of paint into another. This is quite useful, for often a certain softening of edges is necessary. The use of this method can give us exactly what is required, and so prevent our work from looking too crisp and cut-out. The blending of shadows, which rarely have a hard edge, is a good example.

The areas in *C* show exactly the same principles in reverse. Practise these techniques, for they are quite important and will avoid confusion later. As we shall see shortly, a painting is made by building up the whole scene *all* the time, and towards the final stages the practice we have had in these little panels will be put to extremely good use. It may not work first time, but have patience and master it, for it really is well worth the effort and you will find your progress will be all the faster.

Assuming you have mastered the practice pieces, now is the time to reproduce a scene in monochrome. We shall use Payne's Grey with Titanium White to lighten it or heighten the tone. White is not considered by artists to be a colour, for the reason that the addition of white to a blue, for example, will not change it from blue to another colour—it will merely make a series of blues, which get gradually lighter. By the same reasoning black is not called a colour. It is merely an agent which will make a colour darker.

The scene which I have used for my monochrome (*Figure 31*) is a little back street in the old part of an Oxfordshire town. It is basically quite a simple arrangement and if we look at it with our artist's eye we shall see it is really an irregular mass of dark, making a pleasing silhouette against the sky, with lighter shapes in it. There are three vertical areas—the gable end, the right-hand bush, and the flash of light through the old stone wall—whilst there are horizontal lighter areas where the lights dance across the lane. With this basic 'story' in the mind we are ready to begin.

First, with very little paint and turps, draw the scene in a linear way, as I have done in (*a*). Be careful to avoid over-drawing at this stage, as all we need to establish is the placing of the various objects. This part can, if preferred, be done with charcoal (not pencil), but it will need fixing before you start to paint. Too much detail at this stage would tend to make us forget that each and every part of the painting is actually a piece of drawing. The difference is that oil painting is the drawing of masses or areas, and therefore too much linear work beforehand can be confusing. So draw just enough lines to help you to place the scene on the paper, and remember it can have *minor* errors which can be corrected to a certain degree as you go along.

The next stage (*b*) is done by making use of the technique of thin scrubbing strokes we learnt in our first practice piece. Remember, only a tiny amount of medium and very little paint is used. If you go a little wrong, wipe out the offending mistake with rag and a little

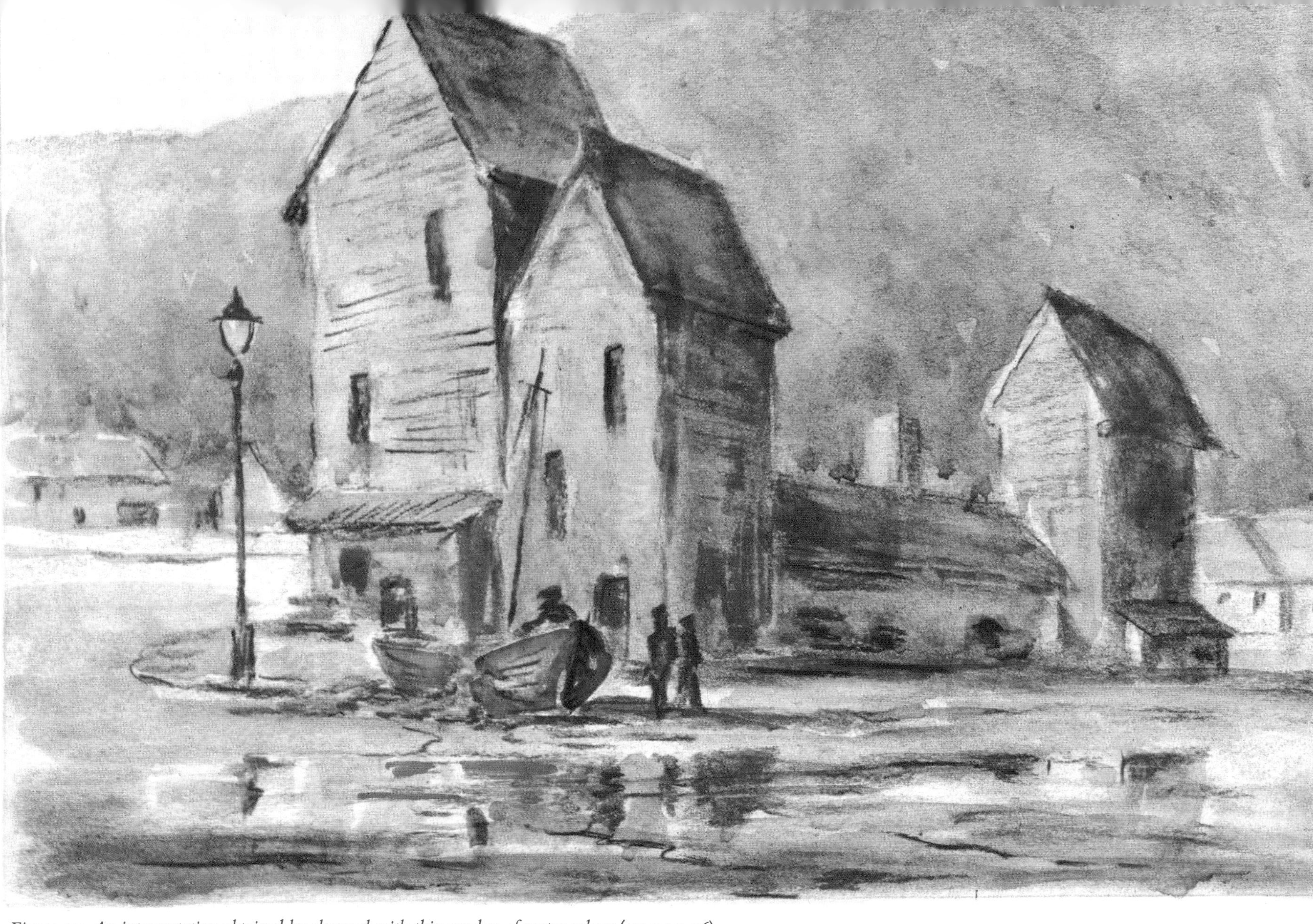

Figure 17. An interpretation obtained by charcoal with thin washes of water colour *(see page 36)*

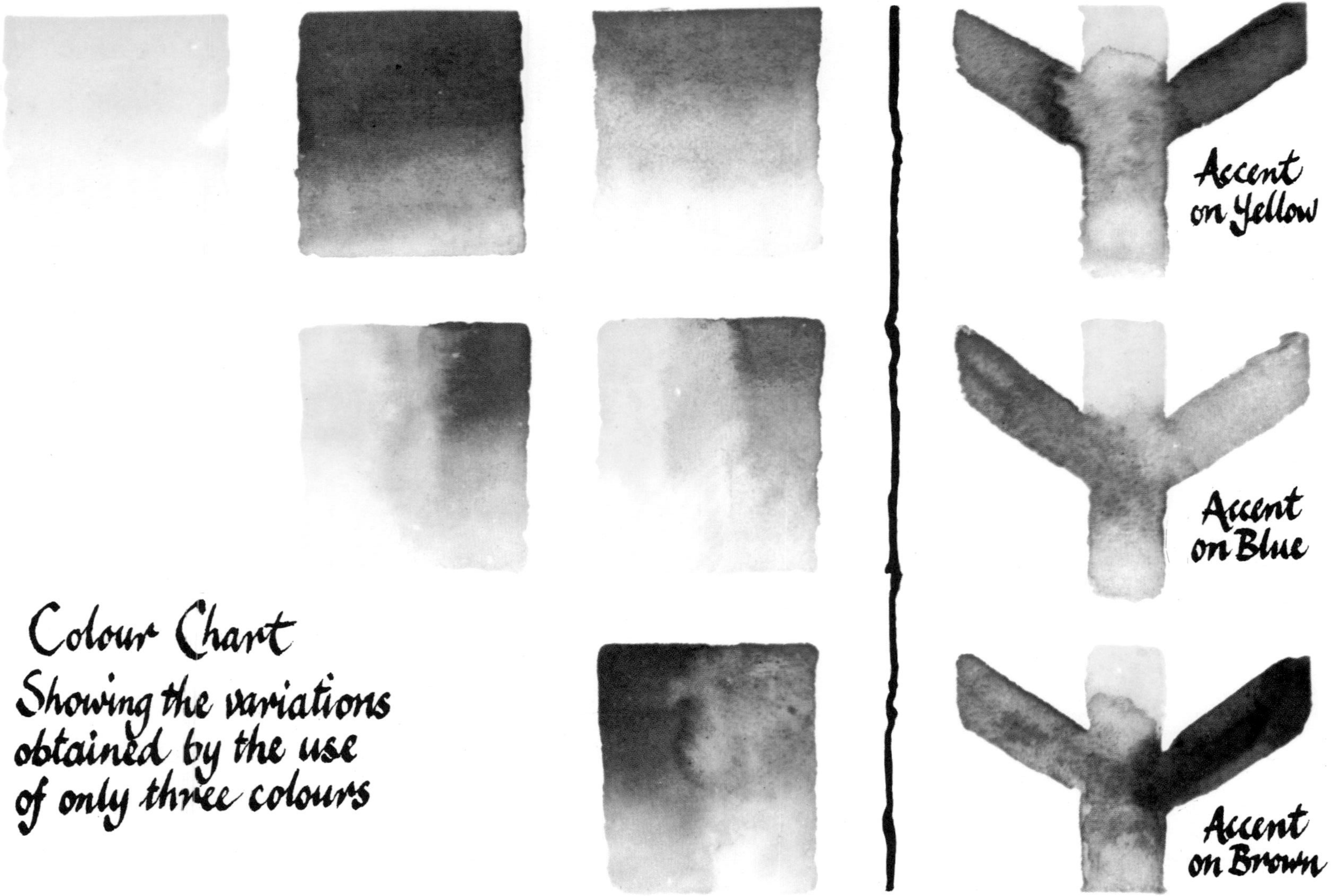

Accent on Yellow

Accent on Blue

Accent on Brown

Colour Chart

Showing the variations obtained by the use of only three colours

Figure 20 (*see page 44*)

STAGE I
Apply the first washes, working from light to dark. Whenever possible, keep the work wet

STAGE II
Keeping the work wet to retain a feeling of foliage, apply the darks. When the work is not quite dry, put in branches and extra darks

THE MEASLE TOUCH
Resist the temptation to suggest separate leaves; it makes the work spotty and unsympathetic to your material

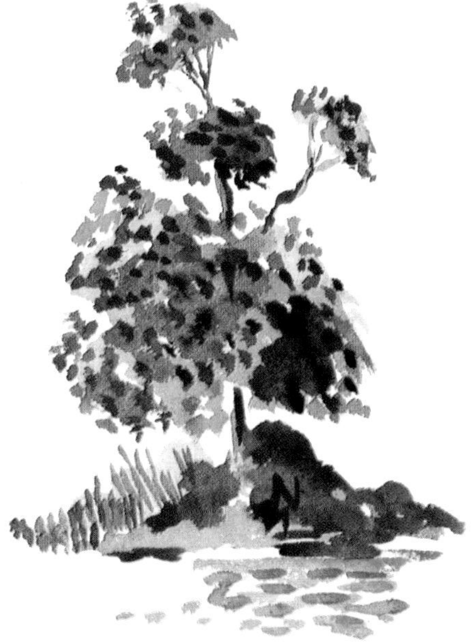

Figure 21 *(see page 44)*

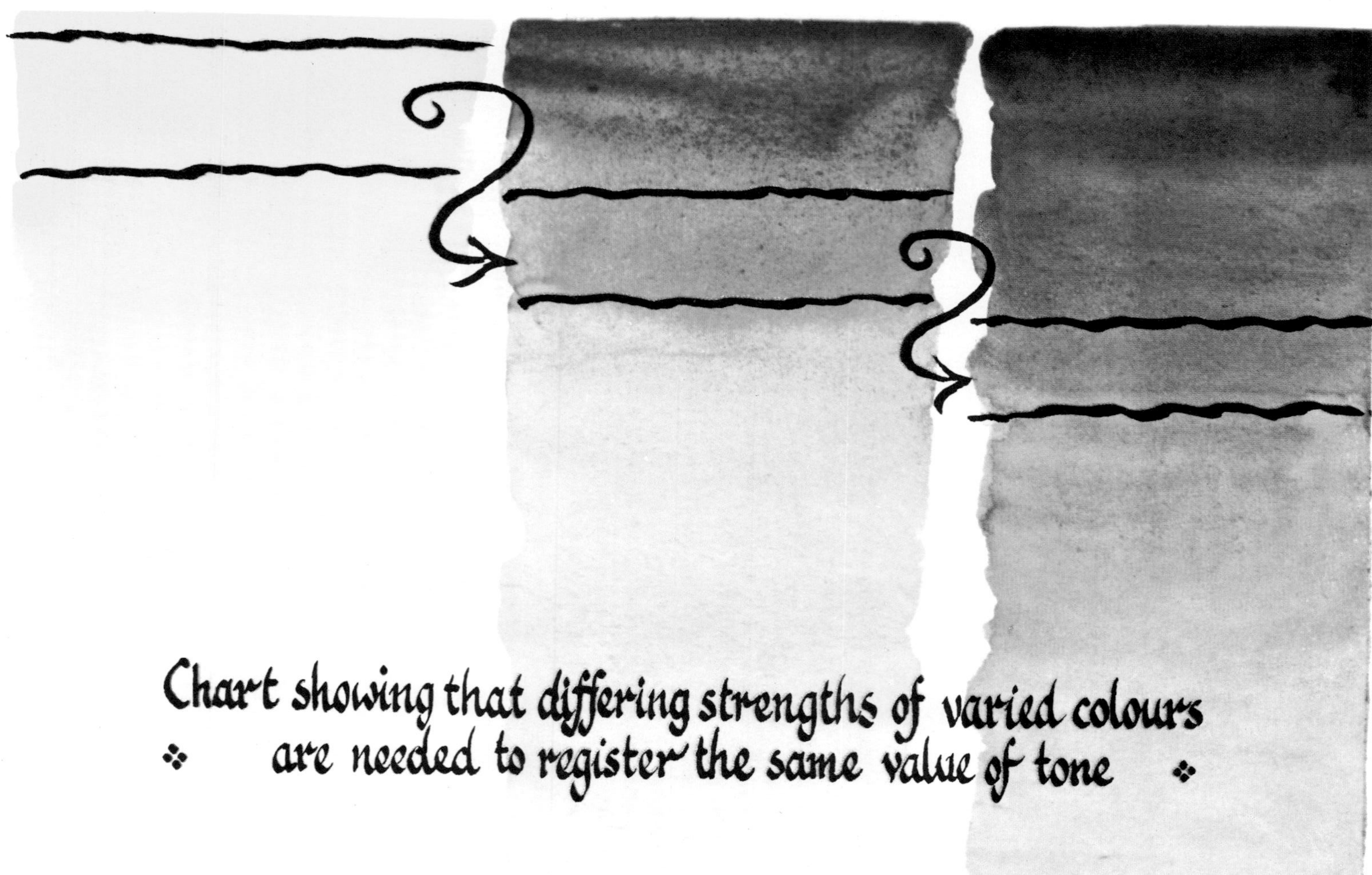

Chart showing that differing strengths of varied colours are needed to register the same value of tone

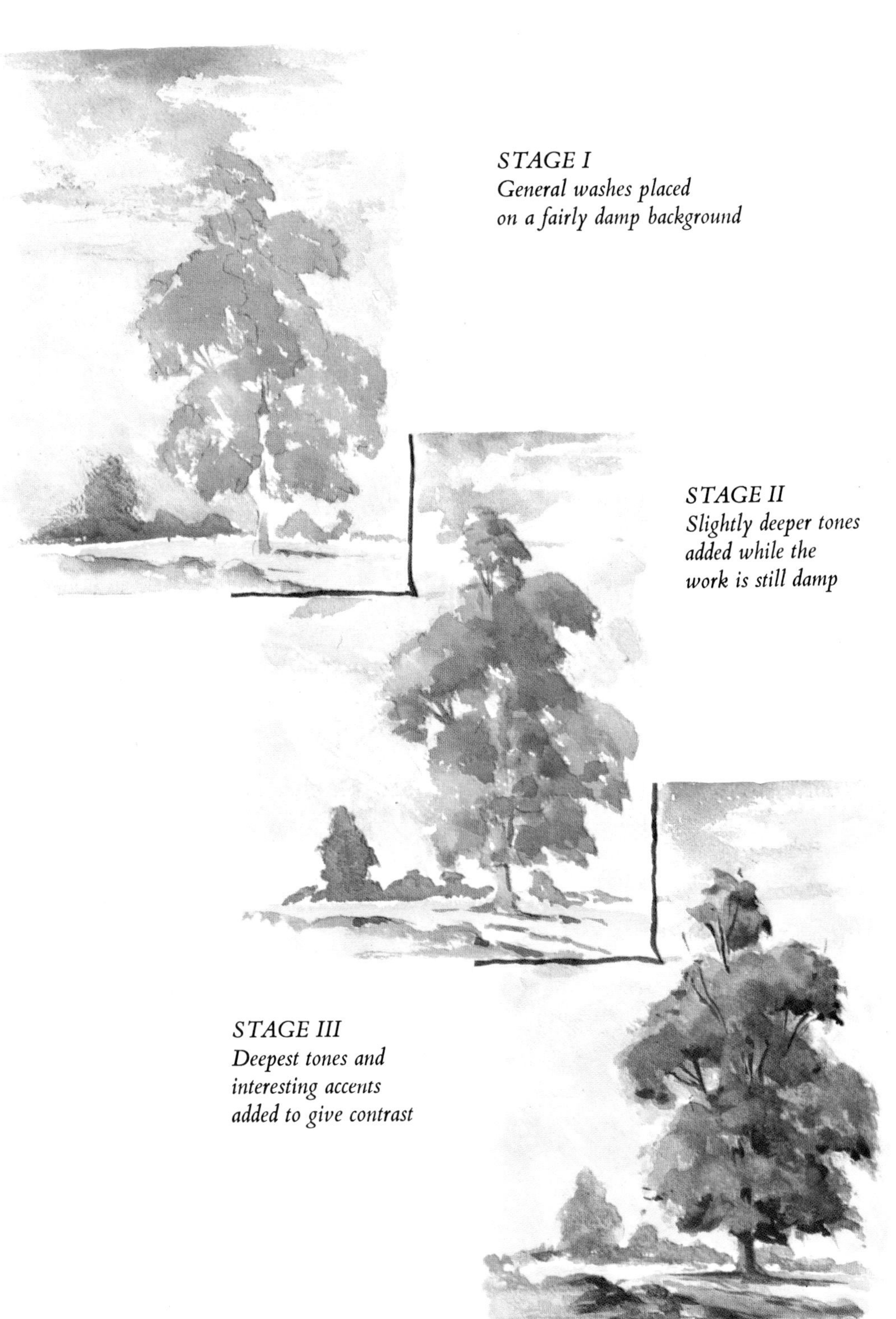

Figure 24. Tree painting: a progressive method which is explained on page 50

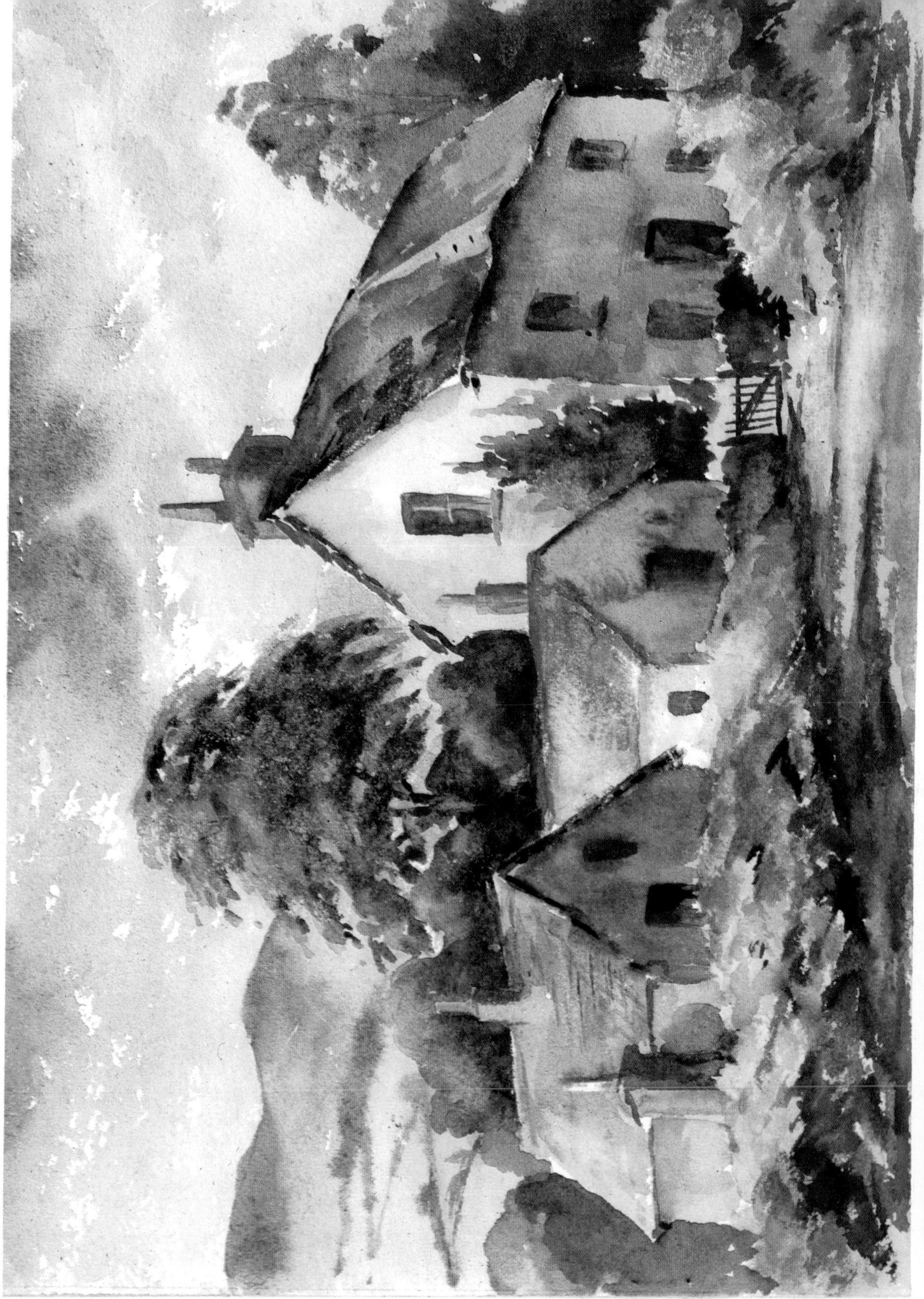

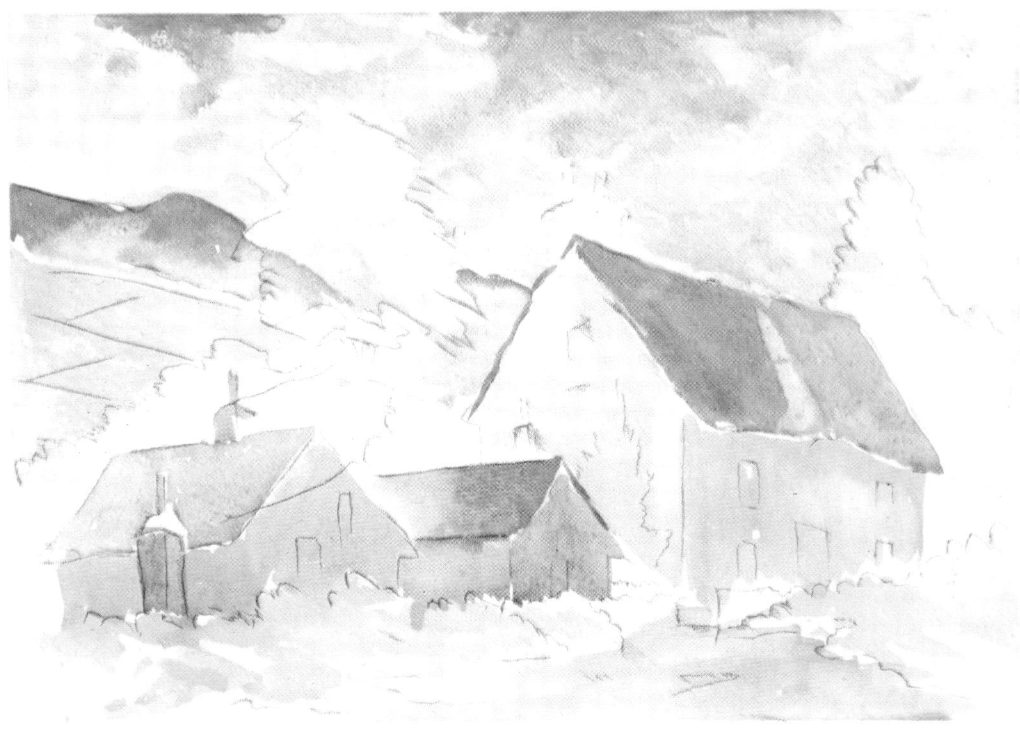

Figure 27. Laying in the washes (see page 54)

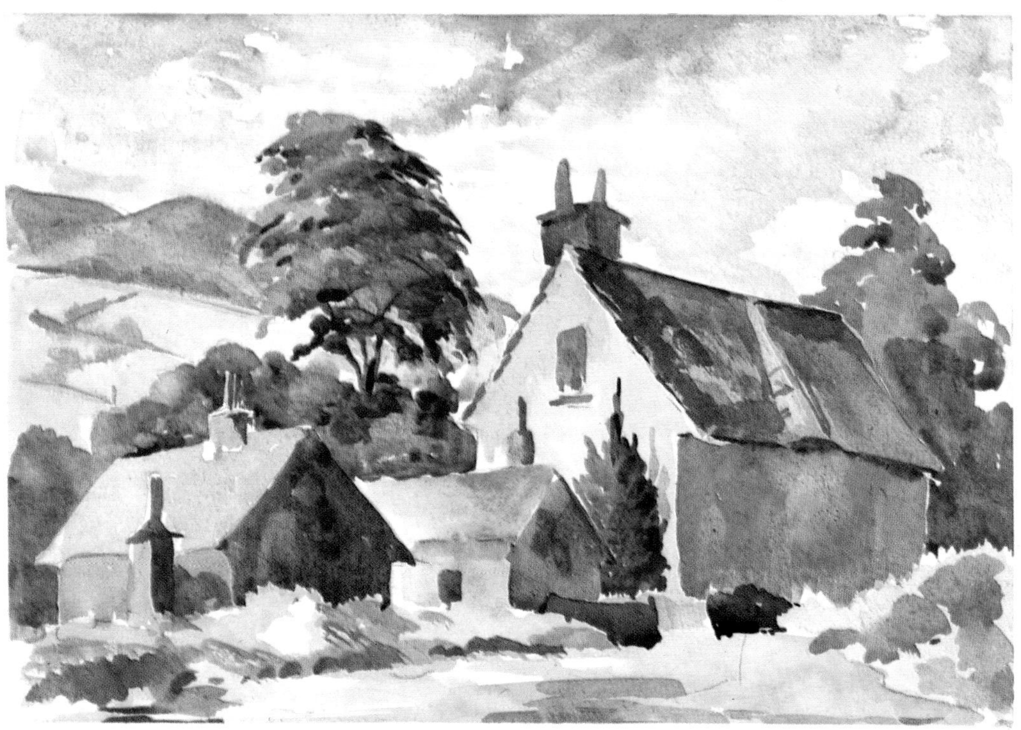

Figure 28. A later stage, when the tree values have been established

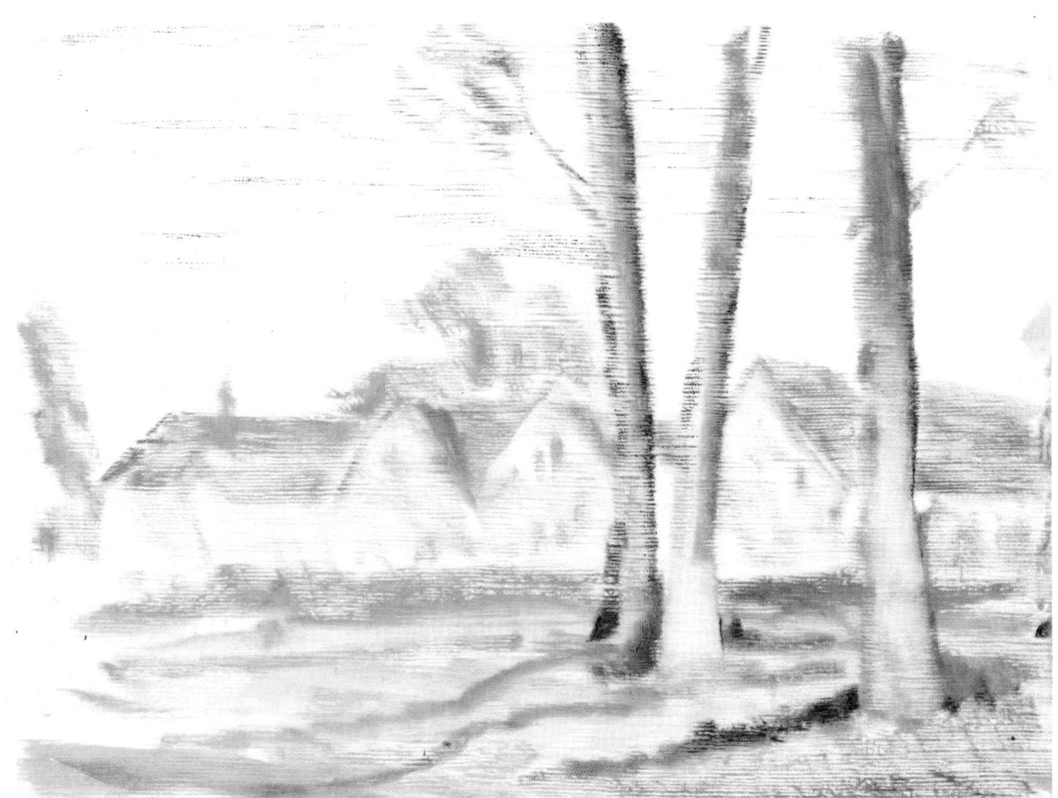

(*a*) *Laying in a scene*

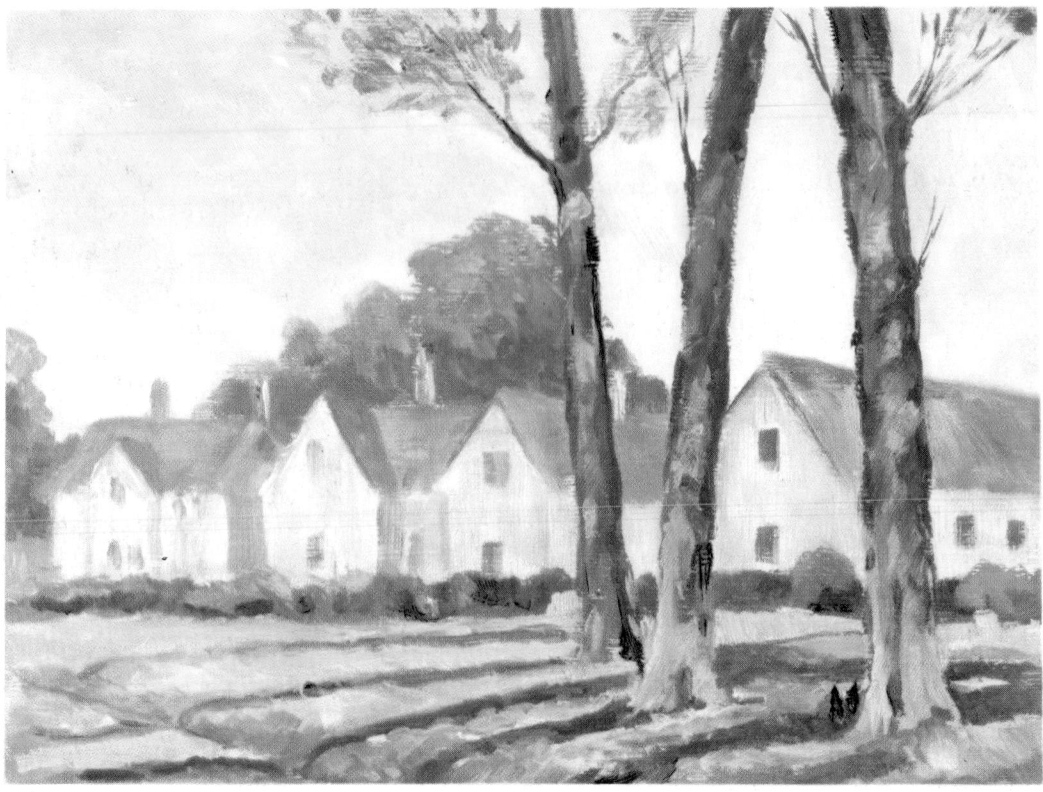

(*b*) *The finished painting*

Figure 36 (*see page 84*)

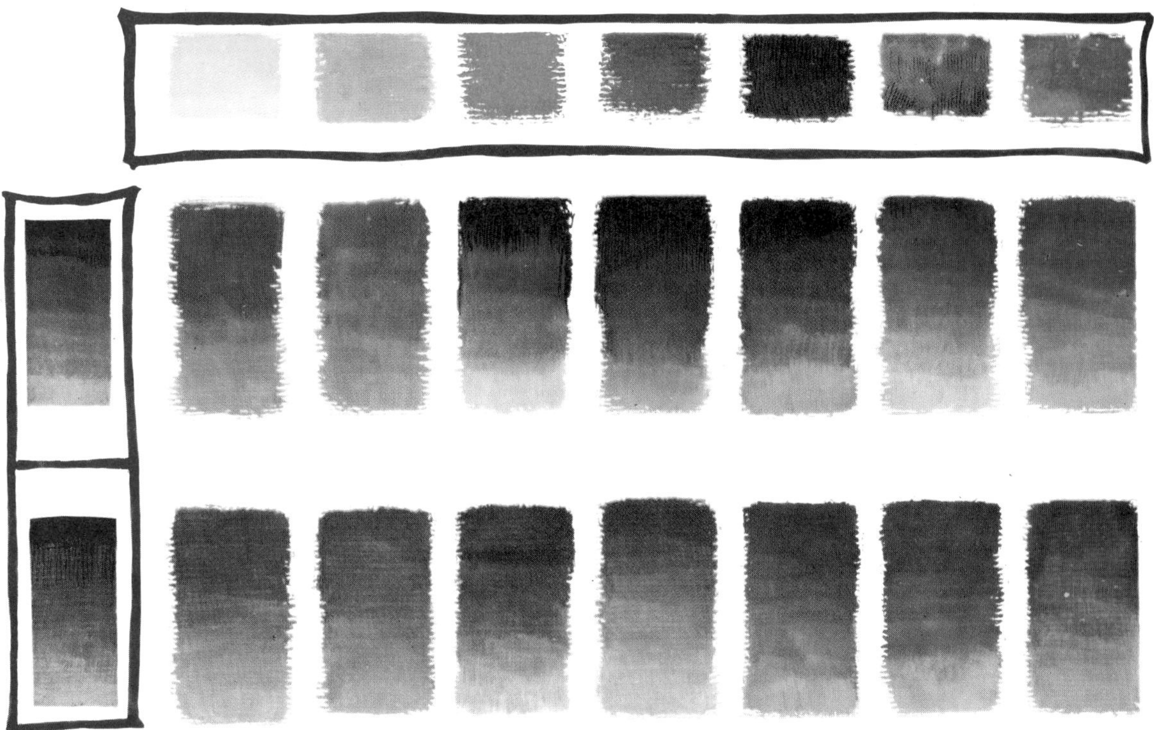

Many subtle greys can be made by mixing the colour on the left with one from the top row

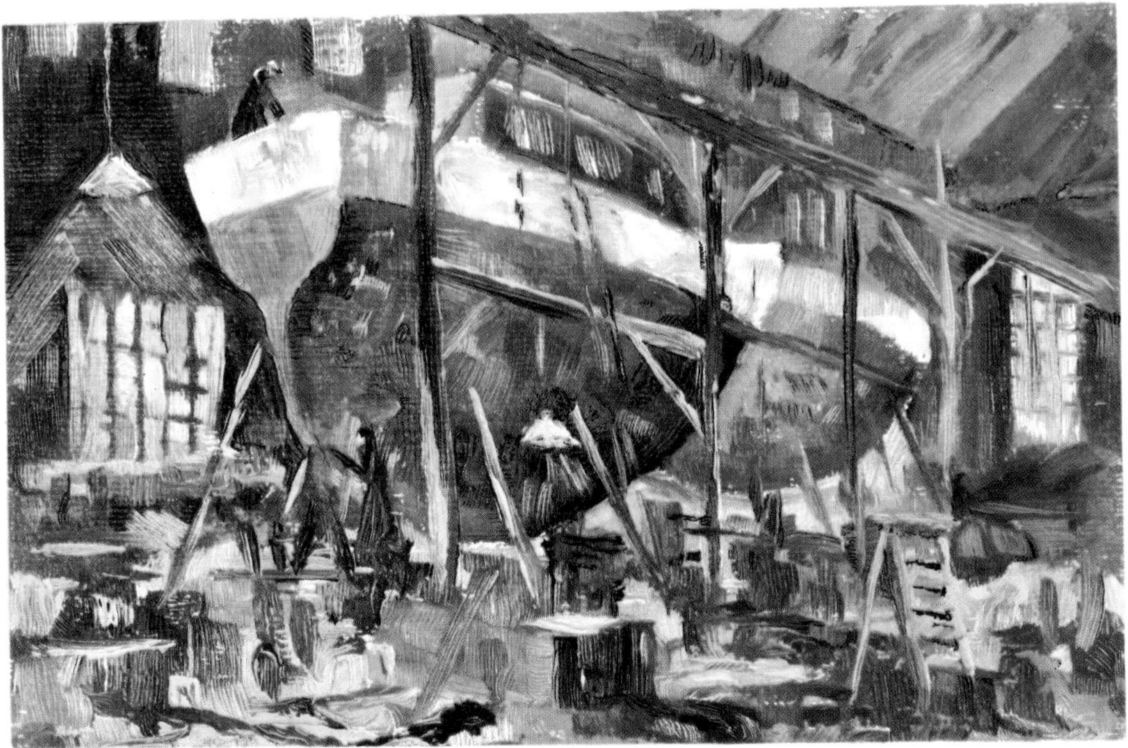

Boat-building—an example of greys used in painting

Figure 38 (*see page 89*)

Figure 39 (*see page 90*). *Experimenting with greens in oils*

Figure 40
A progressing method of tree painting in oils *(see page 91)*

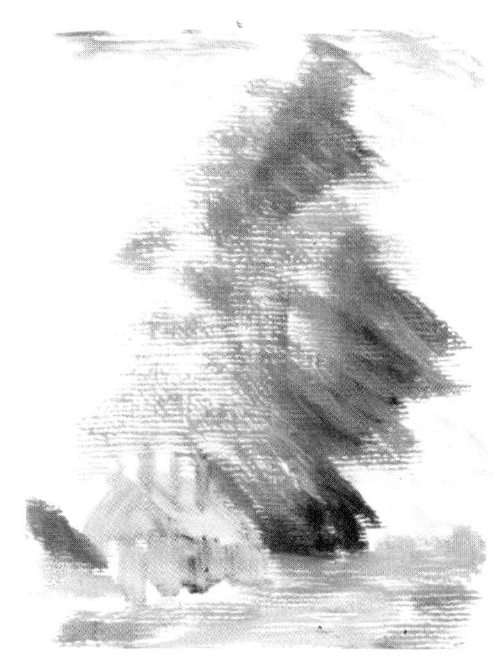

STAGE I
The group is arranged and painted with pigments made quite thin by adding a little medium. No white is used

STAGE II
The darks are established and then the whole area is painted a little more thickly. It has a half-finished look all over

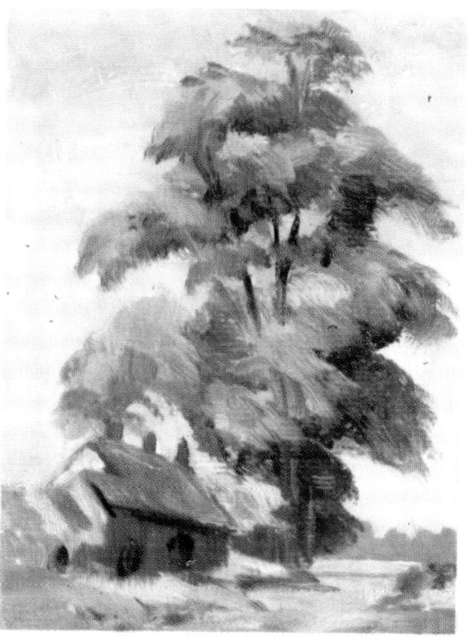

STAGE III
The painting is worked over once more to build up texture and improve the drawing. Finish by putting in any highlights

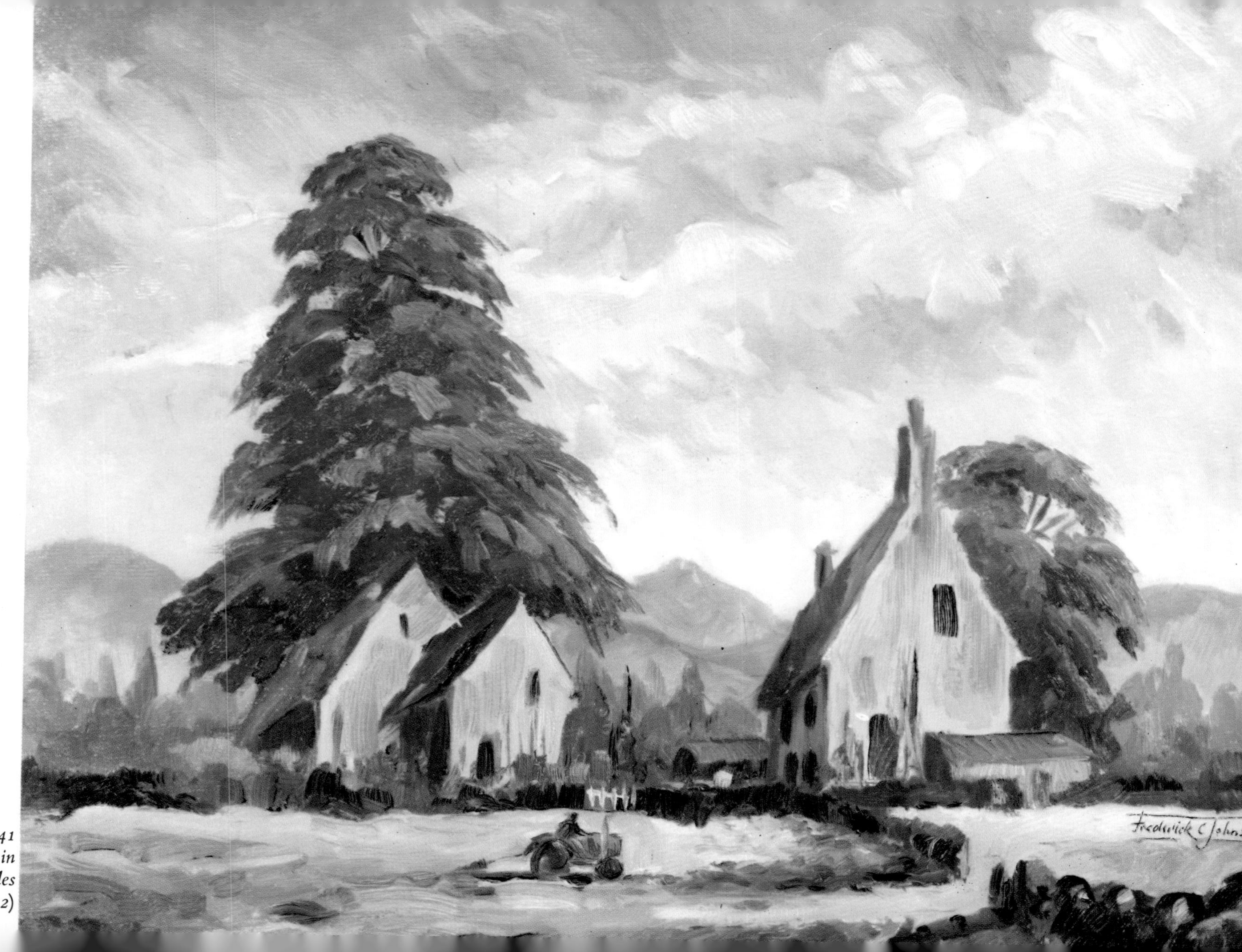

Figure 41
A farm in
North Wales
(see page 92)

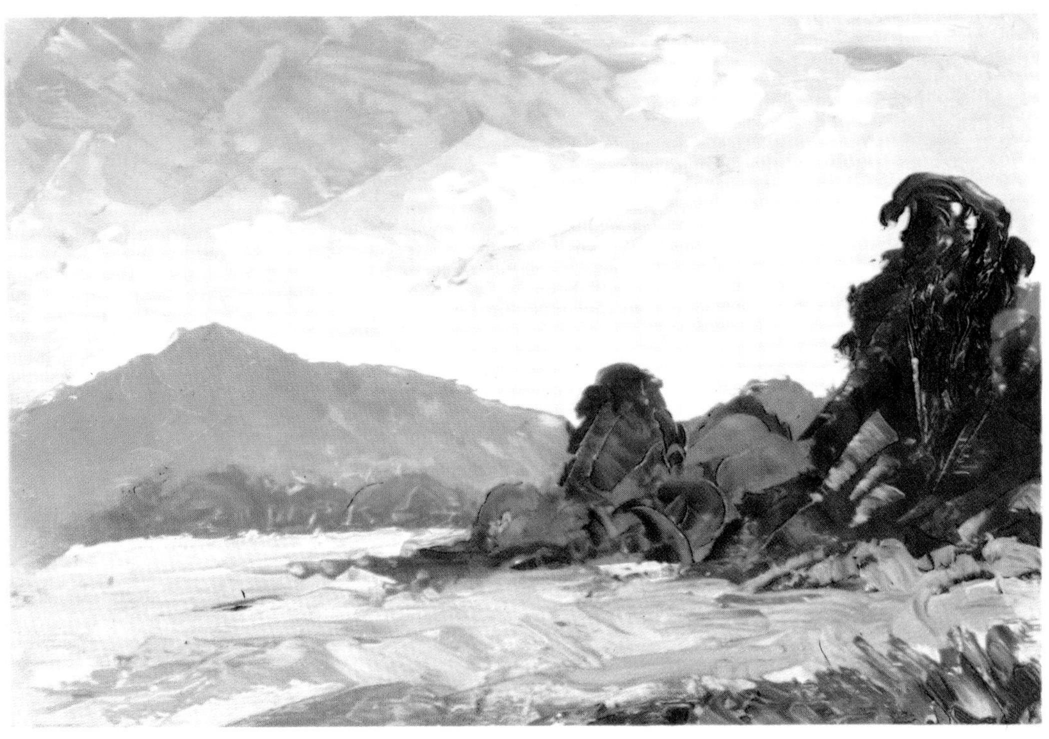

Figure 42. Painting with the palette knife in oils (see page 94)

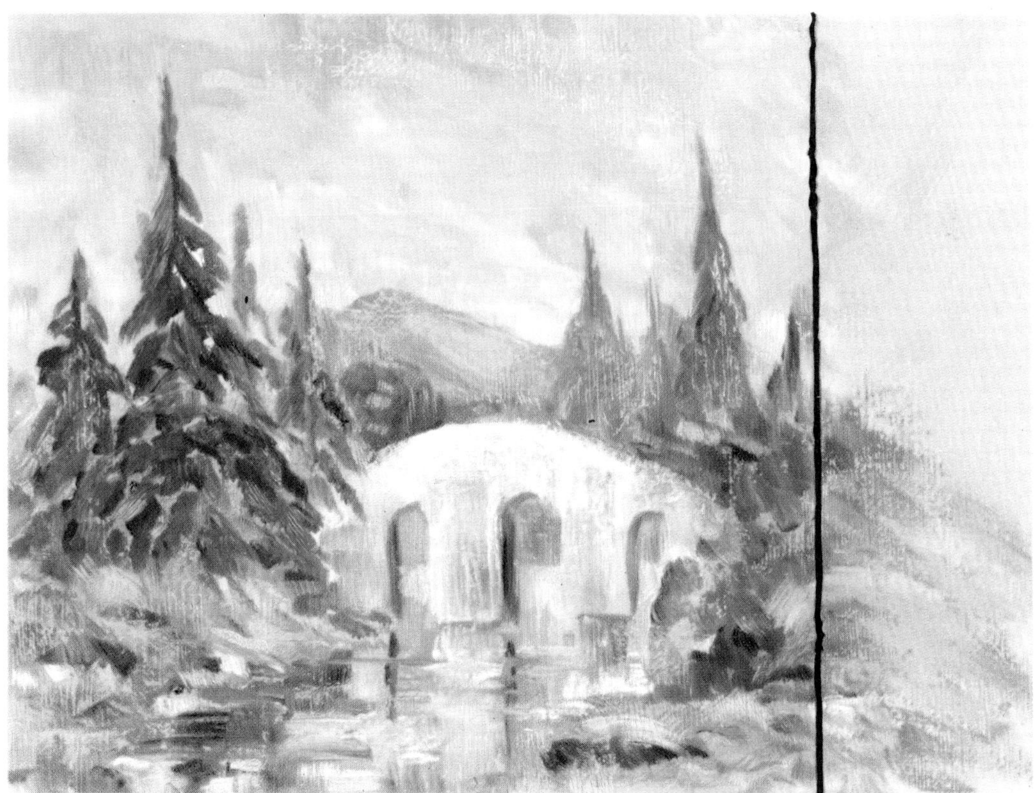

Figure 43. The 'showing-through' method, in which a previously painted background is allowed to show through (see page 95)

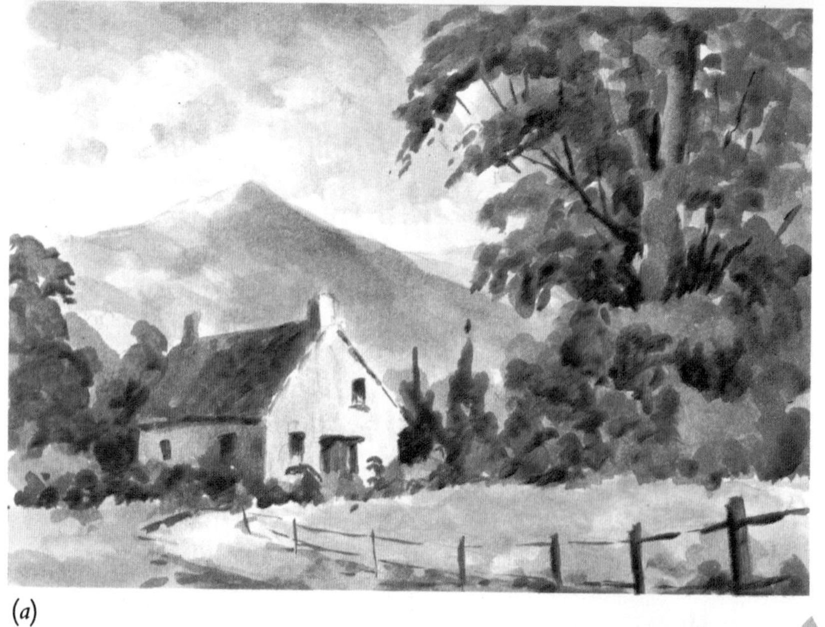

(*a*)

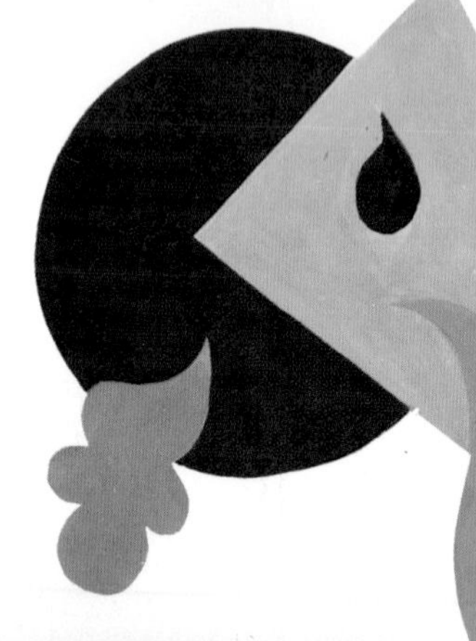

(*b*)

Figure 44. Examples of the versatility of Acrylic paints (see page 99)

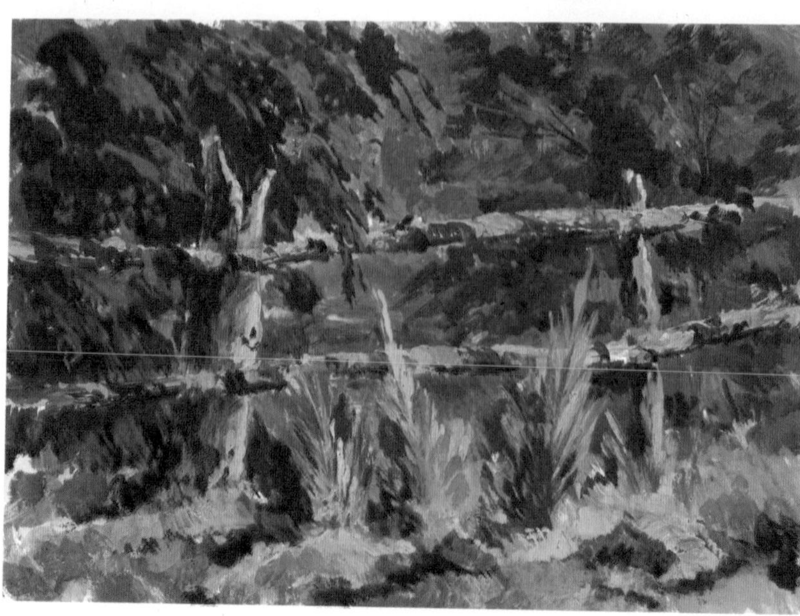

(*c*)

Figure 45. Textual qualities (see page 102) (*a*) (*b*)

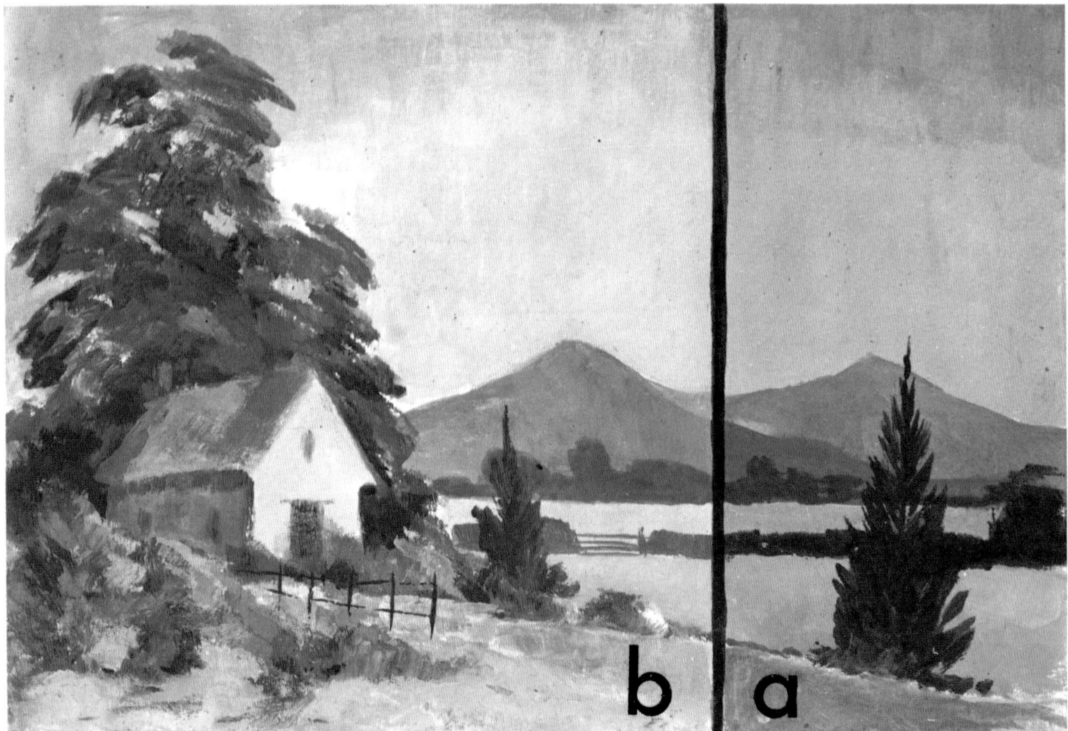

Figure 46. Tonal corrections made by overpainting with thin films of Acrylic colour (see page 104)

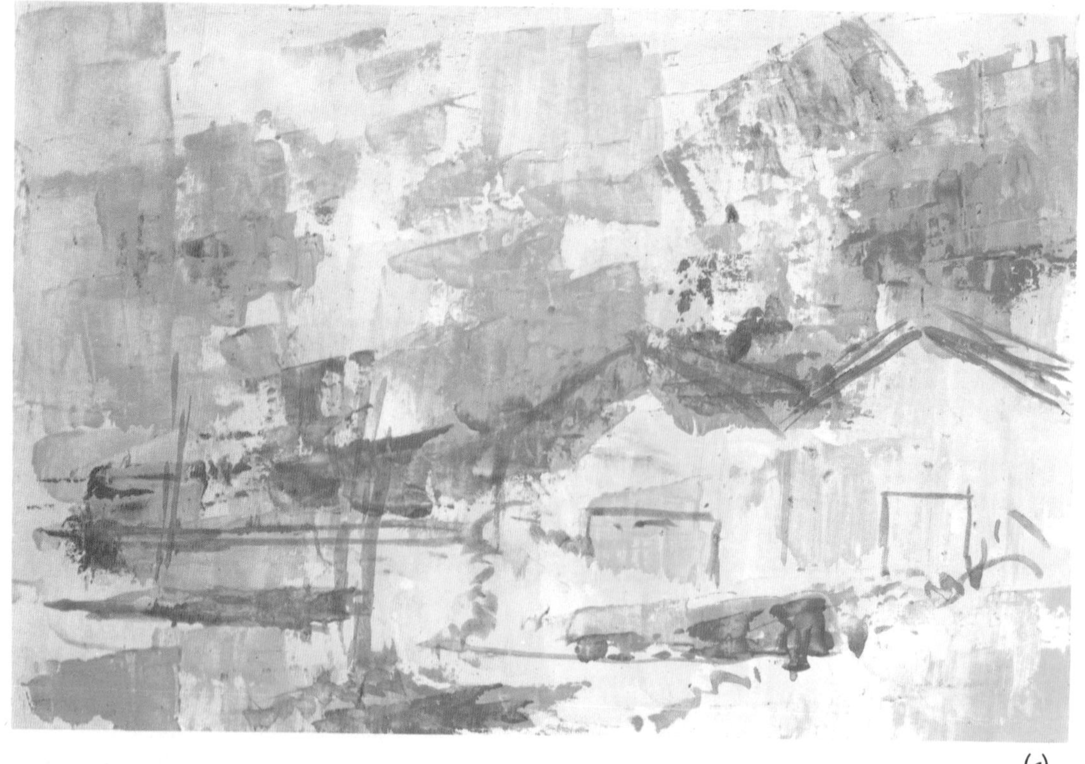

(*a*)

Figure 47. Two styles of knife-painting with Acrylics (see page 105)

(*b*)

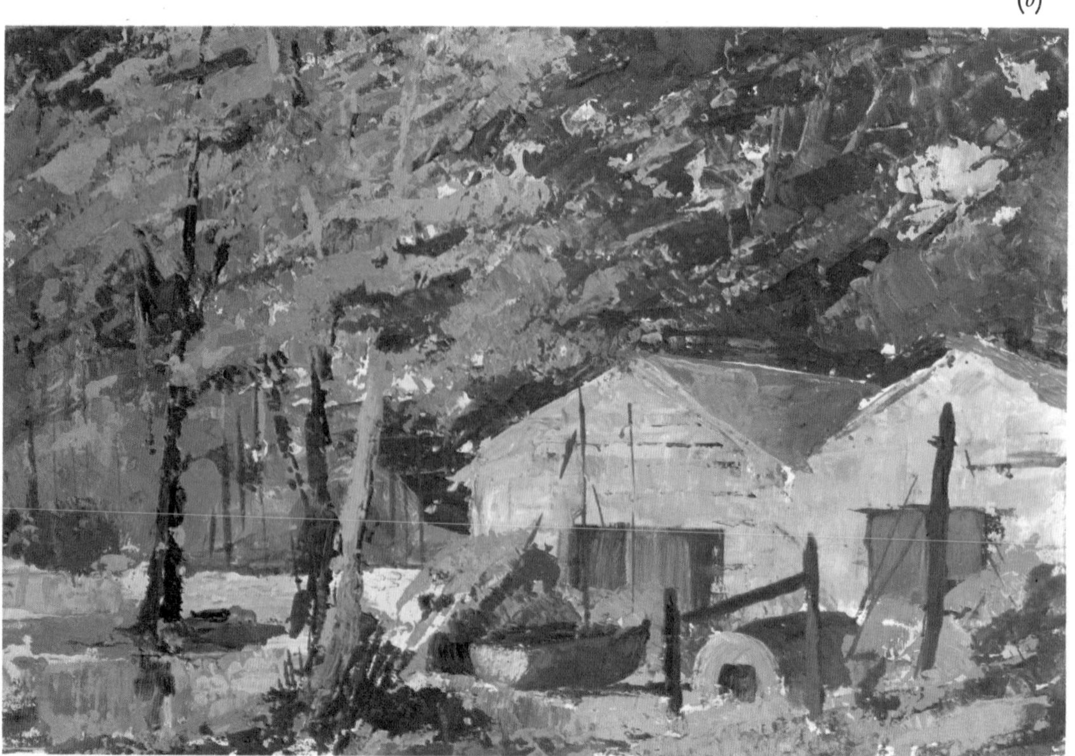

turpentine. Again you will see that at this stage the lightest areas are the white painting paper, and the grey patches are made by letting the paper show through. It is exactly the same method as was used when working with charcoal, except that we are now using thinly applied oil paint. Although the sketch looks very hazy at this stage, take great care, for it is here that we usually capture the spirit of the scene, which very largely dictates how we are to proceed with the next stage.

Having established the picture by the placing of darks and lights, and all the intermittent tones of grey, the final stage is to build up on this with thicker paint so that it becomes richer in quality, at the same time adding emphasis in the more important passages. Thus the whole thing has a better surface texture, a greater luminosity and a richness. Stage (*b*) can be likened to an army blanket, but stage (*c*) becomes a luxurious tapestry.

Comparing it to a tapestry is indeed quite apt, for a good oil painting has short definite strokes which create a texture very similar to this exquisite type of weaving. How do we achieve this result? Merely by working all over the picture in the correct general tones. Make sure the central mixing area of the palette is quite clean, and have three brushes ready, one for the darks, one for the middle tones, and one for the very light areas.

Where one begins matters little, for no attempt is made to finish one piece first. In this case I started with the sky, which was reasonably simple, merely making it a little darker overhead to enhance the dome-like nature of the heavens. I had reasoned also that it would be easier for me to paint the trees and buildings into the sky rather than to dodge in and out of the tracery of the tree in an attempt to put the sky behind the tree. In certain areas I merged the tones, as in the distant belt of trees and in the shadows, and also to a certain degree on the large tree. All the time, by carefully mixing the right tone on the palette, and taking care not to mix up my brushes, I was slowly getting all the picture area covered with a second rich and fairly thick layer of paint. Towards the end I went around the painting once more, enriching any darks which might have got sullied, such as parts of the wall and the trunk and branches of the main tree. The fence and windows were put in very thickly with a clean and constantly wiped brush, followed by the crisp and pure highlights.

I am often told, and I have observed it with my own students, that all goes well until the final round of stage (*c*). Usually the reason is that the brushes and palette are getting dirty and out of control. If this happens, be resolute and stop, no matter how inspired you may feel. Clean the palette. Dip the brushes lightly in the turps and give them a thorough wipe. It is best not to swirl them around; just dip, lift and wipe, and the turpentine will remain clean for further use. However, in case the brushes should get dirty beyond the service of a good wipe, have one or two clean ones ready to serve as reinforcements. It is essential at this point to keep yourself, your equipment and, most important, the work, clean, brisk and sparkling.

Copying my work stroke for stroke is of little value. Use mine to help you to avoid making foolish mistakes in tone, but also allow yourself plenty of scope for expression without destroying the basic qualities of the scene. That is the great joy of painting; it is so personal that ten artists could paint the same scene and although all versions would be similar enough for recognition, each would be quite different and would have about it the individual outlook and expression of the artist.

If you have made a reasonable job of the monochrome you will be anxious to proceed to colour. This is right and proper; but please do not write off monochrome work as something merely for the beginner. A monochrome, with its insistence on correct tonal values, is good discipline; and it allows the artist to produce work of great subtlety.

3. *Out and About with Colour*

Now, for the first time with oils, we are entering into the realm of colour. This is always an exciting experience but it is essential, however, that excitement is tempered with a little caution, for such highly charged sensations can so very easily dispel sensitivity, with the result that colours, instead of bringing an added quality to our work, merely result in something rather crude and garish. In his book, *The Magic Image*, Cecil Beaton states, when writing about photographers who work in colour, that few seem to realize that often the most satisfactory results are from transparencies in which colour is reduced almost to a monochrome. This comment applies just as well to painting, and it is something I insist upon throughout this book—namely that tone is of extreme importance and colour brings additional enjoyment.

Bearing this in mind, it would be wise to try some of the possibilities of a limited range of colours before setting forth. In this way, when you do finally arrive at your chosen site, you will be armed with enough knowledge to proceed smoothly with the real business of painting, rather than spending a frustrating afternoon trying to work out your salvation as the work progresses. Settle down at home and make a small chart showing the various mixtures of three chosen colours. I suggest:

Cadmium Yellow
French Ultramarine
Alizarin Crimson

Using an odd piece of Oil Painting paper, paint the first colour, yellow, and gradually weaken its strength of tone by adding white. Paint fairly thickly but not with so much paint that the brush becomes overloaded and unmanageable. Close by, put down the next colour, blue, in exactly the same manner. Then, with gentle strokes from a constantly wiped brush, merge one patch of colour into the other. You should now have a wide variety of tones and colours, made by mixing the original two at varying strengths. By continuing the sequence and mixing each of the three colours with one of the others, it will soon be found not only that you can quite easily obtain orange, green and violet, but that many subtle variations of these new colours can easily be made, according to the proportions of their ingredients. You will discover also that by working wet paint into wet paint with soft strokes a delightful soft blending can be made. This is a basic technique of painting in oils, and one which can be used quite often when painting passages which must not be over-emphasized.

Theoretically, if red, blue and yellow are mixed together in the right proportions it is possible to make a black, and then, with the addition of white, a grey, which can have a delightful tint of any colour. It is interesting to mix the three colours with a varying bias towards one or another, and it will be seen that some very subtle darks can be produced. Practice of this kind is invaluable. It will ultimately make your progress very much faster, for if written notes are added under the more unusual mixtures, the complete chart will serve as a useful piece of reference to pop in your sketch-bag.

We shall obviously need a few more items of equipment before we set out to make our first landscape painting. The table easel will be of little use, and we shall need a lightweight sketching model. This will be of wood or very light metal, and there are several kinds available. The type I have illustrated in *Figure 34* is quite adequate, and I have had one like it for many years. It is reasonable in price and quite sturdy, but should you prefer something different make sure that it is not too heavy and that it will truly grip the canvas or drawing board. The type on which the board is merely propped is hopeless, even in the gentlest breeze. A blustery day can be disastrous as it is possible for the whole easel to be blown over. Since the unhappy day when I spent long hours picking sand from a wet painting, I have always carried a length of stout string with a hefty metal meat skewer on one end. This I tie to the centre of the easel's tripod, bringing it down tightly to the ground, into which the skewer is thrust. This makes a firm anchor which defies the strongest wind. If the ground is hard I suspend my bag or a brick on the string.

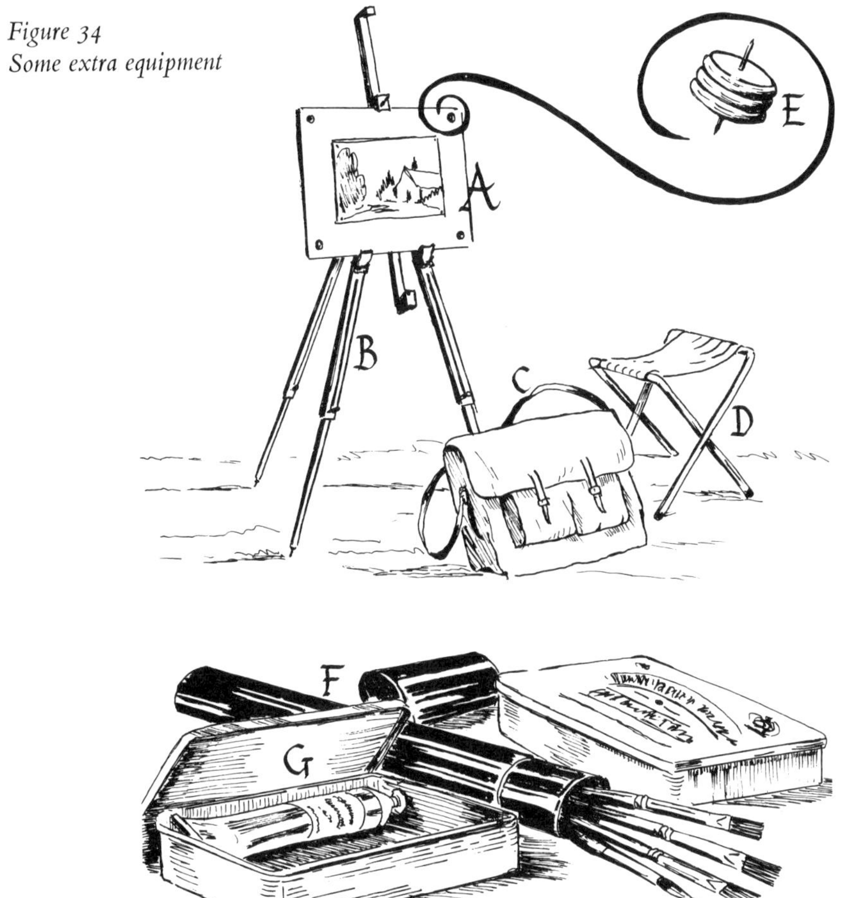

Figure 34
Some extra equipment

A. Thin sheet of plywood; another in satchel
B. Lightweight wooden folding easel
C. Satchel, large enough for drawing board
D. Lightweight metal folding stool
E. Canvas pins, to place between boards when work is wet
F. Metal brush-container
G. Metal boxes to hold tubes of paint

Should one of your favourite pieces of equipment possess bolts and wing nuts, burr the ends of the bolts with a hammer. This will damage the thread and prevent the wing nuts from spinning off, thus sparing you the necessity of combing the countryside on your knees.

If you are working on paper, as I have suggested, a thin sheet of plywood (*A*) serves as a very adequate board on which to mount it. A piece measuring 20 in. × 16 in. is a good size. You will also need a duplicate which can be left in the sketch-bag until the work is finished. It is then that the canvas pins (*E*) come into use. They are placed in the corners between the two boards, keeping a space between them and thus preventing the work from being smudged on the journey home. Of course if you decide to paint on any of the prepared boards which are available, only one sheet of plywood will be needed.

The sketch-bag (*C*) is a great help, as it keeps everything together. It has a shoulder strap for carrying, and straps at the back to hold the easel. My own bag measures 18 in. × 24 in. and has pockets for rags, sweaters, macs, sandwiches and a thermos! All very necessary items, for in order to be relaxed the artist must also be clean, warm, dry and sustained. The stool (*D*) is optional, but if you consider it necessary, as I do, make sure it is of a light alloy and that it will fit into the bag. Always endeavour to carry all your materials together, leaving one hand free to open and close gates and to help when clambering about the awkward places where the good subjects are always found.

A large paint-box can mean carrying a considerable weight, and I find it a much better plan to collect a few robust tins, such as tobacco tins, which take the tubes comfortably, and place a selection of colours in them (*G*). The brush case (*F*) will protect the brushes, and there is room too for the palette knife. Add your viewfinder which proved so useful when making the first introductory charcoal sketches and you are all set to go.

Let us assume that you are all prepared and packed ready for a day's painting and have journeyed to some pleasant spot which you know is rich in paintable subjects. You will probably find that at first you see so many lovely things that you will be completely at a loss as to what to attempt, or how much to include. It is now that your viewfinder comes to the rescue. By holding it a few inches from your eye, you will find that the deep border will mask most of the scene, and through the aperture you will begin to notice delightful little studies. I have carefully avoided the word 'pictures' as this might suggest preconceived ideas of something much too grand and ostentatious.

Having found what we consider to be something worthy of painting, we must next ask ourselves a very important question. It is this: 'With my limited knowledge and experience, could I, with a little luck, manage to paint this?' By all means let us be humble and honest, for if we try to be too clever and ambitious too soon, the result will quickly put us in our place, and we shall go home feeling rather subdued. It is far better to choose something which has a well-defined contrast of light and dark, and has shapes which are not too difficult or complicated. If we do this, and endeavour to capture the essence of this simple scene, we shall produce by our sincerity something very much better than we should by endeavouring to stretch our limited skill too far. Remember that a simple study, well painted, has far more quality than the enormous scene badly done.

If the answer to your question is 'yes', then it is time to set up your easel. At this stage I would advise you not to choose a scene which is merely land and sky, because although this *looks* very simple it actually needs considerable experience. It is far better to choose something which has very definite but simple shapes, with such things as fences, hedges, walls, trees, buildings and hills to simplify the problems of recession. Several things which overlap and create a pattern are easier to paint than a wide open landscape.

As this is our first trip out of doors, I strongly recommend a small preliminary study in monochrome. In this way you will quickly discover all the tonal problems, and you will also ascertain the best procedure to adopt after the initial 'lay-in' with a dry brush. You will also be much better prepared for the larger coloured version. Remember that things in the distance appear a little colder (there is a certain amount of blue in them), whilst similar objects which are nearer have a slightly warmer look (red is included).

A final selection for a subject is shown in *Figure 35*. I chose this little piece because the hedge, the buildings and the shadows had a stronger horizontal movement which contrasted nicely with the vertical lines of the three trees. Moreover it was not too difficult and would therefore allow me freedom to put a pleasant painterly quality into the work.

Figure 36 (*a*) and (*b*) shows how I painted the scene, using the three chosen colours. I am not including the monochrome sketch, as I feel we have already been through this fairly adequately. Having set up my easel, I squeezed out a good supply of paint, making sure that each mound of colour was arranged around the outside edge of the palette from dark to light. In this case blue, red and yellow were supplemented by a larger supply of white. Then, with an almost dry brush and just a little medium, I proceeded to 'lay-in' the scene —only this time with colours which were approximate to those which I wanted in the final painting. You will notice that once again the work resembles a charcoal drawing, except that colour is being used, and that even at this early stage the pattern of lights and darks has been clearly established. From then on it was a matter of mixing and applying the colours until the paint was rich and opaque, and the scene had been satisfyingly expressed.

The colours have first to be *mixed* on the palette, and it is advisable to have the yellowish colours mixed near the yellow, the reddish colours near the red, and so on. If you scatter your mixtures all over the place you can very quickly get into a shocking mess. By keeping some kind of order, you always know where to look on the palette for a previously mixed colour.

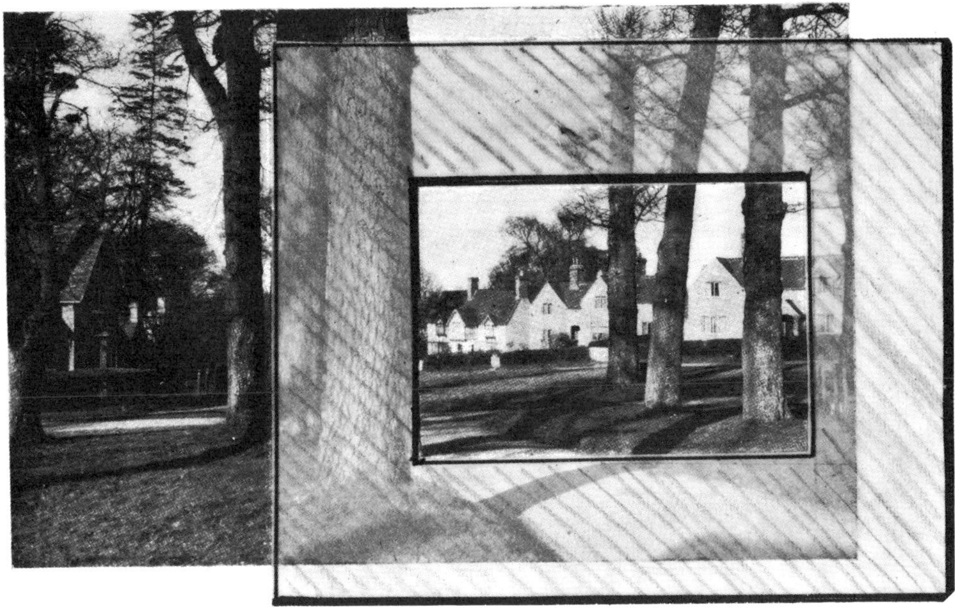

Figure 35

When mixing, drag colours down towards the centre, and mix with the brush. Do this gradually, gently and thoroughly, leaving room for additions and corrections. Always mix completely, as the finished stroke should never be streaky, but thoroughness should not be confused with heavy-handedness. Treat the paint gently, almost lovingly, adding a little of this or that to your mixture until you have what you want. As you are working with a limited palette (only three colours), you will almost certainly find that an exact match of colour cannot always be attained. This should not cause worry, for the main thing in three-colour work is to get the right *tone* in approximately the correct colour. In any case a perfect colour copy is not our aim, for even now little subtle exaggerations and under-statements will make your work delightfully original.

The next stage is to get all round the painting, putting the masses of colour down where they have been indicated by the first lay-in, but making them richer and more opaque, and at the same time getting the tone and colour even more accurate. It is now that use is made of the soft strokes which gently blend the colours, so that the scene has a hazy and ghost-like appearance. In fact a term that is often used is 'ghosting it in'. It is here that the delightful creamy, soft quality of oil paint becomes apparent, and everything seems pleasant and exciting as the scene gradually appears. Now we must take care not to lose this lovely quality by searching for irrelevant and unimportant detail. For example, in my sketch I have made no attempt to put glazing bars in the windows or individual leaves on the trees. Oils are at their best in the painting of *masses*, and it is better to work *with* the material and concentrate on these, rather than try to work against it by making many niggling little strokes.

The final stage is to work a little more thickly still, painting over the edges as before, so that final strokes will ensure a complete coverage with the paint. Which part to do first is best decided by the ease with which it can be done. For example, in my sketch it would be better to leave the finishing touches of the trees till last: it would be much too difficult to paint in a flowing sky afterwards, between the masses of foliage. Any fine lines which are needed can be placed over the wet paint by making the colour slippery by the inclusion of a little medium and by using the brush sideways to give a thin stroke. If you hold the brush from above and merely let its own slight weight do the work, you will find that very pleasing and sensitive fine strokes can be made. Now is the time for a clean-up before the final touches, and then a look round the painting to see where to put any crisp strokes. Last of all, add any real highlights with rich, clean, deftly-applied paint, and the work is finished.

So there you are. You should now be ready for your first painting expedition. Choose your subject carefully, mix the colours gently, and tackle the job thoughtfully, and I am sure you will find both enjoyment and success. And may the weather be kind!

4. *Further Colours to Handle*

It is now suggested that a few extra colours be added to your kit and your immediate response may well be to ask why. This would be quite reasonable for, after what we have discovered already, you might point out that very expressive and successful work can be done with just three colours—so why have more?

Obviously I do not recommend extra colours merely to brighten your work, for to do so might only bring about gaudiness. I do so because a few extra colours can often be very helpful. They save time and worry by allowing you to obtain the more difficult mixtures a little more quickly; they allow a greater facility for the control and variation of the theme and mood of a painting. Lastly, they can give the work an added richness which, if used with discretion, can bring about an even greater unity.

What are these additional colours? There are only four and they have been carefully chosen for their ability to mix well with those I have already suggested and to bring about what is often referred to as a well-balanced colour-palette. They are:

1. Yellow Ochre — A warm and sunny yellow, similar to the colour of French mustard.
2. Cadmium Red — A very pure red, rather the same colour as a pillar-box. It does not contain the traces of purple found in Alizarin Crimson.
3. Burnt Umber — A rather warm dark brown. Not a true 'landscape' colour as it stands, but extremely useful for mixing warm, rich, dark colours.
4. Viridian Green — A powerful blue-green which can hardly ever be used as it comes from the tube, but is a great time-saver when making a wide range of greenish mixtures.

Thus you now have a complete palette which is almost exactly the same as that recommended for water-colour painting, except that when using oils, Titanium White has to be included. The complete range is listed below.

Two yellows	Cadmium Yellow, Yellow Ochre	One blue	French Ultramarine
		One green	Viridian
Two reds	Cadmium Red, Alizarin Crimson	One grey	Payne's Grey
		One white	Titanium White
One brown	Burnt Umber		

Experiment in the blending and mixing of these colours in a cross-reference chart, and from it you can see what happens when any two colours are mixed together, on the principle of the water-colour chart in *Figure 22*. By then adding white to each colour before mixing, to heighten its tone, and then blending the two with soft and gentle brush strokes, a variety of effects can be observed, many of them of great subtlety or excitement. Don't include Payne's Grey, for I intend to deal with this separately. The chart will be an invaluable piece of reference to keep in your sketch-bag, and the making of it will do much to improve your touch and facility of handling. Oil paint needs this delicate touch; sometimes light enough merely to colour the hairs on the back of your hand without actually painting the skin! Make the chart fairly large; about 20 in. × 25 in. would be ideal.

In this exercise the colours are mixed on the actual painting surface, but remember that when painting a picture it is usual to mix the colours on the palette first; after applying them, the brush is used to obtain soft edges and subtle blending, *but the main colours are never mixed on the work*. When the palette is in full use in the orthodox way it is an advantage to have the colours set out in an orderly manner near to its edge, leaving the central area clear for mixing. Keep to the same order and you will always know exactly where to go for the colour you need. As stated earlier, mixtures should always be near to their source and not scattered all over the place. For example a yellowish-green would be mixed near the yellow and red-purple near the red. *Figure 37* explains this. An orderly palette will nearly always mean a more successful painting. I would not advise mixing more than three colours until you are very experienced. Freshness is all important and the use of too many colours can so easily produce rather dirty and unpleasant mixtures. We now come to those all-important greyish mixtures. As I said when discussing water-colours, almost all greys have been influenced, however slightly, by the inclusion of colour. Because of this they help in the creation of the most happy harmonies. Moreover, when the artist uses a strong bright colour, he realizes how much more clearly it will sing if placed within or near one of these delightful neutral areas. It will not have to fight with another colour which is equally bright and demanding. There are, of course, many things which have a natural greyness and to assist in cases like this Payne's Grey has been recommended as a useful colour.

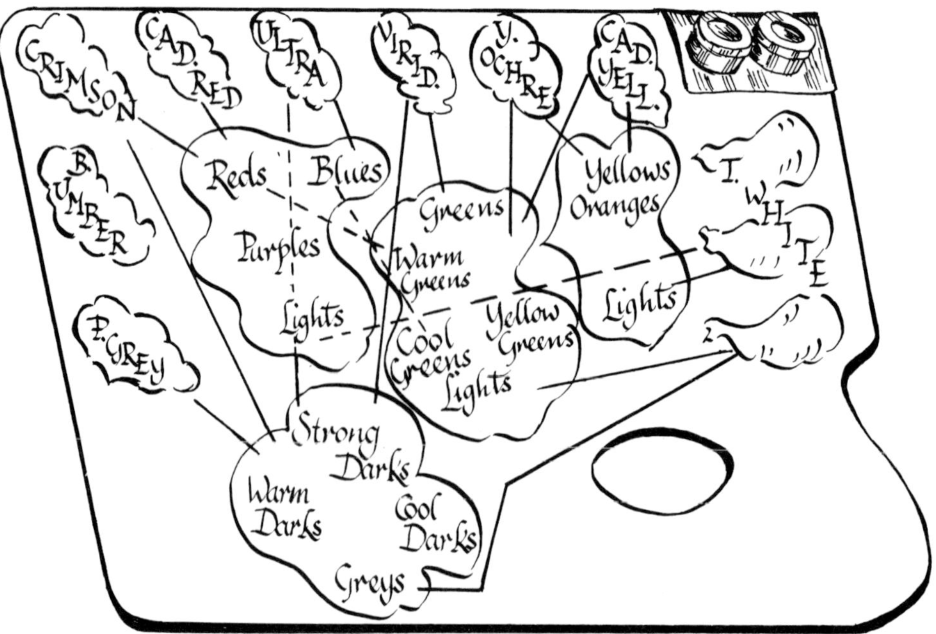

Figure 37. A suggested layout of colours with an orderly arrangement for the central mixing area

An idea of what can be achieved with a little simple mixing is shown in *Figure 38*, page 73. The top row consists of our range of seven colours, whilst on the extreme left is shown first Payne's Grey and, below, a grey made by mixing blue and brown. The first set of mixtures, reading from left to right, is made by taking Payne's Grey and introducing a little of each of the top row of colours in turn. The second row of mixtures follows the same procedure except that the blue-brown grey was used as a base. The two rows of greys, although very similar, are not quite the same. This gives greater variety and scope, but the real advantage of using Payne's Grey is the saving of time. It is most frustrating, when inspiration is running white-hot, to have to mix three colours when the effect could have been gained with two. The making of greys is not all that simple, and the use of a good basic grey makes life a little easier.

The oil sketch below the charts in *Figure 38* shows the interior of an old boat-building yard at Bangor in North Wales. The light was rather diffused, and this gave almost everything the appearance of coloured greyness which we have been discussing. Here you can see the changes within the greys and notice how very telling are the little patches of bright colour when surrounded by large neutral areas. Concentrate on the making and the use of greys. Whether light or dark, they help to unify a painting by their quiet dignity, and they also serve to create happy and telling accents and contrasts. Very many paintings stand or fall by how well the artist has managed to control his use of grey.

Although the aim of this book is to get you out to record the delights of the landscape, I must warn you of the pitfall of only setting out your paints to create 'pictures'. Try to give yourself time to practise mixing colours. Although it is tempting to start painting right away, if you can solve problems quietly at home, it is far better than being brought to a sudden halt in the middle of a piece of work, or even spoiling it completely by trying to overpaint an offending passage. So please keep experimenting and you will gradually come to know all the mixtures and be able to call them to hand almost without thinking.

The effect that the atmosphere has upon colours is important: the slightly blue-grey content of colours will suggest distance and space, and the colours nearer to us should be much warmer. Remember that there is not only a perspective of *size* but also a perspective of *colour*.

5. *The Painting of Trees*

Trees present an enormous range of pattern, shape, texture and colour to the artist. Most would-be artists have a love and sympathy for trees, but when they start painting them they suddenly become confused and frustrated by the vast number of leaves and branches. They also feel that because everything is so dominantly green they will be hard pressed to give the scene any variety. We are really presented with two basic, but quite distinct, problems.

Let us first tackle the problem of how to treat all those masses. At this stage I would suggest nothing more than an exploratory ramble, our intention being to observe the trees in very simple terms, but bearing in mind our special problems as artists. The need for preparatory sketches has already been stressed, but even before these are done it is essential to assess things quietly and thoughtfully. Look for the complete shape of the tree(s), trying hard to think of it or them as a solid mass—not as countless leaves, nor as an outline, more as a silhouette. It is then not too difficult to take note of the smaller masses which break up this silhouette. Do not strain, just look for the large main clumps which enfold the trunk. The final, and very important thing to observe, is that each of these smaller clusters receives a certain amount of light and shade, and that each can cast its own shadow.

This method of looking is recommended for most kinds of painting and the illustration in *Figure 23*, page 51, will help to explain this. When working in oils it is even more essential to paint in these rather broad masses.

Very similar principles of observation are needed for other types of foliage. When dealing with grass, adopt the same method; establish the main area, then separate it into shapes made by the more dominant clumps.

We now come to the second problem; that of the vast variety of greens to be found in any landscape. I suggest we solve the problem in the same way as when handling other colours, by making a chart to show some of the countless variations that can be made from using just one basic green. My own such chart is shown in *Figure 39*, page 74.

Take about half a sheet of Oil Painting paper and in the first two vertical columns show the kind of green that can be made by mixing Viridian with each of our other six colours in turn (excluding Payne's Grey). Thus we have the six new greens shown in column 2. Take care at this stage to ensure that the colour you have mixed is still a green, and that you have not made it change into a brown, for example. At the bottom make a row of the six other colours. Then introduce into each of these two-colour mixtures a colour taken from the bottom line. Again make sure that the resulting mixture still has a definite greenness about it, and add a little white towards the bottom so that you can see what happens when the colour is heightened in tone. By reading the chart as a cross-reference sheet you will not only find the greens that can be made from mixing two colours, but will immediately see the effect of introducing a third.

While on our ramble we would have been aware of many greens. Some were warm, others cold; some veered towards a sandy colour, others had distinct traces of brown or even purple. The elm is a good example for its greens can vary from a distinct Ochre-and-brown-green to one which has a high content of purple. With your chart to hand, all these greens and many more, are at your call. What is more, in one short session, you have conquered problems that still bother many quite experienced painters.

And now the usual plea to avoid the trap of merely *reading* about colour mixing. Please roll up your sleeves and actually *make* such a chart—there is no substitute for experience. It is not easy, but it is far better to have several tries at home first.

We are now well-armed with a knowledge of how to look at trees and also how to make many of the greens which we are liable to encounter. Obviously the next thing to do is to find a nice satisfying tree study which will enable us to put our knowledge to the test. Avoid a vast panoramic view, choose a compact cluster of trees, or even one single tree whose shape and form are of interest. In *Figure 40*, page 75, you will see such a specimen, and I have shown the three stages of painting as a direct follow-on from the three stages of looking.

The first step, as shown in Stage I, was to cover the painting surface with paint made quite thin by the addition of a *little* turps and to establish the general shape of things. No attempt was made to complete anything, for the object here was merely to cover the area and to give a rough idea of how the *whole* thing would look. Ultramarine was used for the sky, and the greens were mainly a mixture of Viridian and Yellow Ochre, with browns and blues added for the darker areas. The whole thing was painted thinly, without using white. Light areas were suggested by allowing the painting surface to show through.

Stage II shows the work painted a little more thickly. The darks have been established more clearly and some of the lighter areas put in by mixing them with white. For example the sky, although not yet completed, has now received sufficient paint to throw the tree forward, and also to allow the tree to be painted into it a little later. Notice the little dabs of colour within the tree which will later become the 'sky-holes'. At this stage attempts were made to improve colour and tonal qualities which will achieve an effect of modelling. This can be seen in the various masses of foliage and on the grass verges. Notice the introduction of cool greens and warmer greens.

The final stage is really a continuation of the process. The paint is a little thicker, but not so thick as to be unmanageable; the tone and colour are improved and by the use of careful brush-strokes the drawing is made more accurate. All the time one looks around the picture to see if any passage strikes a false note. In my case I first worked on the sky; then, taking some of the darkest greens, I 'drew' the tree. The cottages received more paint and the distant grey-green trees were improved. Then I proceeded around the painting with the middle tones, modelling and correcting. Finally any crisp lights, such as the sunlit field and the bend in the road, were painted with clean light colours. The finished effect should not be detailed and photographic, but should have an opaqueness and a surface texture which will help to give the work an appearance which has both life and atmosphere.

Such is the method I normally adopt, for at all times one can see how the painting is gradually progressing. It is most disappointing to spend a long time finishing one part, which looks grand when seen on its own, but obviously does not fit when the rest of the scene is completed. The main thing to remember is that each part should look as if it belongs to the others; the scene must have unity. There are other approaches, some of which I will explain later, but in most of them use is made of this principle of building up gradually, and all of them allow a tremendous scope for personal interpretation.

Paintings can be varnished when dry, but remember that a fairly thick painting is still wet beneath the surface for about six months. A temporary treatment is to use Retouching Varnish when the work is touch-dry. Clear Picture Varnish can then be used when the six months' wait has expired. Alternatively a pleasant matt finish can be obtained with wax polishes specially made for the purpose and simple to use.

6. *An Artist at Work*

You are invited, in this chapter, to accompany me in your imagination and look over my shoulder as I work. My intention is to 'build up' an oil painting gradually, and perhaps as I do so your questions will be anticipated and your problems solved. By such a demonstration I hope to display and explain some of the technique and skills of both seeing and doing, and also show how they are made to work together to produce a result of harmony and unity. One skill is not seeking priority over another; all things work happily together in an attempt to capture the *spirit* of the scene, which is so very important in the painting of a landscape. One false note, and the feeling of being out in the air where skies move, the wind ruffles and the shadows vary, will be lost, and the scene will suddenly become static and dead.

The scene I have chosen is in the Snowdonia area of North Wales. It is reproduced in *Figure 41* (page 76). I motored off one summer morning with a pleasant feeling that happy things were in store. Suddenly in the distance I saw a little cluster of colour, standing on high ground, which later proved to be this farmstead. There it sat before a beautiful mountain backcloth. I settled down to paint.

The only alteration I made, as far as I can remember, was to place the two groups of buildings a little closer together, because their true positions made too large a gap in the centre of the picture. It is not suggested that we should always be making vast alterations, but occasionally little changes can make a great improvement in the composition.

My first task was to settle down comfortably and quietly review the scene, composing and painting in my mind. I noticed the distance between the buildings and decided to lessen it. As the weather was a little changeable, I watched for an interesting pattern in the sky and remembered it, at the same time making a quick mental note of the shadows and observing how such a sudden effect fitted in with the general tones and colour of the whole scene. This is important, for although the landscape artist always has his subject before him for general reference, he must be aware that the mood of the day is constantly changing and he must rely very much on his memory. Without it he will, as an exaggerated example, have morning sun in one part of the picture and afternoon rain in the other.

Having made my observations, which took half an hour or more, I started to paint. I used an O.P.P. board (Oil Painting paper mounted on stout card), and very lightly sketched the outlines of the main masses. This was done with charcoal, which was later flicked with a rag to make it very faint. It could also have been done with paint made very thin with turpentine, using perhaps a very weak blue. I next started work on the masses by applying colour thinned with a little medium. This was done rather sketchily, as I was still feeling my way. No white was used at this stage; the lighter areas were obtained by working with a very meagre film of colour, rather like the technique of the water-colourist. Colours were indicated, but at this stage they were only suggestions, as I was much more intent on getting true tones rather than absolute accuracy of colour. In other words, even at this early stage the darks, lights and medium tones had to be established. Mistakes at this stage can be corrected by wiping the offending area with a well-turpentined rag. As I proceeded I took care to cover the whole of the picture area so that every part of the scene was indicated and any faults in the composition would be immediately obvious and could be corrected there and then.

It is at this point that I wish to correct a fallacy. It is sometimes said that oils are a fairly easy medium *because they can always be corrected.* This, like all sweeping generalizations, is only a half-truth. Of course, as oils are an opaque pigment one *can* overpaint thickly to blot out what is wrong, just as one *can* take a palette knife and continually lift out offending passages, but these are hardly things one should *want* to do. In the later stages, when paint is becoming rather thick, such an attitude can be disastrous. Naturally minor improvements and gentle corrections can be made as the work proceeds, and this is the right method—to build up gradually. The work must progress with care, thought and knowledge, and any corrections should be minor ones, made at once. Major alterations need a great deal of skill and knowledge.

Let us return to the lovely Welsh farm. I now started with the sky, and with a mixture of Payne's Grey/Viridian/Ultramarine I painted the 'blue' areas, gradually weakening the colours with white as they approached the horizon, where a very weak pink was introduced, made from Cadmium Red and White. The bank of cloud was suggested by mixtures of weak Yellow Ochre and all the edges were gently agitated with the brush to avoid hard lines. Having established my sky which, being the source of light, gives meaning to every part of the painting and thus becomes a yardstick, I next went for the darkest and middle tones. The first correction was the colour of the distant mountains. Next came the dark trees, which were mainly variations of Viridian/Ochre/Umber, and these were put in with a little more attention to shape. The dark sides of roofs and walls were also established. At this stage, although the paint was becoming opaque, there were no thick ridges and it was still quite easy to handle. Then I went all over the picture, gradually improving the colour and getting it to cover more thoroughly. Any minor faults in drawing were corrected and the work was moving along nicely.

The completion of the work was a continuation of this process. Usually it is a good plan at this time to work from far to near, as the finishing strokes look better if they overlap their own background. For example, it would be rather difficult to paint the large tree *after* the two barns; to help give the impression that the buildings are in front it was better to paint them last. This far-to-near technique is not a hard and fast rule; the best thing is to decide as you progress which is the simplest and most effective method for each particular passage. It is at this time that I feel a little magic often takes charge of the painting—its voice almost tells us what to do, and suggests little changes and interpretations which are refinements not to be seen in the actual subject. Thus I went round my painting, improving the sky, putting in paint for the 'sky-holes', modelling the tree, blending the background and putting extra brush-drawing into the buildings, the walls and the grassland.

Right at the end came the extra touches which give the work its finished appearance. They are such things as the red touches in the roofs and on the tractor, the patches which resolve themselves into out-houses, and other little splashes of brighter colour. This is always a dangerous period, for it is now that we are sorely tempted to include lots of extra details. To do so would be unwise, for they would destroy the strong, broad simplicity of treatment which is the charm of a good oil painting. Their insertion would make the eye wander and fidget, instead of letting it rest calmly within the picture. Therefore these last accents must be added with care and restraint. Changes of colour were put into the walls of the buildings and those around the fields. Any extra darks which were either missed, or needed enriching, were also put in. The trees were given a branch or two. Lastly, in went the fence and the lovely light patches in the meadow. Then very deliberately, because further work would have spoilt the picture, I put it aside and packed my bag.

7. Further Techniques and Painting Surfaces

Butter-like was the term I used earlier to describe the consistency of oil paints. It is this soft creaminess which gives such pleasing qualities and which allows it to be moved and handled without trickling or running. It has a most gratifying plasticity. Just as butter can be spread with a knife, so can oil colours, and indeed painting with a palette knife is a very old and satisfying technique.

It is not a method normally recommended to complete beginners because it needs experience of colour-mixing and a sure approach, for once the paint is applied it should be left to glow in all its freshness. This obviously gives full scope to a very broad treatment and the artist therefore concentrates on shape, tone, form and colour and deliberately ignores detail. You may wonder, since it is usually considered to be an advanced technique, why I have included it in a book of this kind. The reason is that once students have got over the first hurdles in painting in oils, two main faults appear. They find either that their colours are being over-brushed and becoming dirty, or that too much detail makes their work fidgety and lacking in unity. This muddiness on the one hand and fussiness on the other can often be overcome by a little practice in knife painting.

It is not too difficult, for it is, after all, very similar to spreading butter on to bread and most of us have had plenty of practice at that. The main problems lie in controlling the shapes and making sure the colour is right before it is applied. Do as I have done: find an uncomplicated scene, like that in *Figure 42*, page 77, which is composed of rather definite areas, and see how these can be suggested in a simple and direct manner by merely spreading on the paint after first mixing it on the palette with a knife. Take care to mix gently and carefully. My scene tells a simple story of receding planes, each with a slightly different value of tone. It is similar to the sketch in *Figure 6* which explains how tones vary according to distance. After mixing the first colour on the palette carefully and smoothly, with no streaks, it was spread evenly and boldly on to the painting surface. This method is a very direct one, and rather in opposition to the usual practice of building up gradually, but it is normally a safe procedure to work from far to near. Therefore in this case I started with the sky. Once the first knife-load was exhausted I lifted more paint and carried on, gradually lightening the colour as it neared the horizon and taking it slightly over the area where the hills would come. The pinkish clouds were put in on top of the wet paint. To paint slightly beyond the edges of the areas which are later to be near objects is a good plan, for it means a better coverage and gives a softer edge. It will also leave the majority of these areas clean and unspoilt, and in a good condition to receive their own colour without any risk of it becoming sullied. Once the paint has been applied, a little merging can be done to soften the edges, but in general it is best to leave the work alone once it has received the paint. Remember always to wipe the blade quite clean before changing to a fresh colour.

Palette knife painting can be used in a variety of ways, ranging from one in which the strokes are bold and vigorous, with deep ridges, to one with strokes that are smooth and caressing. It can be used over a brush underpainting, and small patches of this can be left showing, to give a slight variety to the work. It can also be used *in conjunction with* brush painting, but my own opinion on this is that in the majority of cases one should keep to one method only; otherwise the work may look disjointed and uncoordinated. Experiment a little with your knife, for even if it does not prove to be the best method for you, I am sure it will help to loosen-up your subsequent work with brushes and give it a pleasant flowing freedom. Should it suit you, however, you will have to hand a style of painting which is fresh, clean and capable of infinite variations and interpretations.

There is another approach to brush painting. I have included this because not only will it give many delightful effects, but it is also most helpful to those people who have great difficulty in covering the canvas. Although they know it can be disastrous they always seem to fall into the trap of trying to finish little bits at a time. To overcome this I am suggesting they might try what is often termed the 'Wiping-out Method'. This means that at the outset the painting is completely covered with a fairly thin paint weakened with a little medium. Choose a colour which is sympathetic to the general scene; in the countryside perhaps a green made from Viridian/Ochre/Umber. Brush this all over the canvas, introducing, if you wish, a slight change of colour but making no attempt to draw the various shapes. Then, with a rag dipped in turpentine and with a firm bold touch with one finger, wipe clean what are to be the lighter areas. A little practice will soon prove that a variation of tone can be obtained quite quickly. Later, with the same general colour, a little definition can be made with a few brush strokes. The result is much like a charcoal sketch plus colour. The advantage of this method is that the surface is covered very quickly and one can visualise at an early stage how the painting will look when finished. It also encourages a pleasant, flowing and artistic interpretation rather than a brittle record of a number of items. From this hazy veil-like beginning the sketch can soon be built up by the application of thicker and richer paint, but at all times we are aware of exactly how the work is progressing. It is a pleasant method and will encourage the slight feeling of fantasy that is so often experienced when observing the landscape.

The early stages of the wiping-out method are similar to yet another technique, which makes use of the placing of paint over a previously prepared ground so that little patches and granulations of the original colour show through. This gives the finished work a soft and diffused look. I do not think such a method has a proper title. Perhaps we could invent one and call it the 'Showing-through Method'. When we first used monochrome you will remember I said that although the first 'lay-in' had a pleasant transparent quality when first painted, this effect would be lost, as the priming or undercoating would quickly discolour and the work would lose its sparkle. Why not, then, ensure that this essential sparkle is not lost? This can easily be managed by preparing the painting surface with a fairly thick covering of a single colour which seems suitable for the particular subject in mind. Suitable backgrounds would be some of the greens and greys we made when producing the colour charts—not too dark but somewhere near a middle value of tone. A good quality household white undercoat can be used, and the colour added in sufficient quantity to cover the area required. For a sunny scene, a covering with weak Yellow Ochre or very light Burnt Umber would be quite effective. Once the ground is dry it will be found that oil colours can be used on it with very little or no medium and, according to the pressure used, they will either cover completely or else dance over the textured surface and give a lovely effect where the background peeps through. There is some similarity to pastel work, where the tinted paper is continually showing through and virtually does half the work. Although in the 'showing-through' method of painting the background can be seen peeping through here and there, the fact that this consists of a well-covered layer of paint of good quality ensures that it should never fade and lose its initial sparkle and richness.

I have used this method in the sketch shown in *Figure 43*, page 77, and a portion to the right of the black vertical line has been left to show the original undercoat, which was a mixture of white/Yellow Ochre plus a little Viridian/Burnt Umber. I think even in the reduced reproduction the 'showing through' qualities are apparent. May it set you thinking.

The material on which a painting is made is often called a support. The one mainly referred to in this book is Oil Painting paper, of which there are several makes. It has a good texture with a 'bite' to grip the oil colours, and is primed and prepared ready for use. It can be bought in single sheets or mounted on cardboard. There are other papers, but these must be chosen with care, the main considerations being that they must be non-porous and that the surface should not be slippery, as this would prevent gripping and additional brush-strokes would lift up and move any previously applied paint.

Surprise is often expressed when people are told that a good quality water-colour is an ideal support for oils. This is no new idea: Constable used it in many of his smaller works. Choose a paper which is fairly stout and with either a 'Not' or a 'Rough' surface. It does not need to be treated, and painting can proceed straight away. It has a pleasing texture and holds the paint well, although it is advisable to use very little or no painting medium. With this one reservation there will be no penetration. If desired, a few scintillating white spots can be left showing and these will always remain clear and clean.

All the above papers, provided they are mounted on a board before framing, are quite acceptable and are extensively used by artists.

Canvas, the support which usually comes to mind when talking of oil-painting, is a most satisfactory material, for its coarse, irregular weave, complete with little 'slubs', gives it good gripping power. Usually it is purchased already prepared and drawn tautly across a wooden framework known as a stretcher. This has small wedges in the corners of the reverse side which serve to keep the material tight. Canvas can be bought from the roll in various widths, qualities and textures. It is also available mounted on stout card. When drawn across a stretcher it has a pleasing drum-like resilience which allows for delicate and sensitive brush-strokes. It is *not* as permanent as a good quality paper and needs careful handling when being moved or despatched, but its surface is so very amenable to the artist's touch that it will always be a top favourite.

Cardboards are quite satisfactory but as they are extremely porous they need treating before work begins. The easiest and simplest method of preparing any such surface is first to seal it with a coat of fairly thin size and then to cover it with two applications of a reliable household white undercoat. Alternatively, white primer from your art stockist can be used. Strawboard works quite well, as do most stout boards. Builder's merchants often provide ideas, and many artists have found the grey wall-board known as 'Essex' board to be an excellent support, being only about $\frac{1}{4}$ in. thick but very light in weight. There are other similar materials that can be used, the main consideration being that the surface texture is suitable and that they will not crack easily.

Hardboard, a manufactured panelling about $\frac{1}{8}$ in. thick, is often used, as it is considered that the rough reverse side has a texture similar to canvas, but I find this surface much too regular and mechanical to be sympathetic. Furthermore, once it is primed the indentations produce very rough edges, making the covering of it much too worrying an activity for the work to progress with a nice restful rhythm. It is very unkind to brushes too. I find it better to use the smooth side, having slightly roughened the surface with glass-paper before treating it. There is also a thinner quality of hardboard, and the rough side of this is much more pleasant to use.

Another good panel on which to work is plywood. Choose a fairly thin one or it will be too heavy to handle; about $\frac{3}{16}$ in. is ideal. It is better to purchase the marine quality.

Although this may mean waiting for delivery, it has the advantage that it does not part or peel.

It has already been stated that cardboards and panels can be satisfactorily prepared with size and undercoating, but there is an alternative method which I have found quite good. It is a variation on the method of applying a gesso ground. Prepare a mixture of one tablespoonful of gesso powder and one tablespoonful of size and place them in a tin with $\frac{3}{4}$ pint of water. (I usually use an old syrup tin.) Heat gradually and keep stirring. When the mixture is nice and creamy, and still warm, paint the support with firm quick strokes, using an ordinary household paintbrush. Two coats with brush-strokes in different directions should give an ideal surface, but it is advisable to paint the edges and put a large diagonal cross on the back, to prevent warping. All types of boards and panels are suitable for this treatment, and a variation can be made by first sticking a sheet of gauze, scrim, linen or canvas over them, making sure that a little is turned over the edges and on to the back. This can be done with size used as glue. Then paint on your gesso mixture and you have a delightful texture of your own choosing.

The foregoing are a few of many techniques and hints which can be employed by the painter in oils. They make use of previously observed effects which all have their place in the vast story of painting. As you progress you will find strong and definite links between them, and an experienced artist can use various aspects of them in his work according to the demands of the moment. I hope that, with a little intelligent play, these various techniques will help you to overcome certain problems and also encourage you to develop a distinctive and original style of painting.

Part IV
Painting with Acrylic Colours

As acrylic colours have, in many instances, much in common with the properties of both oil paints and water-colours, which have already been discussed, the following chapters deal mainly with the general possibilities and techniques of what, to many, must be regarded as a fairly new medium. The behaviour and possibilities of acrylics are explored and consideration is given to various methods of working to ensure that harmony is maintained, not only with the nature of the new material, but also with the hand and mind of the artist.

There is sure to be a need for further information on such things as colour mixing, the painting of trees and foliage, the making of greys, composition, and general atmospheric effects. All these are carefully explained and illustrated in either the chapters on oil painting or those on water-colour painting.

1. *Acrylic Paints: General Properties*

A fairly recent addition to the range of materials available to the artist is a paint generally known as acrylic, named after the resin which is used in its manufacture. As this paint has qualities which in many instances are similar to those of both water-colours and oil paints, a certain amount of confusion exists as to what it is and what it can do.

On first inspection a tube of acrylic colour does not strike one as being particularly unusual. The tube is much the same as that used for other paints and the colour, when squeezed on to the palette, is very similar in both consistency and appearance to the now-familiar oil paints. Here the similarity ends. For the colour you see was produced by grinding selected pigments into an emulsified resin which, when dry, gives a waterproof film of considerable brilliance and durability. No oil is used in its preparation and therefore it will not mix with oil. In its pure state, direct from the tube, it is thick and brilliant, but it can be thinned down with water to produce delicate transparent washes of great subtlety. Used thickly it can create a richly textured impasto (an intentionally uneven surface); by thinning partially with water, or a specially prepared medium, it is possible to make opaque washes of colour that possess the same qualities as the more conventional gouache or designers' colours. Thus in this one medium are combined all the potentialities of texture, opacity and transparency.

Figure 44 shows examples of these three qualities of transparency, opacity and texture. The scene shown in (*a*) (from a visit to Scotland) was done by using the colours considerably diluted and painting in much the same way as a conventional water-colour. Indeed it would be difficult to tell the difference. The only problem here is that you have to be rather sure of yourself as colours cannot be lifted once the paint has dried as the dry film of paint is quite waterproof. *Figure 44* (*b*) shows the considerable covering power and opacity of the paint; as you can see, it lends itself extremely well to patches of even colouring. In this example a little water *and* medium was used to enable the paint to flow freely. *In Figure 44* (*c*) you can see how, by combining the two previous methods and gradually putting on several extra layers of paint, you can build up quite a heavy texture. It is important not to confuse acrylics with other media, nor to use them merely as a substitute. They will stand alone quite proudly and independently and in no way should be considered as a mere substitute.

It must also be remembered that acrylic colours dry quite quickly. A thick application will dry in about twenty minutes; a thin one even more rapidly. This speed of drying is often thought to be a disadvantage, but this is not strictly true, for apart from the single caution not to be *too* liberal when squeezing the paints on to the palette, any paint which dries speedily has many advantages. Not the least of the problems which face the holiday painter is the worrying business of transporting wet oil paintings. With acrylic paints such problems no longer exist. When working in oils, the work often has to be put aside for a while because it is too thick and slippery to accept any further applications of paint; with acrylics any such waiting time is reduced to mere minutes and one can continue to build up the thicknesses of paint either when it is at the right stage of tackiness or when it is quite dry. When one is working at full stretch with hand, eye, intelligence and imagination all working in coordinated harmony, it is comforting to know that the work can progress with such a happy continuity.

Now for the materials that are needed. These can be obtained by purchasing a large boxed outfit, but as these so often have to be modified to suit personal needs and tastes, my own recommendation is that you build up your own kit item by item. Below are the things needed:

1. Colours:
   Cadmium Yellow
   Yellow Ochre
   Cadmium Red
   Alizarin Crimson
   Titanium White (a much larger tube)
   French Ultramarine
   Viridian Green
   Burnt Umber
   Payne's Grey
2. Small bottle of painting medium
3. Mixing palette
4. Two or three brushes
5. Two water pots
6. Painting surface (paper, board, etc.)
7. Drawing board
8. Rags
9. Easel, stool and sketch-bag (if working out of doors)

The colours need little or no explanation as they are the same as those recommended throughout this book and although changes can be made, the above list should be more than adequate for a happy and successful start. Be quite sure to get a very much larger size tube of white, as the acrylic colours are very strong and many mixtures will need considerable lightening.

Should it be preferred, a specially produced painting medium can be used for mixing instead of water and this will give the work a slightly eggshell finish. Alternatively one can thin the paints by using a little of both water and medium. Whatever method is adopted plenty of water should always be on hand for the various cleansing purposes.

Owing to the quick drying and powerful adhesive qualities of the paints, care has to be taken over the choice of palette. Hardened paint is difficult to remove from the normal wooden palette and for this reason it is best to use a hard plastic one from which the paint can more easily be scraped. Glass is quite satisfactory although a little dangerous, and I have even seen an enamelled plate being used.

A water pot is absolutely essential and should have a wide opening so that brushes can be vigorously swirled as the work proceeds. Remember if working out of doors that this container must somehow be attached to the easel. Remember, also, to have a second container so that brushes not in use can be left to soak.

The choice of brushes is very individual, but a small pointed one with a couple of flat ones of different types should be quite adequate. It is important that brushes be constantly washed (and wiped if necessary) while work is in progress. At the end of each painting session brushes should be washed thoroughly with soap and cold water, rinsed, wiped gently, and re-shaped. Brushes left to harden are usually no longer serviceable, but with good fortune they may be saved by agitating with methylated spirit.

On what can we paint? All kinds of surfaces can be used without any preparation. Wood, hardboard, strawboard, cardboard, plasterboard and all kinds of paper will readily accept acrylics. Shiny or greasy surfaces are not suitable. On canvas, hessian and the more absorbent materials, a coating of acrylic primer is advisable, but only on extremely porous materials will a second coat be necessary. Primer (or priming paint) is sold in tins and is similar in appearance and application to ordinary household paint. Should a very smooth and brilliant white surface be required, for a particular effect, two coats of priming are usually sufficient. Work can soon commence as the priming dries very rapidly.

2. *Texture: Making Use of Opaque Qualities*

Most artists who use acrylic agree that it is particularly effective when the work has plenty of texture; this is achieved mainly by laying one colour over another. With this type of paint one can put down a colour and, within a few minutes, paint almost all over it with different kinds of brush strokes; some thin, some thick, some in one direction, others in another. Immediately one is aware of an extra enriching quality. The work is elevated and improved, and displays attributes impossible to achieve by a single application of colour.

For a first exercise it is suggested that you get several odd sheets of paper about 6 in. square and cover them with a fairly liberal application of paint, having first mixed the colours on the palette in much the same way as when using oil colours. Do not be too liberal with the water or you will find the paint so slippery that you will be lifting it off rather than putting it on! Have several mixtures, similar to those shown in the examples in *Figure 45* and remember to wash the brush and wipe the palette when this first stage is completed. We shall shortly be painting over these areas but before doing so it is interesting to note that already white paint has been used in making these earlier mixtures, for with acrylic painting the white paint can be introduced at any time. Having read Part III on oil painting, you will know that it can be dangerous when using oils to use white paint too soon as its comparatively slow-drying properties allow it to become brushed into other wet areas; with acrylics, the white can be used from the outset and the fast-drying qualities permit a passage of the wrong tone to be over-painted quite rapidly, with no danger to adjacent areas.

Let us continue with our practice. Our 'underpainting' is now dry and we are ready to put on more colour. In my first example, *Figure 45(a)*, there is a purple-grey background, made with Burnt Umber/blue/crimson, and over it were painted variations on yellow, including mixtures involving reds, browns, ochre and even greens. Such a method might be most useful for such things as a cornfield, or any other very sunlit passage. Notice that this area, although still very much yellowish, is certainly more interesting than the adjacent panel which was merely stippled in tones of one single colour.

In the next trial piece, *Figure 45(b)*, the background was perhaps a little more interesting, being a variation of pinks, oranges and very light greens. Over this I placed some much darker greens made with varying mixtures of Viridian/Burnt Umber/Yellow Ochre. Thus we have an area which might well represent some fairly dense foliage, with incidental lights either shining through or striking an occasional patch. Again, it is worthwhile to compare it with the rather solid all-green mass shown in the panel alongside.

Please do several more of these trial pieces, for it is all too easy to accept what is shown and demonstrated through reasoning, but it is often a very different matter when it comes to the actual handling of the material.

When putting down a fairly shadowy underpainting in preparation for your landscape studies, be careful to be subtle. Do not be casual for no one would want a bright red showing through a tree—unless it was a sunset, and we are certainly not ready for anything quite as ambitious as that. By all means experiment in the underpainting, but take care to avoid stridency. Then, when you are working direct from nature, you will be prepared to search for and find the many delicate and all important 'peeping-through' colours and thus bring to your work a genuine feel for the atmospheric qualities of the subject. What is more you will be handling the paint in a much more sensitive manner.

Having a paint which is so responsive to texturing opens the way to many exciting possibilities and experiments. In a single sitting quite a heavy build-up of impasto can be made, with a variety of gentle colours showing through. The paper can be tinted first, either with some harmonious colour, or dappled with two or three. The drawing is then gradually built up and improved upon by painting one colour over another, with patches, ridges and spaces making the whole thing lively and sparkling. Sometimes, right at the end, extra colours can be dragged across the surface of the work with a brush laid very flat, so that the paint merely dances on to some of the ridges and high spots. As the work develops, all manner of possibilities suggest themselves and the experience becomes absorbing and very exciting.

Textures of all sorts can be created by using a flat brush with a sideways stroke, a series of rectangular strokes, or diagonal strokes, giving the work an almost tapestry-like quality. Whatever strokes are used they should be made with the brush held comfortably and naturally, and not too near the bristles. Be quite prepared to vary the grip for there are many ways of holding a brush other than the normal pen grip.

Always make strokes which come almost instinctively, for paint should always be applied in strokes rather than in stiff and heavy-handed dabs. Try also to be consistent in the textural effect you create; to have one part of the scene very rough and another very smooth could easily be somewhat disconcerting.

3. Using the Transparent Qualities

The principle of laying a fairly transparent wash over a painting can be used to considerable advantage when working with acrylic paints. The method of application is very much the same as when using water-colour, except that we need not be so cautious as the surface is waterproof and so there is no danger of disturbing what has already been painted. Thus we can, by adding water (and possibly a little medium too, to retain the waterproof quality), make a translucent colour and float it over a previously painted area to give a particular effect. This was a method used quite extensively by artists before the Impressionists, but as they were working in oils, a considerable amount of waiting was necessary to allow each film of paint to dry. This is now no longer necessary. Thus we can scumble (place a thin dark) or glaze (place a thin light) over our work, with only a few minutes' waiting before doing so.

Such a technique can be most useful in helping to suggest some difficult effect, such as the warm colours of a building showing through a superimposed cool shadow, or indeed anywhere where one colour is required to glow through another. It can also be most useful for rectifying those parts of a painting where the total statement is incorrect.

Often the results of placing one colour over another can be quite surprising. It must also be noted that once the paint has dried it cannot be removed and should you do the wrong thing, it must be sponged off very quickly. Better by far to try things first, and for this reason I suggest you paint various colours on odd pieces of paper and put a transparent wash over half of each piece so that you have a 'before and after' sample. Try putting a blue over a yellow and then reverse the process by putting a yellow over a blue. The results are quite different. Continue this idea with many other pairs of colours and you will then have an informative collection to keep for reference until you are very certain of yourself.

I said earlier that these transparent and semi-transparent applications of colour can be extremely useful for making alterations to those parts of a painting which are tonally incorrect. Careful mixing and application can slightly lighten or darken an offending area to give it exactly the desired subtlety of brilliance, mistiness, dustiness or shadow. An example of making such corrections is shown in *Figure 46*, where it can be seen that the whole of the background and middle distance in the part marked *a* is too dark. In fact the distant trees are so deep in tone as to appear part of the tree in the foreground. In *b*, corrections have been made. All the distant areas, including the sky, have been made to recede by mixing some fairly light, but watery colours, and floating these over the offending passages until the desired effect of distance was achieved. The sky was treated first, because it needed much more of a glow properly to illuminate the scene below. This was done by using, at the top, a scumble made with Ultramarine/Viridian/white and, lower down, a mixture of Burnt Umber/Cadmium Red/white. The hills, the distant trees, the water and the hedge had no feeling of the slight mistiness that distance always gives to a scene. These areas were corrected by the application of a blue-grey film made with Ultramarine/white. Even the pathway needed a little improvement, and this was achieved by applying extra patches of thick sandy colours in the manner explained in the previous chapter.

Thus it can be seen that the two techniques of texturing and the applying of transparent colours can readily be used in the one painting, even to the extent of using one method over the other in fairly quick succession. What is more, even when a transparent wash is floated over a textured passage, the brushmarks and colour changes are still visible.

4. *Knife Painting*

Because acrylic colours respond so well to the making of textural effects they become particularly alive and expressive in the hands of the palette-knife painter. In this respect they bear a strong similarity to oil colours, for the consistency of acrylics is very much the same as oils when it is used direct from the tube with little or no medium.

However, in all types of knife painting, be it oils or acrylics, it needs a reasonably good knowledge of colour mixing, an ability to draw in mass rather than line, and also a rather definite approach, for once the paint is applied it should not be worked or smeared. To do so would mean the loss of the essential glow and freshness that is the very essence of this type of painting.

Obviously you cannot undertake the inclusion of fussy details when working with a knife and for this reason it is wise to choose subjects that allow for a rather broad treatment and interpretation. Make the application in a very direct manner by spreading on panels and patches of paint of the right shape, tone and colour. As with oils, always mix the colour carefully on the palette first, and then apply it—never indulge in the hit-or-miss method of trying to mix the colours on the actual painting. If a wrong colour is put down it is better by far to lift it off quickly and make a fresh attempt. To work into colours already applied can be a very dangerous business and is almost certain to produce results that are nasty, muddy and uncertain. The only time that you can work into strokes already made is when you have to merge one colour into another, but even here you must be careful to work very gently with a delicate touch, as too much agitation can so quickly spoil things.

As a first exercise, try a simple scene depicting a series of receding planes, similar to the one shown in *Figure 42*, page 77, painted in oils. The explanation relating to this sketch will also be helpful, for at this stage the techniques of working in oils and acrylics are very similar. The main thing to remember is to keep the work simple and broad in its approach and, whenever possible, to use the blade as flat as possible. Too much work with the tip of the blade can so easily tempt you to be fussy and the lovely economical freshness, which is so essential, gets lost in a maze of irrelevant stippling.

With knife painting even more exciting and interesting results can be achieved by having some sort of underpainting put down first and with acrylics this first coat will soon dry. Such a preliminary stage can be done with either brush or knife, but if the knife is used it is advisable to leave a comparatively smooth surface because too many ridges will impede the progress of the next stage. Such an underpainting can either be a simple indication to establish what colours are to be applied at the next stage, or, which is more interesting, it can be a carefully thought-out patchwork type of background representing all the distant atmospheric colours that are present in the scene. These were mentioned in an earlier chapter and I referred to them as the peeping-through colours. An example of this is shown in *Figure 47(a)*. Firstly, using the knife in this instance, a very flat, dappled groundwork was established, employing a variety of delicate pinks, yellows and greyish purples. These were the colours which would show through the various small gaps made when the next stage was completed. It is at this point, should you find it too difficult to draw directly with carefully shaped masses, that a series of construction lines can be included by using a fine brush and some very thin, weak blue paint, but be careful not to get carried away with detail. Over this came the additional knife painting, shown in *Figure 47(b)*, which not only further established the drawing, but also helped to create the right atmosphere for the scene.

In all there are some two or three extra layers of paint so that the colours are broken into hundreds of quite small areas. And peeping through all these tiny gaps are the sparkling colours of the original underpainting. Once the method is under control it is a most exhilarating method of working.

Another interesting effect obtainable when working acrylic colours with a knife, is that of producing very light colours without the use of white paint. If you work on a very smooth, well-primed, white surface (heavy-weight photographic paper works well) very light colours can be produced merely by using the knife firmly so that an extremely thin film is applied. No white paint is needed because then the white ground will show through and the resulting colour will be so light and brilliant as to be almost transparent. The result is really surprising and very beautiful, reminding one of the effects of stained glass. If a little less pressure is used the colour becomes darker. Such a technique produces a marvellous luminous quality and is particularly suitable for abstract or semi-abstract interpretations where there is a strong need for an emphasis on shape and pattern. With this type of painting you need not be confined to the traditional kind of knife but can make, or improvise with, all kind of spatulas. I have even known a decorator's paint-scraper and a rubber door stop being used to great effect.

Knife or spatula painting can be an exciting and very satisfying experience, but with acrylic paint you need plenty of practice to get thoroughly acquainted with its own particular behaviour and qualities. What is more, because of its twin demands for deliberate colour mixing and the simplification of detail, it usually leads to a general improvement when a return is made to working entirely with the brush.

Reference has already been made to the powerful adhesive qualities of acrylic paint, for, providing the surface is free of grease, it maintains a most tenacious grip on most materials. This leads us to collage, which is the method of producing a picture by sticking all manner of carefully chosen objects on to an already painted area, thus giving the work something of a sculptural quality. Such objects can, if necessary, even be embedded into quite thick mounds of moist paint. You can use almost anything, providing the materials are grease free, preferably have some grain, or 'bite', and convey what the artist intends. Various fabrics, seeds, twigs, wood-blocks, screws, wire, string, paper, hair and card can all be stuck down quite firmly.

It must be stated, however, that really good work by this method needs considerable thought and a great deal of imagination. It also demands an appreciation of the principles of design and an understanding of working in relief. Generally speaking it works best for decorative panels which freely interpret a motif or a theme, or else for purely abstract arrangements. To use the method for the translation of the landscape (which is the real aim of this book) needs considerable knowledge, flair and experience, but it *can* be done if great care is taken over the choice and suitability of the various materials.

Collage, if it is well done, can be extremely rewarding to both artist and viewer; if it is not well done it becomes either ugly, or else unpleasantly naive. So take care. However, if you feel the need to branch out, and we all do at some time or another, the choosing and arranging of the various components must automatically develop the appreciation of both texture and composition.

Part V
The Art of Sketching

Using a Pencil

Because it is so familiar, the pencil is often considered to be easy to use for sketching. This is not entirely true. It has a far greater range than is generally appreciated, and is more difficult to manipulate with expression and sensitivity than one might first think. From childhood we have used a pencil for writing, and because handwriting consists of stretches of continuous line there is a tendency, when sketching, only to make outlines. If some areas need to look more solid, they are 'filled in' by scribbling. This method was used in *Figure 48(a)*. I think you will agree that, mainly through lack of variety and contrast, it looks rather insensitive and ordinary. It has no sparkle. The scribbling could have been made denser here and there to darken certain passages, but this would only have produced a polished, shiny look.

Bearing in mind that a pencil is only really efficient when drawing lines, and remembering that a continuous outline somehow fails to please, the artist has to effect a compromise. Now look at the lower sketch (*Figure 48(b)*. Notice how the whole scene has been built up of separate strokes—some thick, others thin; some close together, others widely spaced—but always with areas of paper showing between them. Pencils of differing degrees of softness (or blackness) were used, and the strokes were made with varying pressures and in different directions. This method gives a much better representation of solidity of form and of the light, medium and dark tones. It helps the artist to capture the atmosphere of the scene, and the pencil is employed in a way which suits its own particular characteristics. Gentle handling for the background trees has given an impression of distance. Darker tones and stronger strokes show the proximity, and the rough and powerful texture, of the larger and nearer tree trunks, and also give depth to the shadows. The delicate light areas on the ground almost suggest we should walk in and test the spring in the turf. Such feelings could hardly be evoked by the limited methods used in the first sketch.

Having learned something about the technique and effects of pencil work, let us attempt to use our knowledge. First we need to know a little more about the essential materials. The following items are easily obtainable from most art stockists:

1. Pencils—HB, 2B, 4B
2. Cartridge paper
3. Plastic rubber (sometimes called putty rubber or kneaded rubber)
4. India rubber
5. Penknife

It is always wiser (and ultimately cheaper) to buy good quality pencils. The wood is straight-grained and easy to cut, and the leads are of a regular density throughout. A pencil which resists sharpening, or a lead which is gritty and makes scratches, can be most frustrating. A good pencil has its grade (the degree of hardness or softness) stamped at one end. Medium grades are B and HB. The harder leads range from H to 9H and the softer and blacker ones from B to 6B. I have listed only three grades because I wish to show what can be done with a minimum amount of materials but it is quite a good idea to buy some of the others, and to carry the experiments further than will be shown here.

It is not generally known that there are hundreds of grades and types of paper. By all

Figure 48

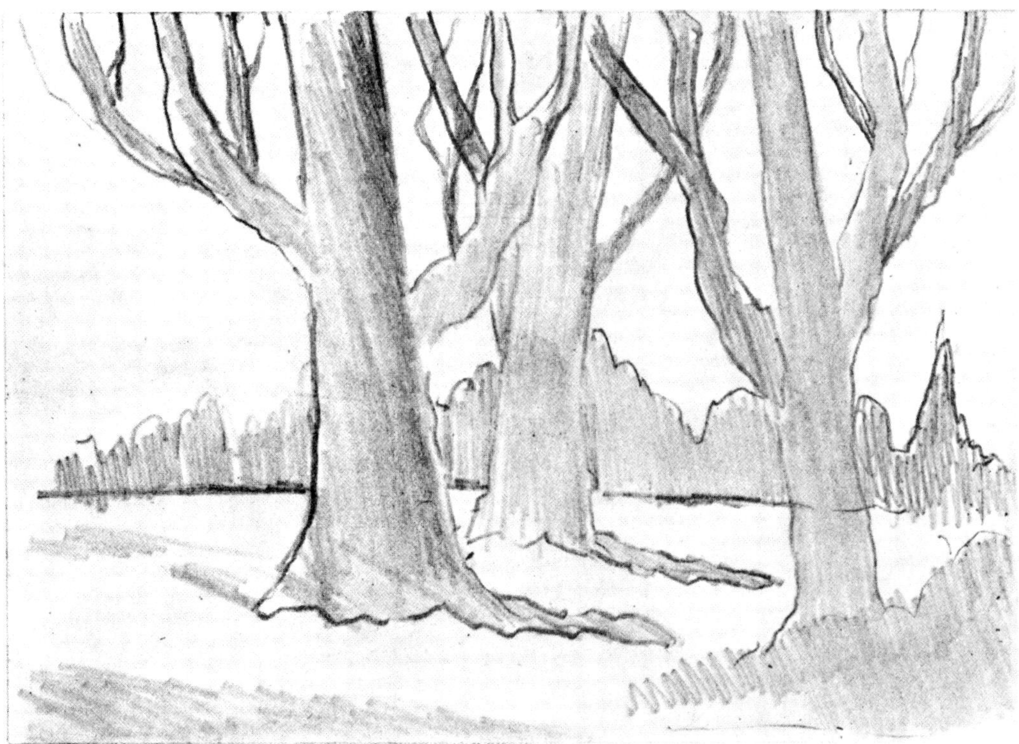

(*a*) *Good shapes and grouping, but not enough use made of the pencil*

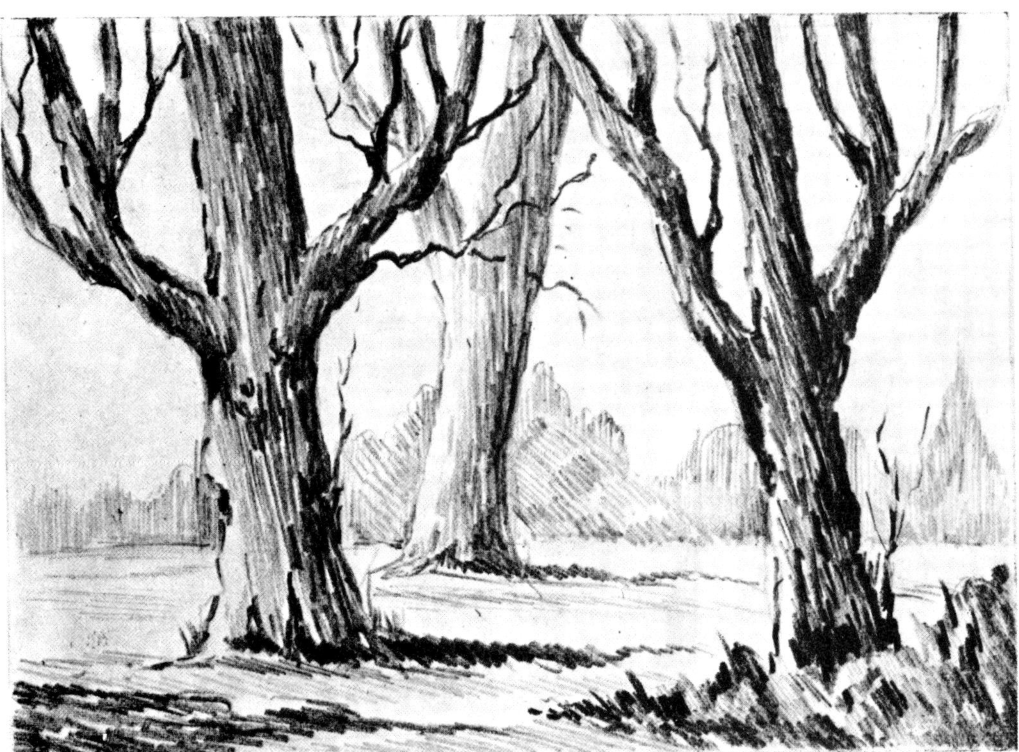

(*b*) *A similar subject but with a greater variety of pencil treatment*

means try using other varieties, but for our present purpose a good quality cartridge paper will serve very well. The effects of other papers will be shown later. A pad or a book with a stiff back is recommended, and it should be fairly large—say about 14 in. × 10 in. If separate sheets are preferred, they should be attached by clips or drawing pins to a thin board ($\frac{1}{4}$ in. plywood is ideal) of the above dimensions. The size and firmness are essential to support the hand comfortably while you are drawing. This means that the sketches will usually be smaller than the pad or board on which they are made.

The plastic rubber will lift off most of the pencil marks, leaving the paper ready for a more thorough clean with an India rubber. If you do not use the plastic rubber first, the India rubber will make nasty smears and streaks. Plastic rubber is soft. Break off a small piece the size of a cherry and constantly mould it in your fingers; then it will remain clean and work well.

The penknife is for sharpening the pencils. There are a number of ways of doing this. Some artists like a very long flat lead, rather like a screwdriver; some have the tip cut off at an oblique angle; while others prefer it long and blunt. To avoid confusion, I suggest that we keep to a long pointed lead which has a slight flatness on one side. This will enable us to make either a broad or a fine stroke (*Figure 49*). Remember, however, that there are no rigid rules, and that all the best ideas have come from someone experimenting. The only thing to avoid is a lead which is both short *and* blunt, for this prevents a sensitive and clean stroke, and needs constant sharpening, which is most disturbing to the rhythm of one's progress.

One final item, which is not on the list as it is optional, is some fine-grade glasspaper. This is a great help to those who cannot wield a knife with sufficient dexterity to get a nice clean and regular point. If preferred, it can be bought in small pads specially produced for this purpose; otherwise the normal sheets from the hardware shop are quite suitable.

Having collected our materials let us now see what we can do with them. As a first exercise, rule out a series of rectangles on the cartridge paper as I have done in *Figure 50*. I suggest you make these about $1\frac{1}{2}$ in. × 2 in. (Mine have been reduced in size during reproduction.) In the first column I have taken the pencil indicated, and made some thin sharp strokes by holding the pencil in a typical pen-grip. Beneath these strokes, in the same panel, is a series of broader strokes made by holding the pencil much flatter. The second column is very much the same, except that the pressure is *slightly* heavier and in every instance the strokes appear a little darker. The third and fourth columns help us to appreciate and experience the results that can be obtained with each grade of pencil. I am sure you will

Figure 49

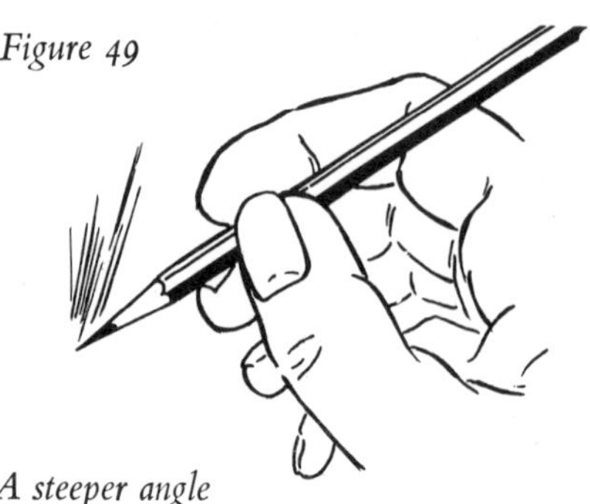

A steeper angle produces a finer stroke

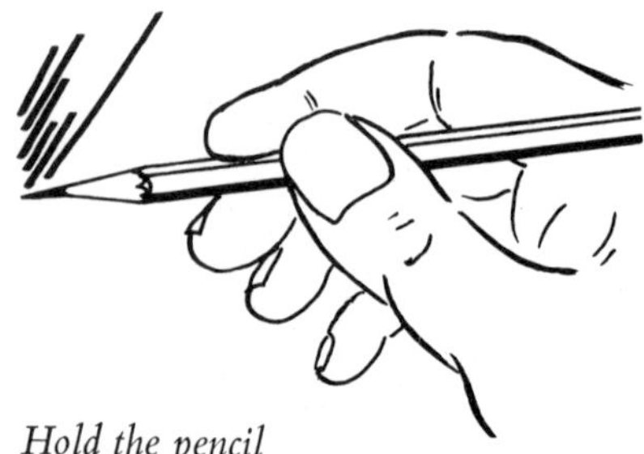

Hold the pencil flat for broad strokes

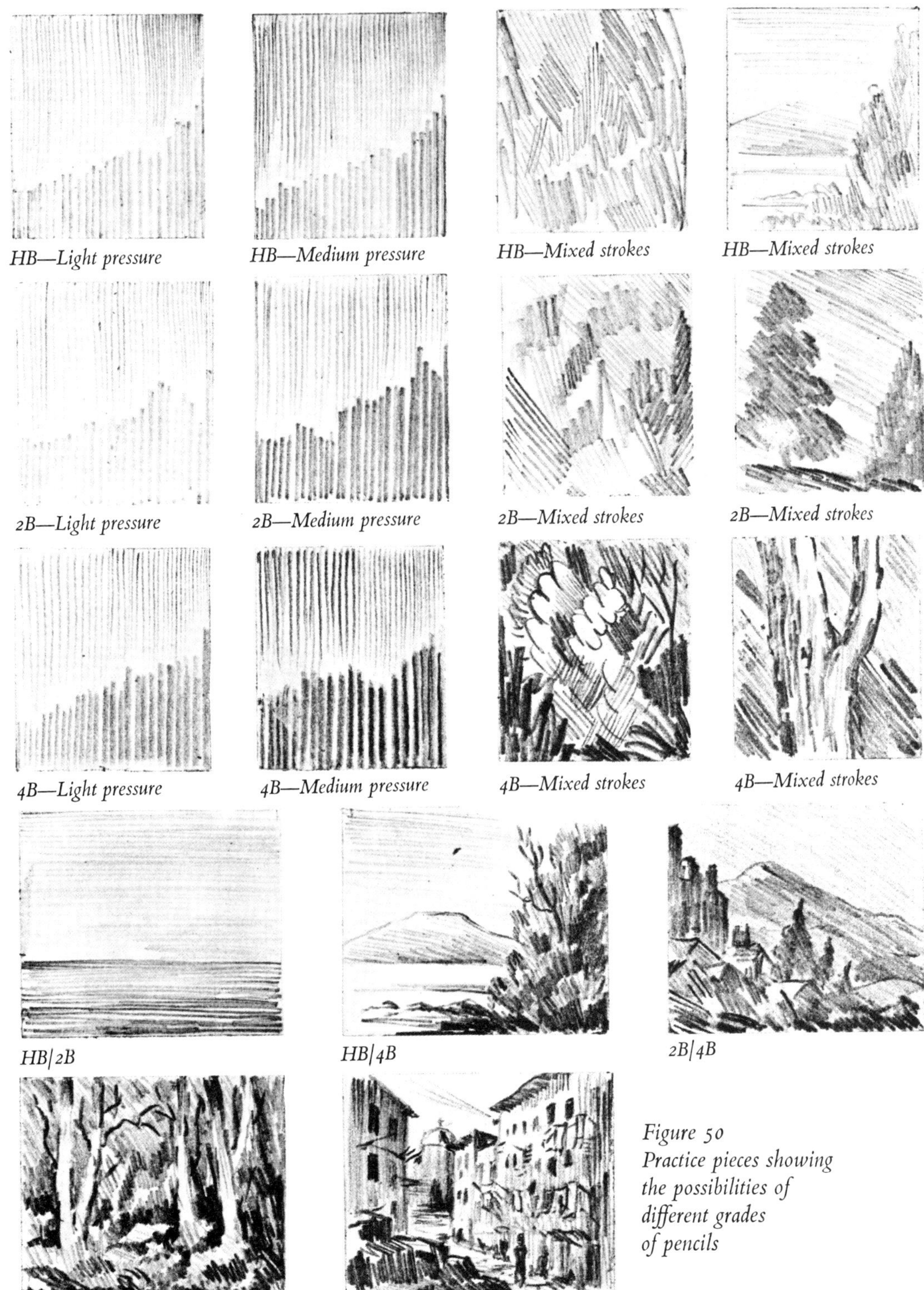

Figure 50
Practice pieces showing the possibilities of different grades of pencils

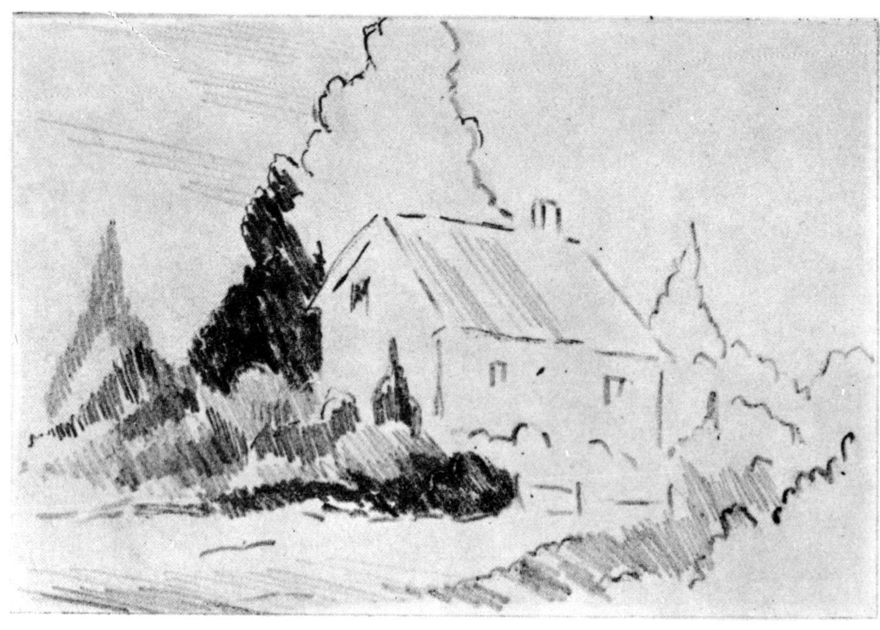

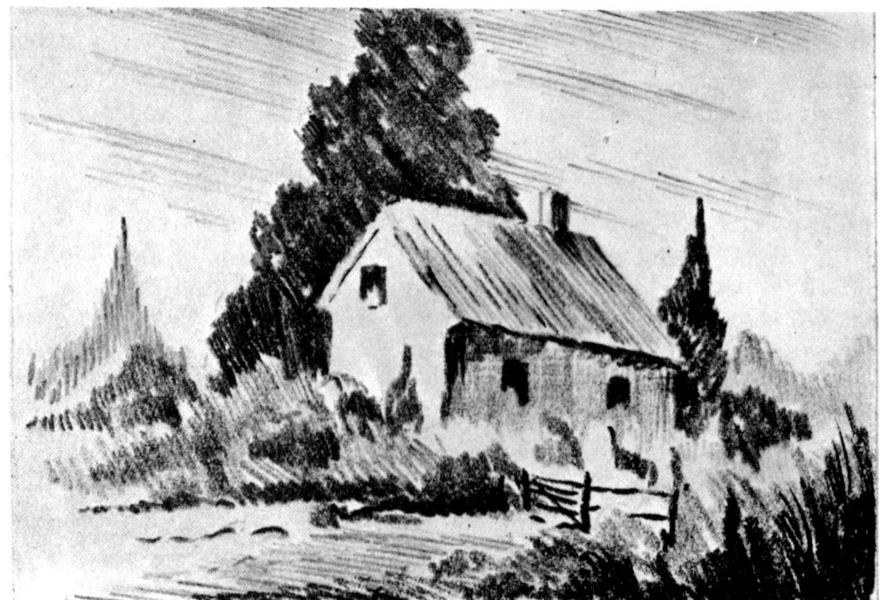

Figure 51. The two stages of making a pencil sketch

notice that the best effects and greatest variations are made with the soft leads, or a mixture with the emphasis on the soft ones. Observe also that the HB tends to obliterate the tiny variations in the surface texture of the paper; the 2B, and particularly the 4B, do not.

All this may seem very obvious but I most seriously recommend you to work in this way. Practise plenty of strokes in every direction—reading is no substitute for experience.

There is an enormous difference between knowing about something and really understanding through one's intelligence *and* through one's hands. With a little practice you will soon be able to make your pencil produce the effect you desire.

When you have achieved a fair measure of control you will be keen to sketch something, using the strokes you have practised. I suggest you copy the illustration in *Figure 51*. Look at it carefully first. Notice how the scene is arranged—how much area is devoted to the sky, the cottage, the foreground foliage. Observe how very light areas are nearly always thrown into contrast by darks which are near them. It is important to have this overall view and not to tackle one piece at a time without comparing it with adjacent passages.

Now, with an HB pencil, make a faint outline of the main areas. This can be done very lightly and mistakes can easily be corrected without any need for heavy rubbing out. To ensure a clear reproduction, my outline had to be a little heavier than I would normally use.

Next comes the problem of where to start. This does not matter a great deal, except that it is advisable not to keep returning to the top of the sketch because completed areas at the bottom will be smudged. The best plan is to look for a well-defined area of dark and get some of this established as a sort of yardstick with which to measure the other parts. In my case, using a 2B pencil, I started with the dark trees behind the cottage as I felt that these, together with the mid-grey of the bushes beneath and the white of the building, would give me an interesting and helpful relationship of tones. (*Note:* As I am left-handed there is a tendency for most of my diagonal strokes to go from top-left to bottom-right. There is no need to copy my work stroke for stroke and be uncomfortable: the finished sketch will be equally satisfactory with these diagonals in the opposite direction.)

Still using the 2B, the background trees and the left-hand bushes were completed. You can create the effect of one area overlapping another by using a variety of strokes to alter the tone. Thus the light will appear to be catching the tops of the bushes and the lower parts will seem lost in shadows. I then changed to an HB pencil, finished the sky with sharp clear strokes and put in the pale grey areas of the walls and roof. I returned to the 2B for the rest of the darker areas, including the windows and the shadows and variations in the roof and chimney. Lastly, the 4B was used for any crisp darks that were needed. You will soon spot them: there are just a few in the background trees and at the corner of the wall. The fence and the foreground grasses also needed a very soft pencil.

Although you have only made a copy, I am sure it has helped you to realize how delightfully sensitive and expressive the humble pencil can be. As you proceed you will appreciate that the strokes always look better if they are made direct, even when they are placed very close together. Keep the pencil sharp so that every stroke is distinct and definite, and always aim to retain the contrast between darks and lights; then your work will have lift and sparkle.

Unless it is merely an exercise to facilitate handling, there is little to be gained in copying because the copyist is not putting his own interpretation to the test. So having mastered some of the technique the next step is to work direct from a scene, or one or two objects. At this stage, rather than attempting large pictures, the wisest plan is to look around you and make a series of simple studies. The sort which are most useful are the little pieces that can be seen in, near and around your home.

The first and greatest difficulty for the pencil artist is to translate a subject which is rich in colour into terms of white, greys and black. The simplest way is to imagine it as an ordinary black and white photograph. View the scene through half-closed eyes: this tends to take away the colour and make the very dark and the very light areas quite distinct. A preliminary careful look also makes it easier to avoid the tendency to finish one piece at a time without having regard to its contribution to the whole. The greatest and most common fault of all who start sketching is to draw in infinite detail and be almost unaware of the pattern of light and shade.

With such experience behind you, and after referring back to Chapter 3, Part I, which deals with the selection and arrangement of subjects, you will be well prepared for more ambitious studies made around the countryside. So off you go! Remember not to use the same pencil *all* the time, and keep the penknife handy.

2. *The Pencil: Further Possibilities*

We are now ready to set forth to capture the charm of the countryside. As these are still early days beware of over-keenness. Do not choose a vast panoramic scene which is mostly land and sky; such views are extremely difficult. Nor is it wise to attempt a subject so complicated that you are continually bothered and confused. Select something which when seen through the viewfinder has an immediate appeal and which you feel that, given a little good fortune, you could manage comfortably.

After making the choice of subject, there will be other decisions to make. The most difficult one is how much detail to include. The soft nature of our pencils does not lend itself to drawing every brick and stone of a building or every leaf on a tree. If we use a harder pencil, the result will be so diagrammatic and laboured that it will look 'tight' and fidgety instead of free and flowing. Therefore the first essential is to ask ourselves how much detail we need for the scene to be recognizable, and what method we should use to capture its intrinsic qualities.

The woodland depicted in *Figure 52* is near my home in Hertfordshire. Once more, cartridge paper was chosen. As the scene had a rather soft and gentle look, I felt that hard and sharp lines should be kept to a minimum. Therefore the pencils were mostly held at a very flat angle to give the broadest possible strokes, but care was taken not to allow these strokes to merge because this would have given too much solidity resulting in a loss of scintillation. I was greatly tempted to draw very careful studies of the foreground weeds and grasses but decided to keep them slightly out of focus, by treating them as loosely as possible, so that the eye could travel unhampered into the picture. Here again there was a certain amount of interpretation and the diagrams next to the sketch explain some of the points to look for.

It is always fun to experiment. During a trip to East Anglia I found I had a different kind of paper with me, which I used. The result is shown in *Figure 53*. This paper has a pleasant crêpe-like surface and is normally used for water-colour painting. It can be obtained in various thicknesses with three textures—Rough, NOT (medium) and H.P. (smooth). In *Figure 53* we see the results on a NOT paper, and I feel that the ubiquity of texture prevents the sketch from becoming spotty and helps to retain unity. The composition was ideal. The radiating lead-in of the perspective of the cottages contrasted nicely with the frontal view of the church tower, and the rich darks of the right-hand tree were helpful too, as they held the eye firmly within the picture.

When working on a rough paper like this, care must be taken not to use too much pressure; otherwise the lead will powder and it will be difficult to prevent the work becoming smudged. As has already been stated, there are a great number of papers and although a very rough one is unsuited to pencil work, many of the others can be used to considerable advantage. Often the subject will help you to decide which paper to choose and after a few trials you may discover one or two which are sympathetic to your own style and method of working.

There are many coloured and tinted papers available to the artist. They are normally used when working with pastels but are eminently suitable—indeed flattering—to the strokes of a pencil. They can be purchased either in large single sheets or in blocks and pads of various sizes. Many of the pads contain a mixture of colours and these are most useful, as you always have a suitable colour available. Just imagine what suggestions of time of day, weather, and general characteristics can be conveyed by the use of subtle variations of cream, blue or purple paper.

Choose the colour of the paper to give a pleasing and restful influence in harmony with the subject. The brilliant highlights supplied by a white ground cannot be obtained from a coloured one, so a white chalk has to be used. Sometimes the chalk is applied with a gentle stroke which lightly brushes the paper and reveals its texture. The pressure can also be gradually varied until an opaque and really dense white is produced. I have found it best to break off about $\frac{1}{2}$ in. of chalk and use it flat with broad strokes, only occasionally turning it on end for a more linear application.

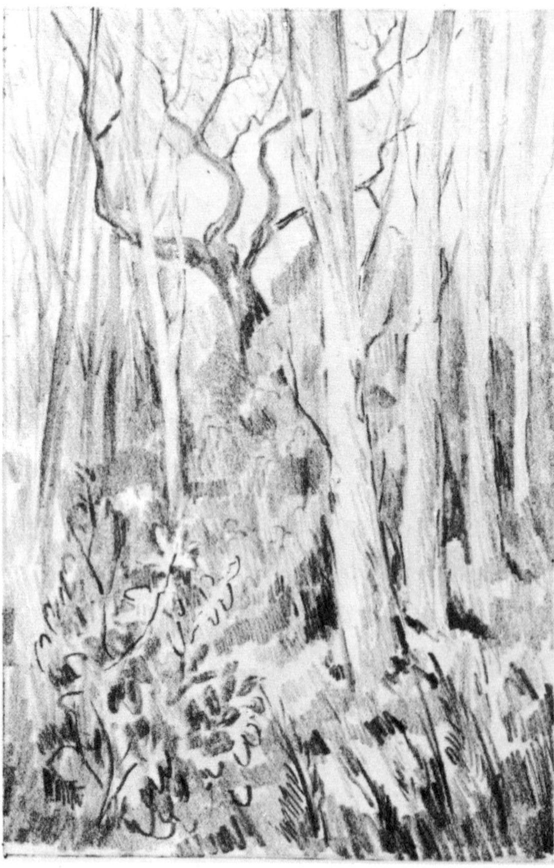

Figure 52
A simplification of the intricate detail to be found in any woodland scene

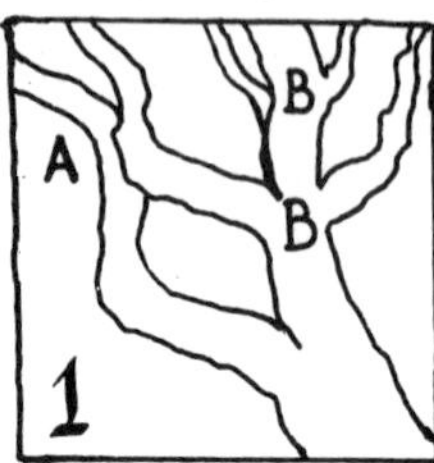

Have the courage to make occasional alterations. On the left is a fairly accurate sketch, but it was unfortunate that only half the branch was overlapping at A, while at B the forks were directly opposite. The right-hand drawing shows the alterations and omissions that can be made

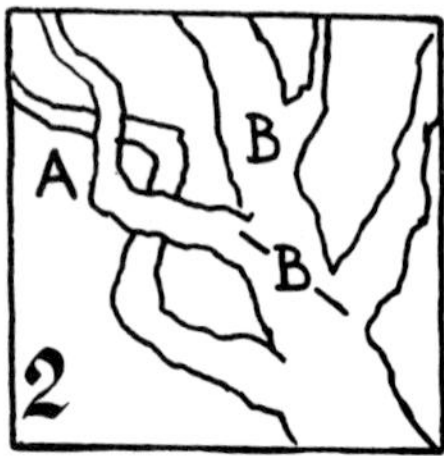

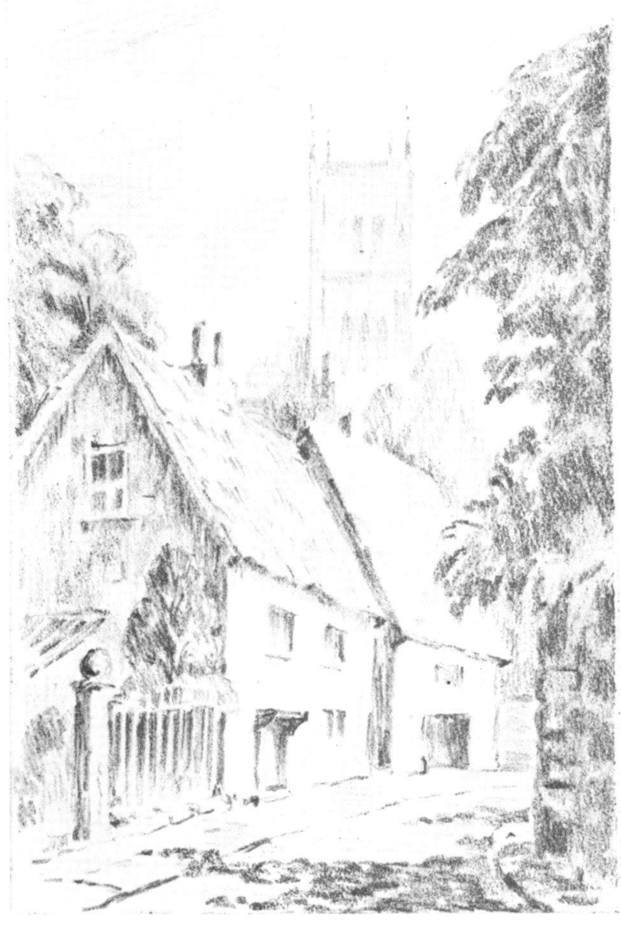

HB

2B

4B

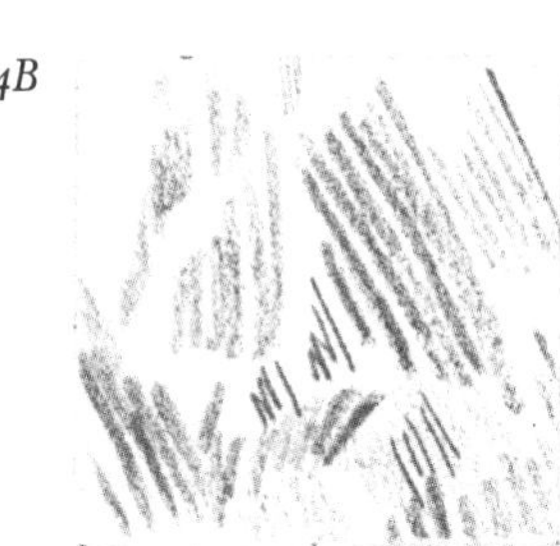

A sketch and practice pieces on a medium textured water-colour paper. A rough surface often gives an effect which is in harmony with the subject

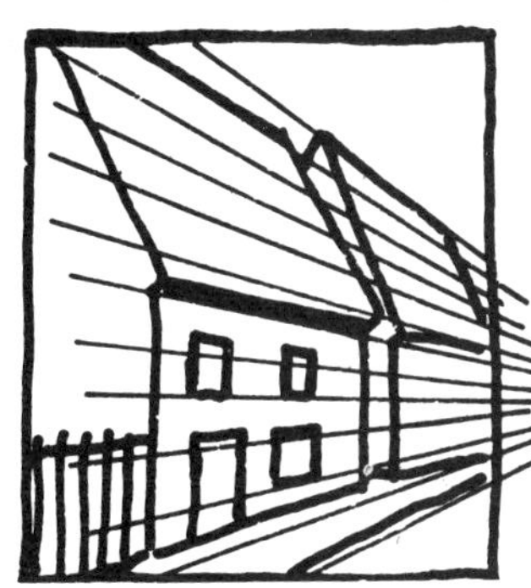

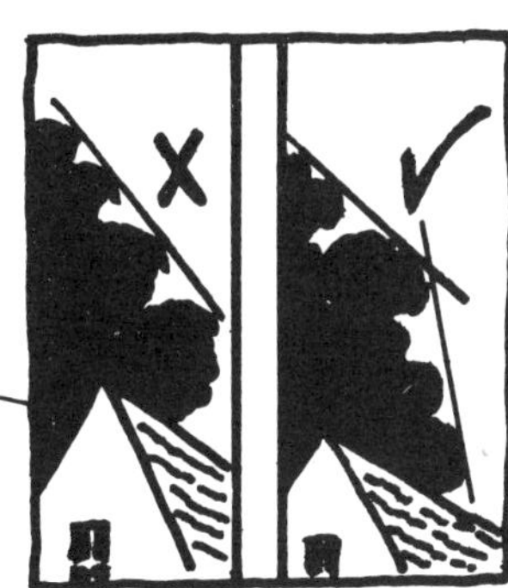

A diagram to show how converging lines of perspective can be used to advantage. In the pencil sketch (top left) they lead the eye into the picture

Two diagrams to show how much more effective is the silhouette of a tree when it follows an irregular line. Both examples are from the pencil sketch (top left). Notice that even a simple diagram like the right-hand one looks better than that on the left because a few 'sky-holes' have been included

Figure 53

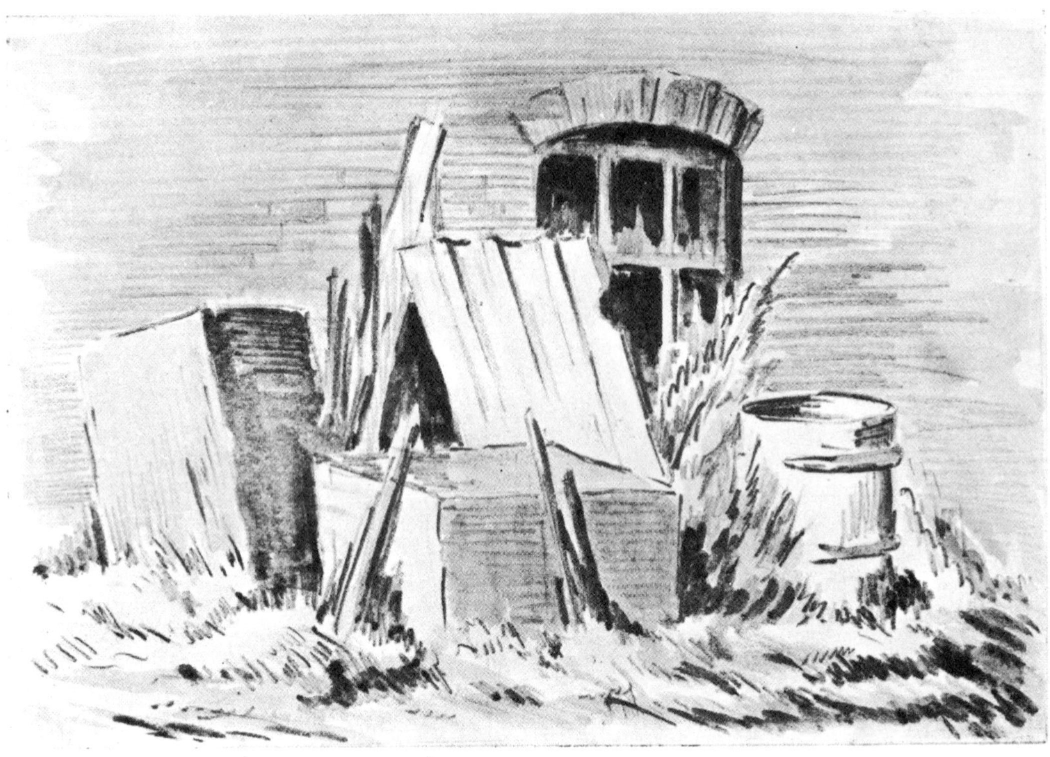

Figure 54. A pencil used in conjunction with transparent washes of water-colour paint

This is a happy method of working because it allows freedom of treatment. The paper now becomes the tone mid-way between light and dark, which means that far fewer strokes have to be made with pencil and chalk. Such economy enhances the freshness found in sketches of this type. They can usually be executed very quickly and almost invariably gain from such speed, provided it is controlled. One slight disadvantage is that the chalk can easily be smudged, but this can be overcome by spraying with fixative. (Full information about fixative is in Chapter 1, Part I). Even normal pencil drawings can receive this treatment if it is felt there is any danger of rubbing, or 'setting off' from one sheet to another.

Many people are unaware that transparent films or 'washes' of water-colour paint can combine very well with pencil work. There is no need to become heavily laden with equipment. Tiny paint-boxes, complete with brush, are easily obtainable and are small enough to fit into a purse or a waistcoat pocket, but remember to have one which incorporates a few depressions in which the pools of colour can be mixed. Water can be carried in any small snap-lidded watertight container, providing it has a wide enough neck to allow the brush to be vigorously swirled for cleaning.

Although you now have some experience in handling water-colours, it is as well to practise controlling these washes of colour, for they look unpleasant if they are too 'dry' or if they are over-handled. Make sure that you can really control them; not only the simple monochrome ones, but also those which make use of one colour being dropped into another.

These washes can be most helpful. They can quickly cover areas which need a fairly even layer of tone, and which could easily become laboured if completely covered with pencil. The strength of colour—that is its degree of lightness or darkness—can be altered as you proceed, simply by adding a little more paint or water. The sketch reproduced in *Figure 54* illustrates this method. There are no set rules of procedure, but I usually find it best to get about halfway with the pencil and then gently apply the washes, taking great care always to keep them semi-transparent and never making them dense or inky. When the final and more telling pencil strokes are added, they have a crispness which might be lost if all the drawing were done first. In my sketch I have used Payne's Grey, but of course other single colours can be used—or you could use more than one.

Pencil-and-wash allows for an infinite variety of individual treatments. My main advice is not to overdo the colouring. Use it subtly; aim for the general effect rather than for reality. I have always found that colour says much more if it does not shout. In fact the result is invariably more satisfactory if one limits oneself to three, or even two, colours.

3. Studies in Pen and Ink

The strokes made by a pen have a firm decisiveness which is immediately exciting—they are so clean and sharp. The clear contrast between the ink lines and the paper gives the work a sparkle and crispness which is difficult to equal with any other media. Because the pen can convey an air of scintillation so rapidly, it can create a wonderfully spontaneous effect when used with sensitivity, intelligence and control. The sketch reproduced in *Figure 55* was made during a trip to Lincolnshire. You will notice that the technique is very similar to pencil work but whereas in a pencil sketch degrees of tone are achieved by using different pressures and grades of pencils, in a pen sketch they can only be suggested by varying the proximity and thickness of the strokes. This makes the technique a little more difficult to master, but the effort is well worth making.

For our initial experiments and work we shall be using ordinary steel nibs, as my aim is to keep all material simple and easy to carry.

This is what we need:

1. Sketchbook or cartridge paper
2. A selection of steel pens (nibs)
3. Penholder(s)
4. Black waterproof ink
5. HB pencil
6. India rubber

The paper is usually cartridge, but there is no need for wild expense: almost any paper will do providing it is non-porous and has a fairly smooth surface. Avoid anything fluffy, as this will be picked up by the pen and will quickly cause clogging and blotting. Very rough paper is also unsuitable because it prevents a sharp continuous stroke and is liable to flick the nib, giving your work an unwanted spray of fine dots. As you progress you may wish to try other papers. Very pleasant effects can be produced on a fine white high-quality paper known as Kent, and also on Ingres paper, which is often used for pastels and can be obtained in white and a large number of restrained colours. For something really special, the smooth card called Bristol board has a most sympathetic surface and is beautifully white.

Penholders can be of any pattern, the main criterion being that they must grip the nib firmly with no trace of wobble and be comfortable to handle. I suggest you purchase a selection of nibs and find one that suits your hand. I recommend using a fairly large nib because it holds plenty of ink, is firm in use, and although slightly sensitive is not too flexible. A rather tiny springy one is tricky to control at speed and can so easily catch in the paper. My own particular favourite is a large 'J' type, which gives fine or broad strokes according to the grip or direction and has a slight flexibility which can be controlled by a gentle change of pressure. I have attached a metal 'reservoir' to it and this provides a lot of ink from one dip.

We will work first with waterproof or Indian ink. In *Figure 57* you will see the various strokes I have obtained with my favourite nib and I suggest you do something similar with the one you have selected. Rule out some panels about $1\frac{1}{4}$ in. square and in the first one try making long continuous vertical strokes, endeavouring to keep them parallel and of even

Figure 55. A pen sketch showing a variety of strokes used to create a feeling of distance and perspective

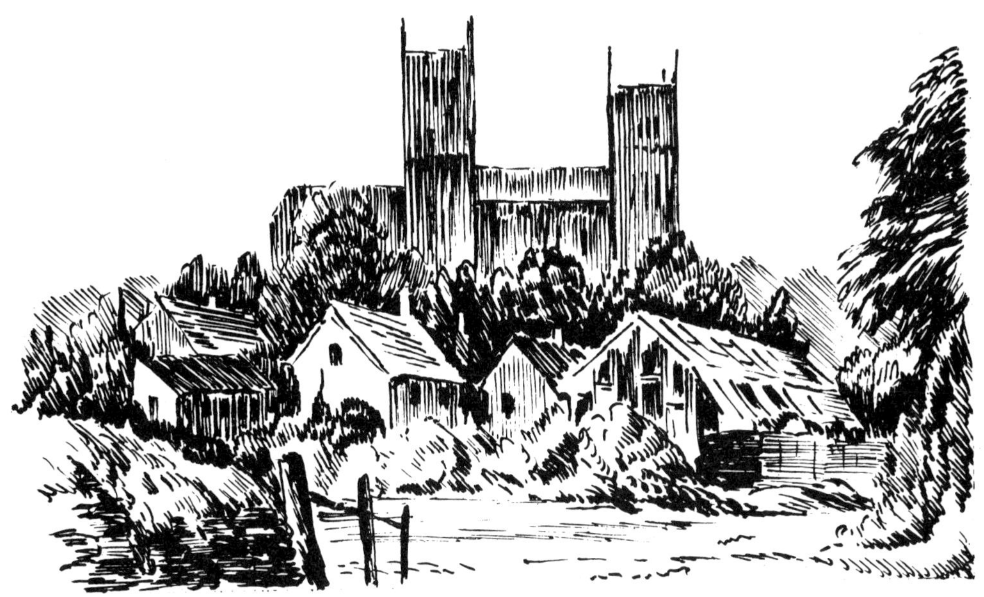

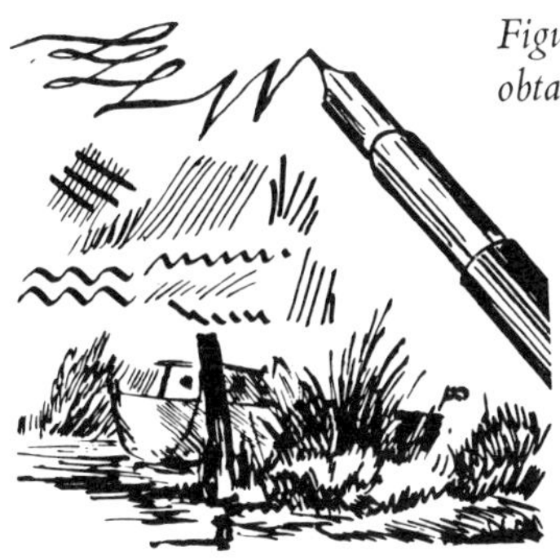

Figure 56. Some of the strokes obtainable from a normal 'J' type nib

pressure. Use the pen as you used the pencil, making it behave as an extension of your forefinger and moving your hand round until the action is comfortable. The first panel shows equally-spaced lines which give an even covering of tone. In the panel to its right the tone is made darker by placing the lines much closer together: this is a most important technique to master. The third panel, reading horizontally, shows how effective a broken line can be, whilst the fourth contains a simple application of the three previous examples.

The next two rows follow a similar progression, except that the strokes are diagonal. These slanting strokes are usually the most comfortable to the hand and are in the majority in most sketches. The fourth row of panels deals with horizontal strokes and the fifth with curves and wavy lines. The latter can look rather false if overdone, but they can be useful when a change of rhythm is considered necessary.

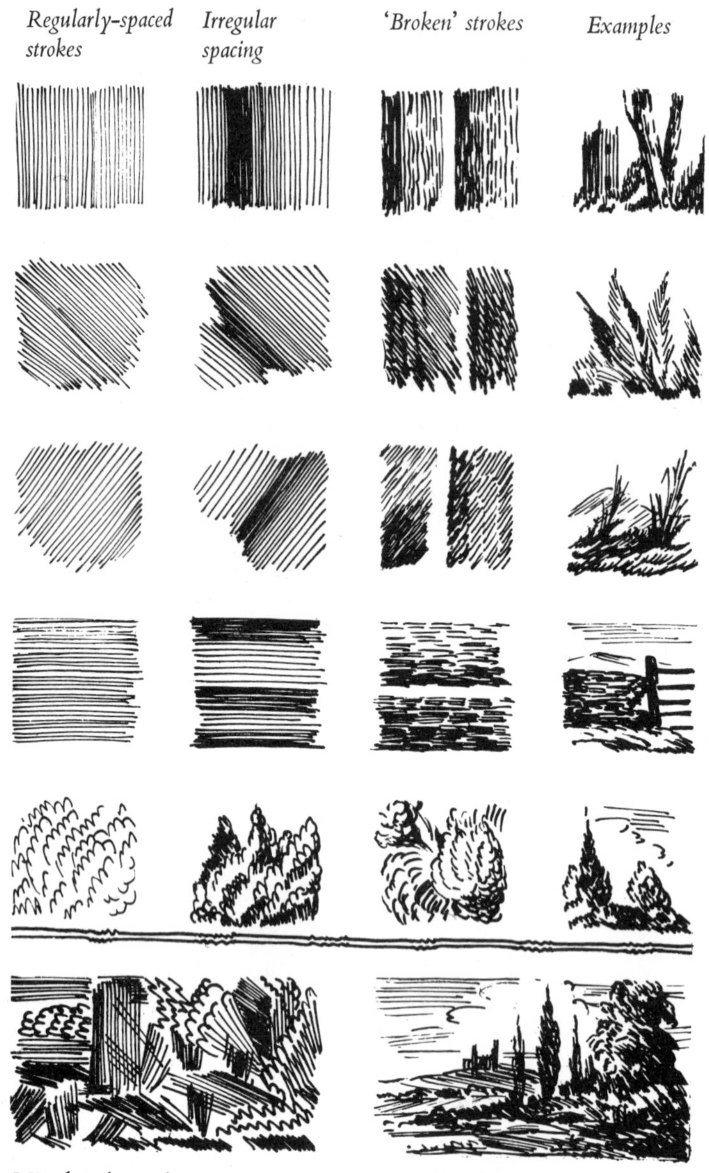

Figure 57

The large panel on the left at the bottom is an abstract design made with these five strokes. This is excellent practice because you are merely filling the paper with various shaded areas, without any thought of reality or recognition: it is solely a question of the beauty and contrast of the strokes, for their own sake, and building them into a pleasing arrangement. The final panel shows a scene in which all the previously practised strokes have been used.

A few exercises like these will save considerable time, for fewer sketches will be spoilt through lack of facility. It will not take long to learn to control the strokes and I think you

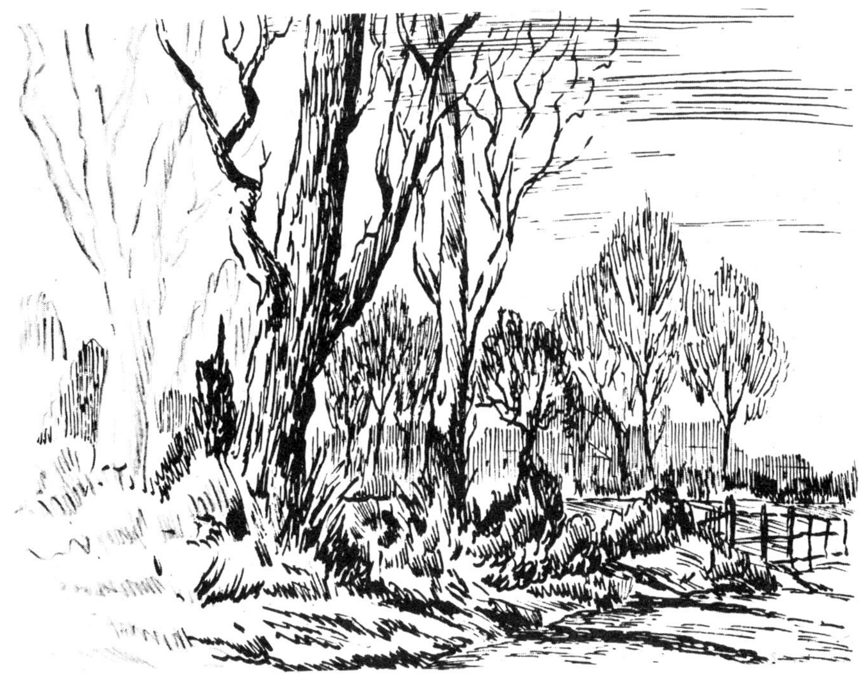

Figure 58. An unfinished sketch showing some of the original pencil guide lines

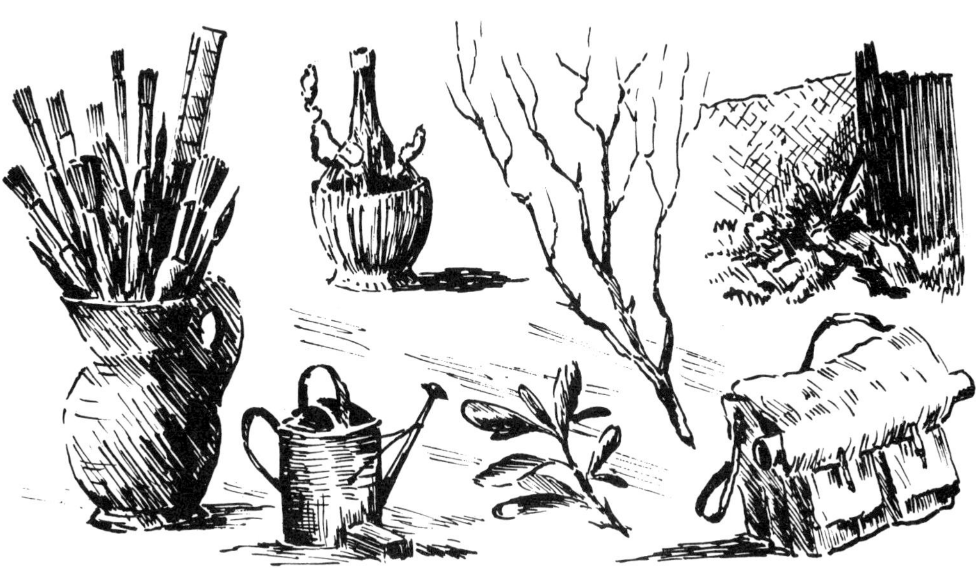

Figure 59. Practice pieces to get the feel of the materials

will find the experiments quite enjoyable. Do not be despondent if things go wrong occasionally; better by far to fail on a trial effort than in the middle of what promises to be an accomplished and thoughtful piece of work.

Once a reasonable mastery has been achieved, it would be wise to copy something to further your skill. The sketch in *Figure 58* should help, for here I have made use of a wide variety of strokes. As you can see, the sketch is not quite complete. I have left some of the pencil marks showing to point out that, unless you are extremely sure of yourself, it is wise to have some indication of what you are aiming at before applying the ink. Normally I use

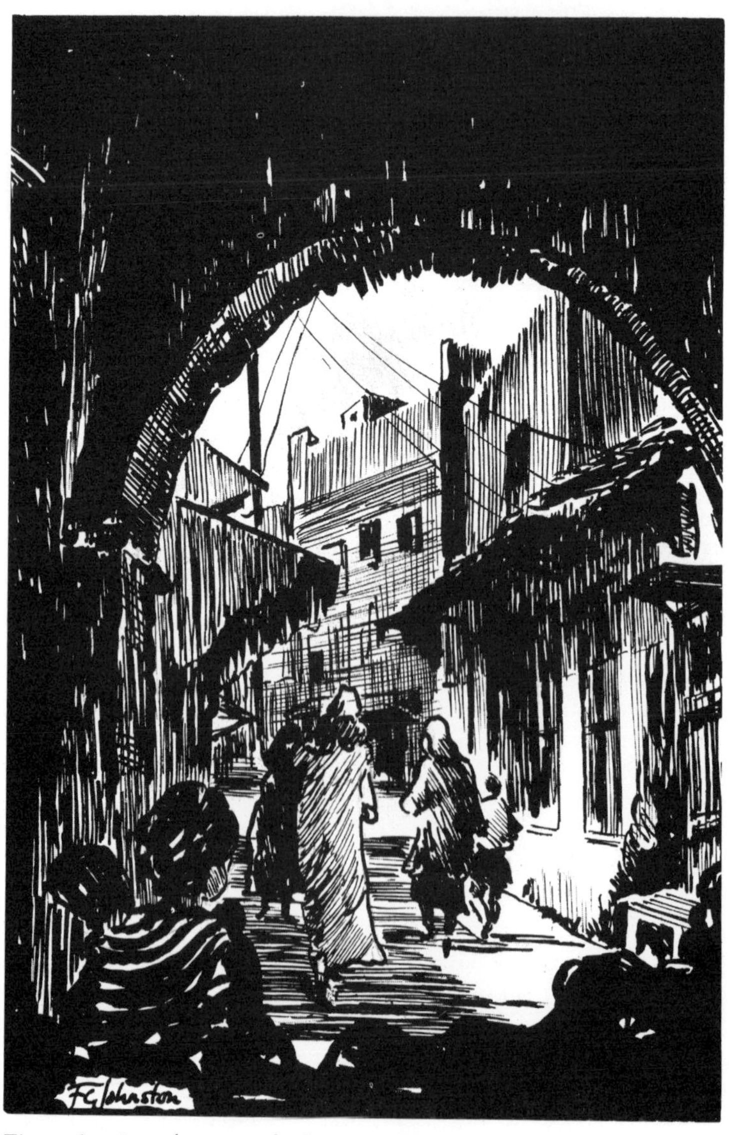

Figure 60. A combination of ink, pen and brush is useful when the dark areas are fairly solid

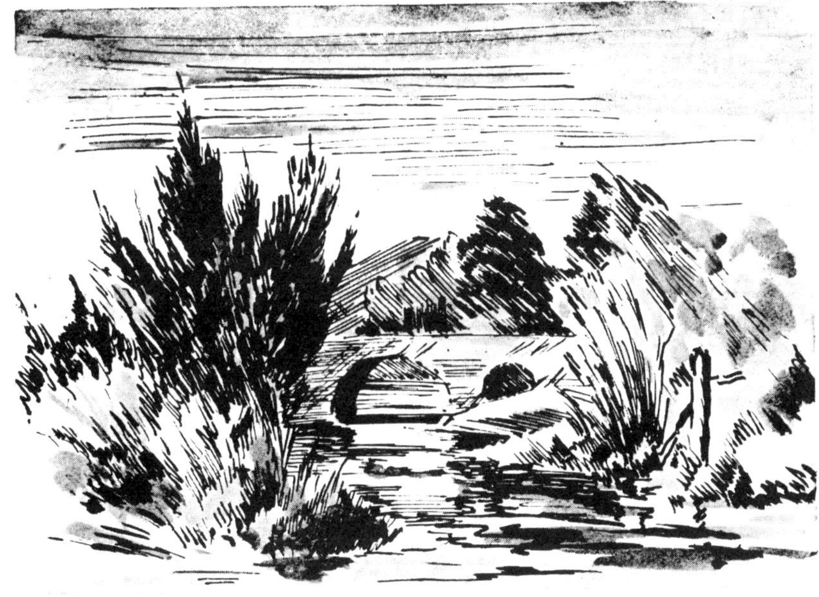

Figure 61
Washes of watered-down ink over the pen strokes help to give solidity and allow for occasional passages of free brushwork

an HB pencil, as this is soft enough not to bruise the paper but sufficiently crisp to indicate clearly where the final strokes are to be made. It is not necessary to make this preliminary drawing too definite; an intelligent suggestion to help you start will suffice. When the ink has dried the pencil lines can be erased.

The main aim in this sketch was to give the appearance of recession. It has been achieved by using much finer and more delicate strokes for the distant things and treating them with great simplicity. The buildings in the background show this quite clearly. Notice, too, how the bolder strokes on the largest tree bring the trunk forward. Try something similar, without slavishly copying, and I am sure you will quickly get the idea.

As with pencil sketching, the next step is to wander around the house and make a few sketches of familiar things. Several examples are shown in *Figure 59*. Remember the basic principles of all the previous work on composition and on the effects of atmosphere and light, for these are of utmost importance whatever the medium. Remember, too, to make a slight pencil sketch first before committing yourself to the finality of ink. Now you are well prepared to set out and capture the beauty of the landscape.

Later on you may like to combine a certain amount of brushwork with the pen strokes, still using the ink exactly as it comes from the bottle. This is particularly useful if your subject has very dense areas of dark, which would need a lot of rather frenzied scratching with the pen to cover them completely. A No. 6 water-colour brush—the type which is round and comes to a nice fine point—is recommended. One made from sable hair is well worth having because it is so springy and well shaped, but almost any brush of this type will do, except a very cheap one whose point is blunt and whose hairs are lifeless and floppy. The sketch in *Figure 60* shows how useful the brush can be in covering large masses of fairly solid dark. It is a good idea to outline the tiny light patches within these dark areas with a pen, and use the brush only to fill in. This keeps the edges sharp and crisp.

Now that a brush has been included in our equipment, we can develop pen sketches in a slightly different direction by placing washes of either ink or water-colour paint over (or under) them. You will remember that this technique was used with our pencil work, and the result is equally effective and delightful when working with ink. *Figure 61* shows gentle washes of watered-down Indian ink added to an existing sketch. One pleasant feature of this type of work is that the areas of brushwork need not be kept rigidly within the already-drawn areas. One can insert happy little touches of free brushwork. My sketch shows such treatment on the right-hand side. There are also a few of these free strokes elsewhere and they can be seen quite clearly in the movement of the water.

Water-colour paints will produce a similar result but with the added charm of a hint of colour. Should you find it too difficult to add colour on the spot, it is quite a good plan to make the sketch and then take a long and careful look to memorize the colouring, possibly adding a few very faint pencil notes to your sketch. The colour can then be introduced, after careful deliberation, in the comfort of the home and away from the demands of absolute realism which can so easily sap our courage and prevent us from making our own thoughtful and individual interpretations.

A normal fountain-pen is quite a satisfactory instrument for sketching, but care must be taken to use the correct ink, which is soluble. (Fixed inks, which are waterproof, will quickly clog.) With this one reservation such a pen will produce satisfying and pleasing work. Good use can be made of the fact that fountain-pen ink mixes so readily with water. If we were to place a few strokes on to paper, allow them to dry, and then brush clean water over them, we would observe two things: one would be that some of the ink would be picked up from the lines and would spread itself across the paper as a weak film of tone; the other would be that the strokes receiving such treatment would become softer—less crisp. We would also discover that, once the paper was dry, further strokes could be placed over these areas. Slight differences of tone in the brushed areas are obtained by occasionally agitating the brush a little more vigorously to remove more ink from the original lines.

This method was used in *Figure 62*. It is taken from a sketch of Chiddingstone in Kent. First a faint pencil sketch was made, and then most of the work was completed with an oblique-nibbed fountain pen. The paper is a very smooth one which I think is sympathetic to this particular method. Every endeavour was made to keep the strokes vigorous and lively in order to maintain harmony with the rather flowing quality created when the water is applied. Immediately the drawing was complete the background trees were treated with water; you can see how these now appear solid, with very few patches of white paper remaining. Almost at the same time, the water was swept down over some of the tiles and into the walls, but care was taken to leave the sunlit areas untouched. The brush now held enough 'colour', with a little water added, to give a slight tint to the road, fence and sky. The larger tree was agitated with greater energy to make it darker. Finally, when the sketch was dry, a few crisp pen strokes were added. There are several under the eaves and projections and in the tall chimney. More can be seen in the large tree and there are a few in the right-hand foreground. From the point of view of composition, it is as well to notice that the foreground has been simply treated and is shallow in height. One very good hint when dealing with architectural subjects: let buildings rise up proud and not too cluttered at their base, and they will almost invariably have a greater grace and dignity. I hope you will like this method: it is one of my favourites. I have found it captures the elusive airiness of the landscape and is quick to use.

In *Figure 64* you will see a sketch made with another type of fountain-pen, which is

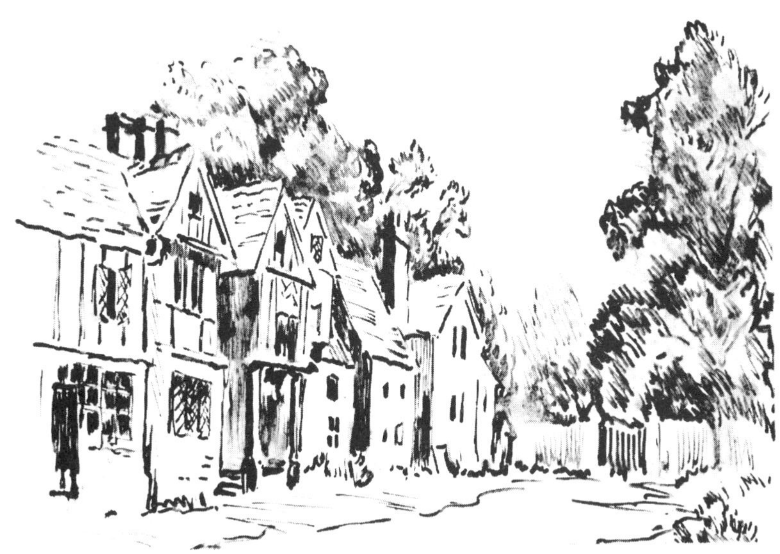

Figure 62
An example of soluble ink brushed over with clean water

Figure 63
The type of pen designed for use with waterproof ink

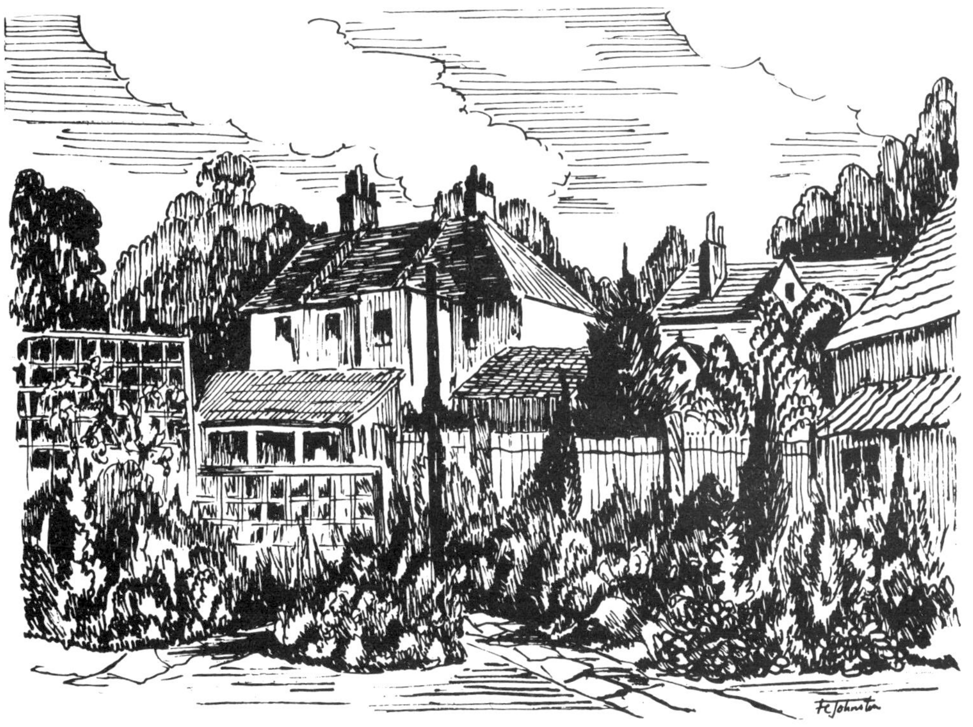

Figure 64. A view of the garden—a sketch made with the rigid nibs of Rapidograph pens

especially produced for use with waterproof ink. In this instance I used one called a Rapidograph which works on the principle of a fine wire inside a rigid metal tube. It can be obtained with tips of varying widths, which are often interchangeable so that the thickness of the line can be altered when desired. The resulting stroke is very even and true but as there is no flexibility, there is no graduation. I used a Kent drawing paper, which has a well-defined texture and tends to 'break' the strokes and give them variation. The scene is from my studio window. I took one liberty. By bringing the distant buildings very much closer and therefore drawing them larger, a more interesting skyline was obtained. Two pens were used—a No. 4, which is fine, and a No. 6, which is broader.

Finally, please remember that there are many methods and techniques. In this chapter I have explained some of them, allied to a few basic principles. I hope you will continue to practise and experiment with all kinds of implements and surfaces. Beautiful work is possible with prepared quills and reeds. I even knew an artist who produced the most profound and delightful work with sharpened twigs and blotting paper!

4. *Pens without Nibs*

Not long ago there appeared a new kind of pen, in which the nib has been replaced by a felt or fibre tip fed with ink from a supply stored in the barrel. Normally the ink-flow is maintained by gravity and absorption, but in the more expensive models it can be varied by applying pressure on a spring-loaded plunger.

Early types were apt to be erratic, and blobs and scratches were hard to avoid, but great improvements have been made and pens of this kind must now be recognized as efficient drawing instruments with a special character of their own. They are not just substitutes: the lines they make are less sharply defined than those made with a conventional pen, but sensitive and thoughtful work can be produced in a style which cannot be achieved with any other instrument. The free-flowing nature of the strokes and the constant supply of ink make them ideal instruments for rapid working, and when speed is allied to sureness of touch the result can be very pleasing.

As you can see from the illustration (*Figure 65*), there are many types of these pens. They can be divided into two categories: those with felt tips and those with hard-wearing fibre tips. In general it will be found that a fibre tip gives a thinner and sharper stroke than a felt tip, which produces a line with a slightly fluffy appearance. Whichever is purchased, it is always wise to ascertain whether or not the ink is waterproof, as this may ultimately determine your method of working. As the fibre-tipped pens are well pointed and sharp, and only a little different in appearance from the pencils and pens with which we are already familiar, we will deal with them first.

Following our usual procedure, let us practise some intelligent 'doodling' with the new pen, in order to get the feel of it. This is what I have done in *Figure 66*. The top row shows fibre-tipped pen strokes on three different kinds of paper. As you can see, it works well even on quite a rough surface, but it must be remembered that rough textures will soon wear away the tip. At first I would recommend using cartridge paper, and avoiding the special

Figure 65

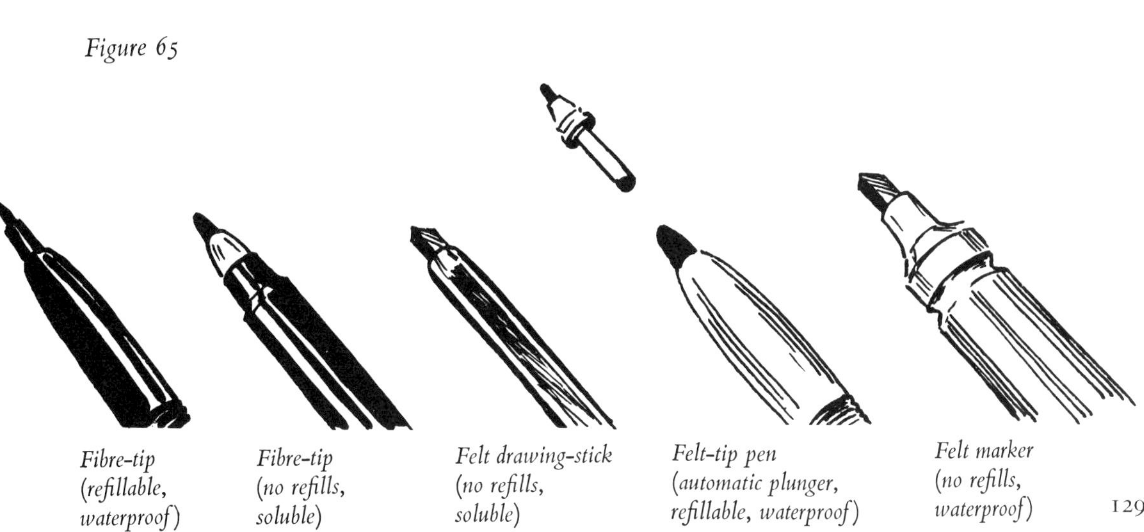

Fibre-tip (refillable, waterproof)

Fibre-tip (no refills, soluble)

Felt drawing-stick (no refills, soluble)

Felt-tip pen (automatic plunger, refillable, waterproof)

Felt marker (no refills, waterproof)

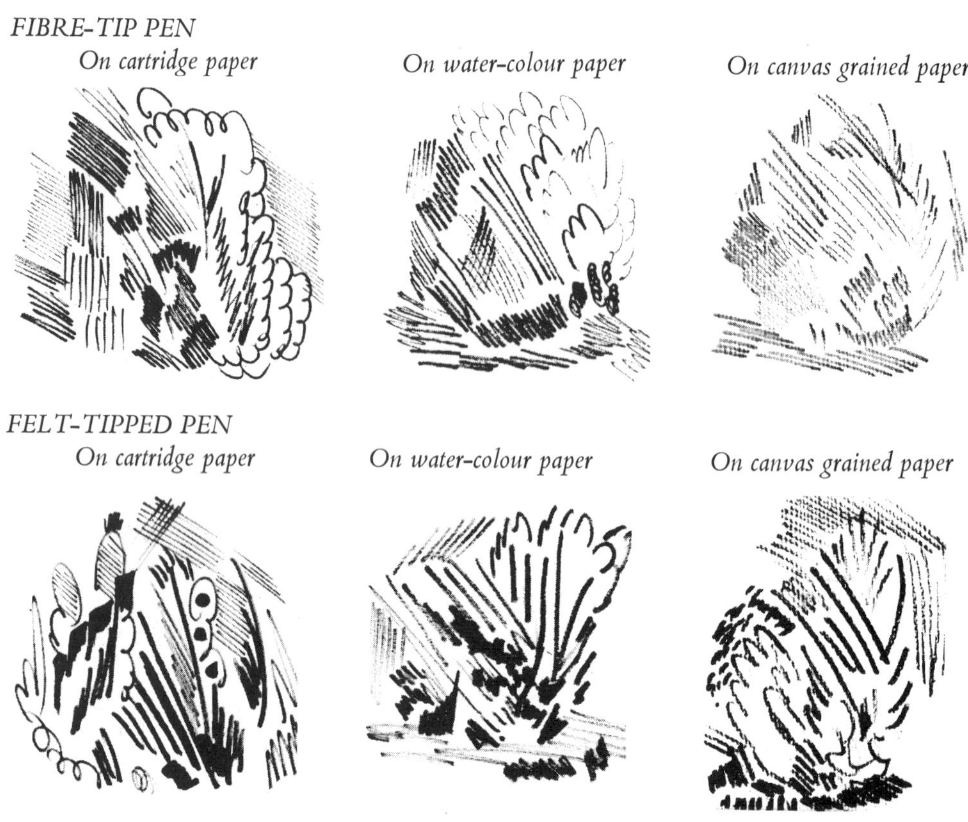

Figure 66

textured effects until you have gained some facility in handling the pen.

Next I would suggest 'hastening slowly' by once more making several simple studies of familiar objects. Only when you feel confident that you have a fairly competent mastery of the instrument is it time to attempt more ambitious studies.

Figure 67 shows a busy side-street in a Mediterranean town with the ever-present washing and half-hidden shops which make this type of scene so attractive. (As mistakes cannot be erased when using these pens, a faint guide-drawing was put in first with an HB pencil.) The sketch is included in this book because it is a good example of the quality of free-flowing strokes which start, stop, and start again, giving a far more interesting effect than bold and continuous outlines. It also shows how we can produce both fine and broad lines with these pens, by holding them at different angles as we did when working with a pencil. The rather strong foreground, with strokes in all directions, helps to take the eye well into the picture; and to maintain this accent on recession, the distant shadows have been treated much more lightly and delicately. A comparison of the technique and general effect of this illustration with that of the steel-nibbed pen sketch in *Figure 55* will help to show both the similarities and the differences in the use of the two instruments.

It is sometimes a good plan to include a few figures to give animation to the scene. These should not be detailed portraits. The essential thing is to endeavour to capture stance, proportion and scale, and to make the figures an unobtrusive part of the picture. Simplicity of treatment brings a unity and harmony to the sketch which detailed and laboured figure drawings would completely destroy. Should you find these figures rather difficult to draw, make plenty of studies in your sketch-book. At first it will be much easier if they are treated almost as silhouettes. This will help you to get them in proportion, and as progress is made the effects of light and shade can be indicated. A few examples of such practice pieces are shown in *Figure 68*.

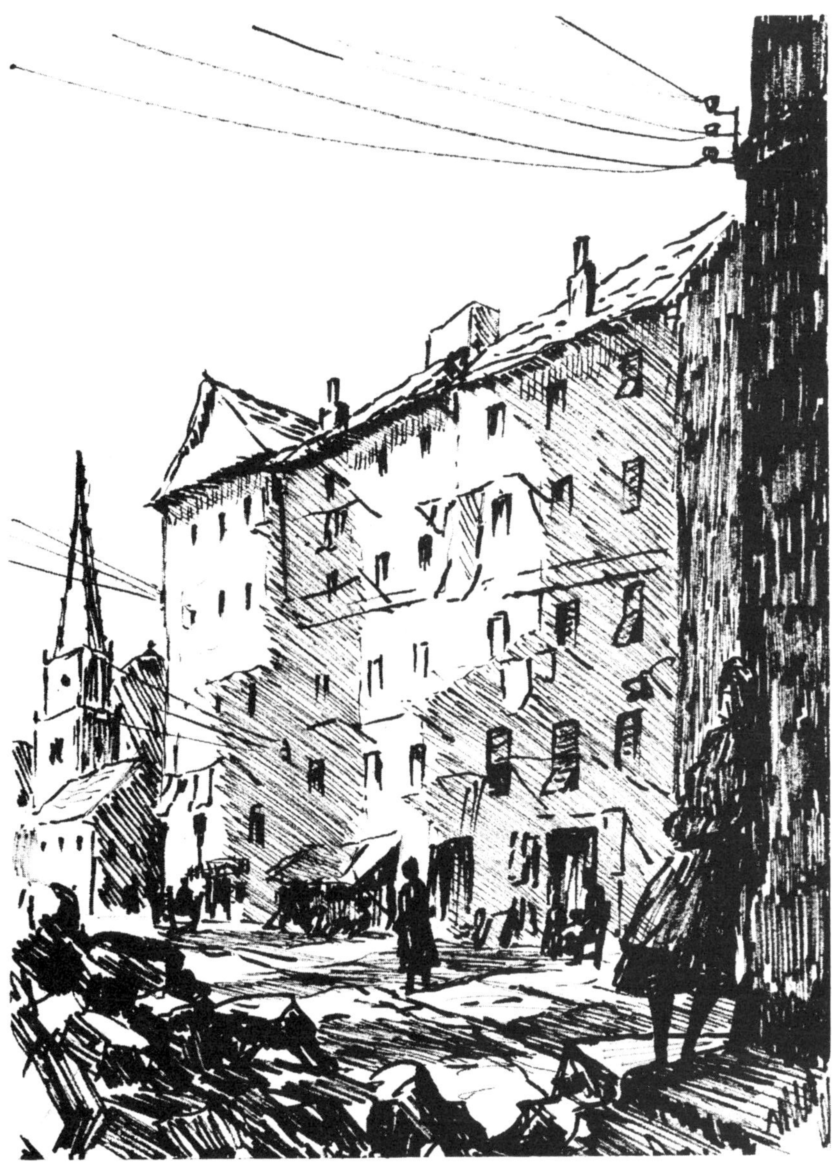

Figure 67. A Sardinian side-street. An example of the use of a felt-tipped pen on a smooth paper

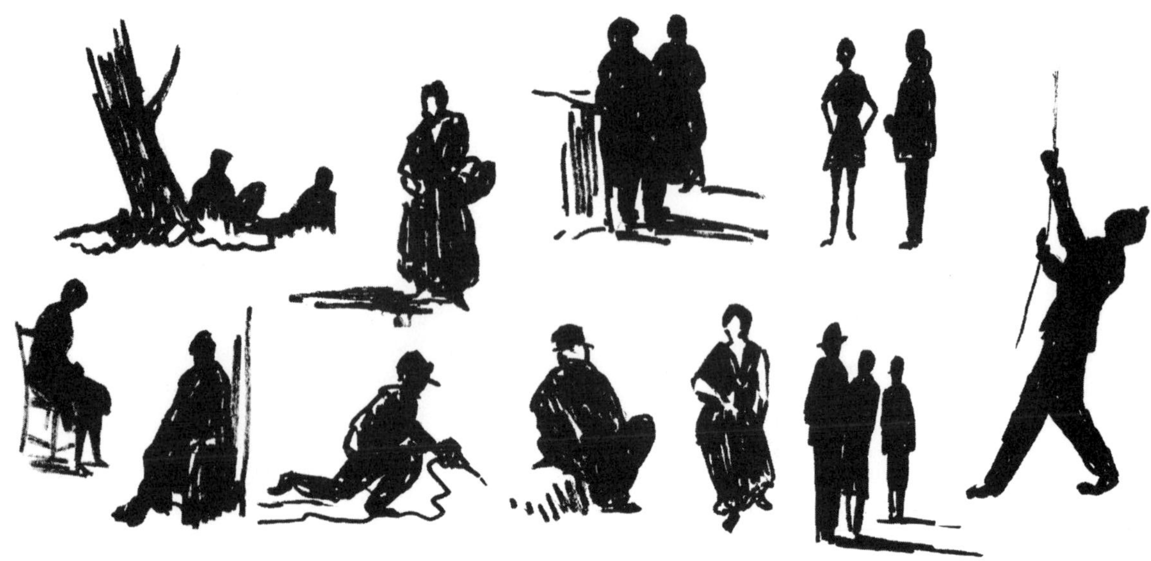

Figure 68. Drawing figures in silhouette will develop the observation of size, stance and proportion

If the pen you have been using contains waterproof ink, fresh and lively sketches can be made by adding a few pale washes of water-colour to your drawing. This is pleasant work and can be particularly useful if the sketch is to be used as preparation for a future painting. However, in this book we are concentrating more on the value of sketches as a means of expression in their own right, and I am sure you will agree that these coloured ones have an individual charm. *Figure 69* is a study of the odds and ends which can be found in a boat-builder's yard. I discovered this interesting corner when wandering around the delightful confusion of boats and tackle in a yard at Woodbridge in Suffolk. I have often found that these corners, where busy people stack their materials, offer naturally good compositions. They are like huge still-life groups, and even if we were able to move all their components I doubt very much if we could improve the arrangement.

If your pen is filled with a water-soluble ink, you can apply clean water to your sketch with a brush, thereby spreading some of the ink over the surface to give the appearance of a monochrome pen-and-wash drawing. I used this method when I was working with an ordinary fountain-pen, and the same system can be employed when using any instrument containing soluble ink. It is a method which lends itself admirably to subjects of a soft and gentle character which need very few bold lines. The country lane in *Figure 70* is a good example, as too sharp a treatment might have spoilt the gentle merging softness of the foliage and the undulating landscape. A few final crisp strokes were added when the work was dry, but these were kept to a minimum.

The reproduction in *Figure 71* shows another sketch from my holiday in Sardinia. The paper I used is slightly textured, and is called Bockingford. If this sketch is compared with that shown in *Figure 67* it will be seen how the lines and strokes have a certain granulation —particularly noticeable in the foreground—that cannot be obtained on a smoother paper.

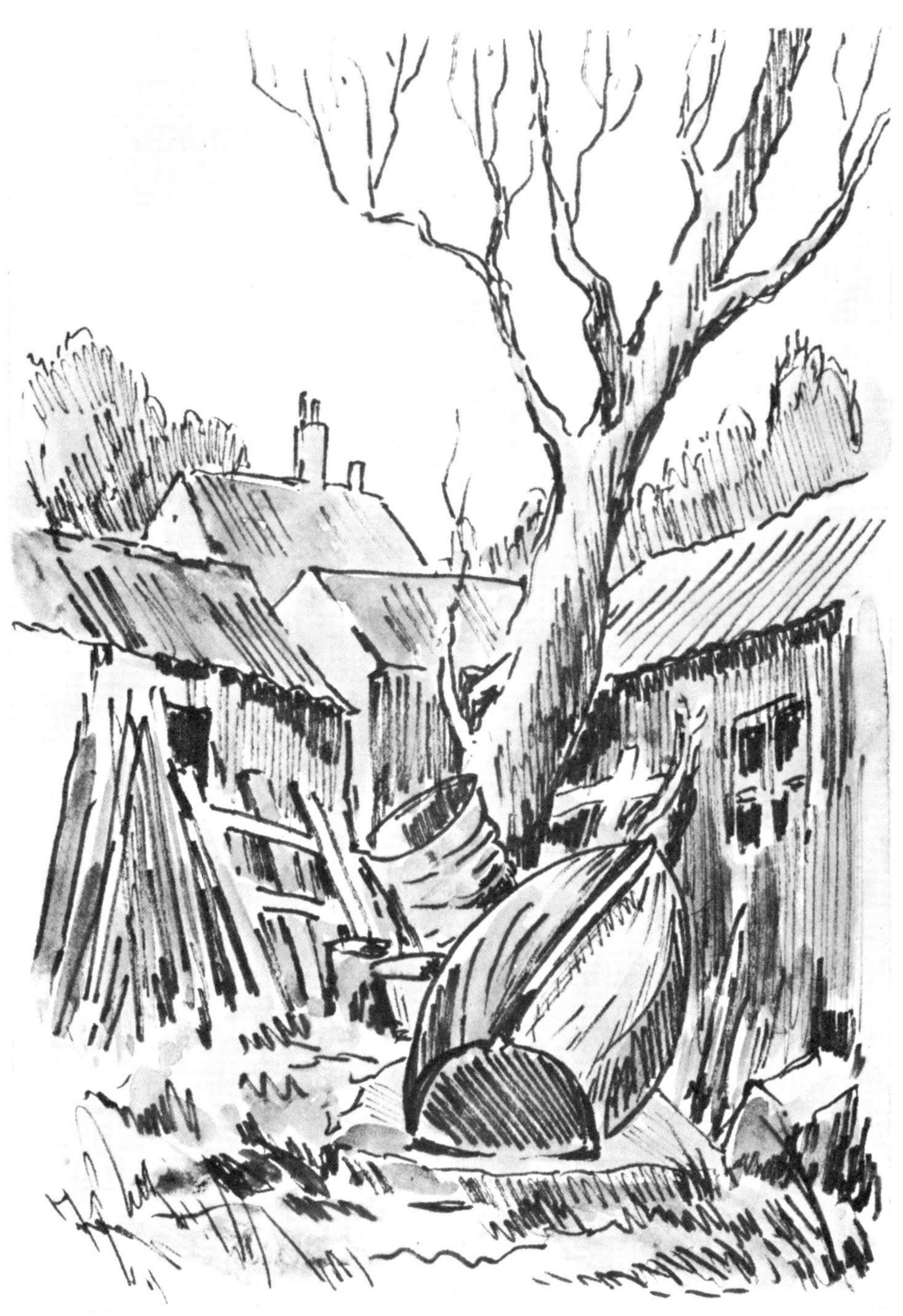

Figure 69. Odds and ends at Woodbridge, Suffolk.
Water-colour applied over a sketch made with a fibre-tip pen

This effect is very suitable for some subjects. From the point of view of composition, *Figure 71* proves the advantage of finding a good viewpoint. I am sure the factor which immediately made me want to possess a record of the scene was the overlapping of the various blocks of buildings, each different in shape.

Now let us explore the potentialities of the felt-tipped pen. If we try some experimental scribbling we shall find that, although the strokes are not as fine and sharp as those made with a fibre tip, it is possible, by varying the pressure or by dabbing the pen first on a piece of rag to reduce the supply of ink, to produce strokes which are grey instead of the usual dense black. Now, with one tool, we can have the variation obtained by several grades of very broad pencils. Admittedly, if we wanted a sketch with fine draughtsmanlike lines, this

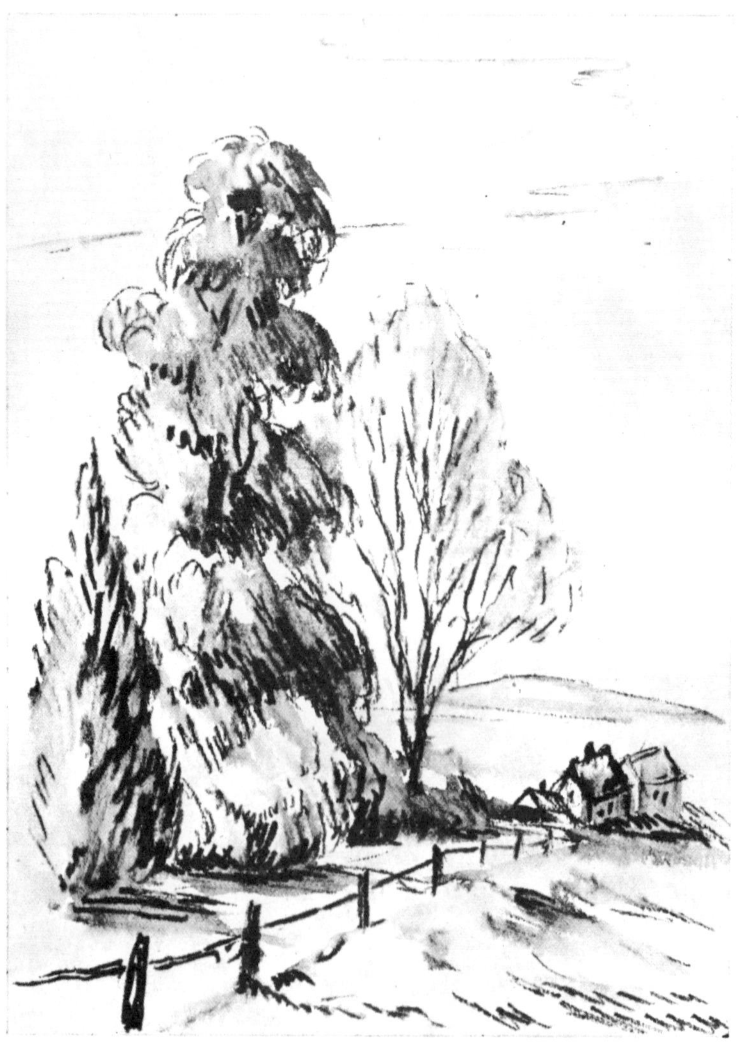

Figure 70. A sketch made with a soluble-ink type of fibre-tipped pen. Water has been added with a brush

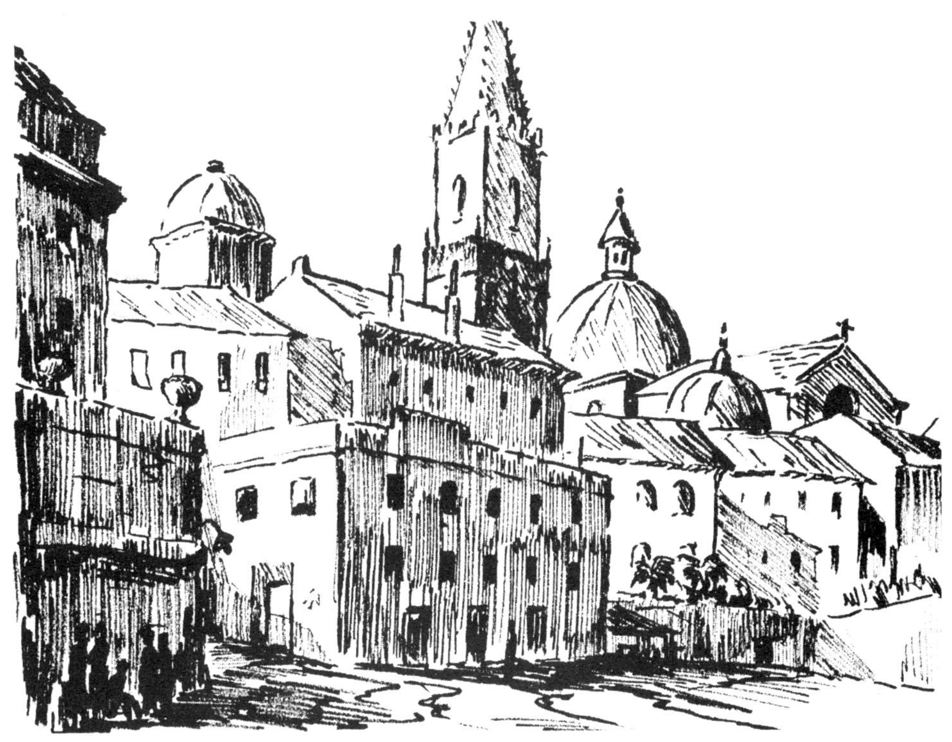

Figure 71. Alghero, Sardinia. Using a fibre-tipped pen on a slightly textured paper will 'break' the strokes and create an old, weathered look

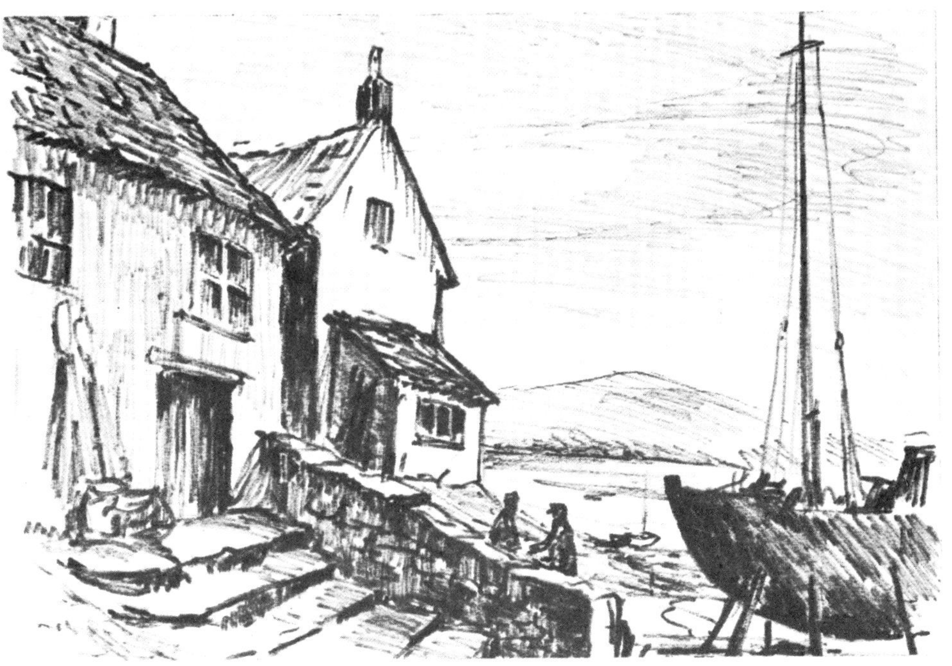

Figure 72. Kirkcudbright, Scotland. A felt pen on a slightly textured paper

would not be our instrument; but if we desired a result which was loose, free and imaginative, this type of pen could suit our purpose extremely well. Again, as any marks made are permanent, it is wise to start with a slight pencil drawing until you are absolutely sure of yourself.

The scene illustrated in *Figure 72* is a corner of Kirkcudbright, a delightful Scottish town which is rich in subjects suitable for sketching, and where an interest in art and artists is a normal part of daily life. I felt that the rough-cast nature of the architecture, the flow of the water, and the sweep of the hills lent themselves to a broad interpretation with a felt pen. The sketch not only shows similarities to work done with a very soft pencil, but also demonstrates certain extra and elusive qualities that can only be obtained with this kind of pen. The model used in this instance had a spring plunger to control the supply of ink, which was very useful when less distinct passages were being expressed. Notice how the one instrument is capable of producing a wide range of tones, from the very soft quality of the sky to the extremely dark areas where the boat and steps are in shadow.

Because this type of pen contains a spirit-based ink, the sketches made with it are eminently suitable for a later application of water-colour. You can treat studies in a very free manner, and although the drawing should be accurate it must not be overdone. The bareness of an understated drawing is often a little worrying to the less experienced sketcher, but before you are tempted to keep adding to your drawing may I suggest you lay on some colour washes? In nearly every case, the addition of colour immediately holds everything together and there is no need for a lot of extra pen-strokes.

As a lover of the beauty and dignity of well-formed handwriting, I believe that good calligraphy is only possible with a pen which by a natural movement is capable of producing both thick and thin strokes. For this reason, I find a ball-point unsympathetic as a writing instrument, but it can be used very successfully for sketching. The only disadvantage is that the work must not be exposed to strong light for long periods, as this can cause fading.

Figure 73. An ordinary ballpoint pen on smooth paper can be an adequate sketching instrument

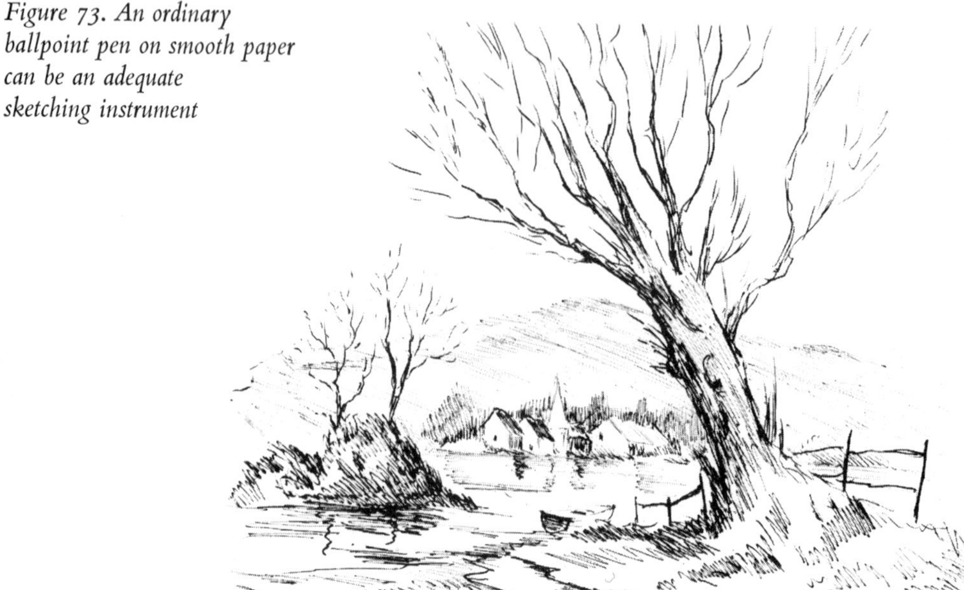

Figure 73 is a sketch made near Pulborough in Sussex. I only had a ball-point pen with me and the illustration shows an on-the-spot effort taken directly from my sketch-book. It is possible to produce extremely faint lines with a ball-point pen, and these were put to good use in suggesting the distance of the range of hills and the village. The bolder strokes needed a rather heavier and more vigorous action; they were particularly useful in the large tree. These bolder strokes, combined with the larger scale, gave a feeling of recession. As the action of the ball-point is so very smooth, my method of working was to use countless rapid strokes in a manner which could be described as premeditated scribble. In other words, although the movement of the hand is very fast and free, care should be taken in getting shapes correct and in deciding which particular features should be ignored, which need only slight suggestion, and which should be accentuated. One final point: colour washes can be added to a ball-point if desired.

We now have some knowledge of a range of pens a little different from the ordinary metal-nibbed variety. Whether you choose a felt tip, fibre tip or ball-point; whether you prefer the softening influence of clear water or the unifying charm of colour, you now have many combinations of material and technique from which to make a selection. Try them all on various surfaces and you will eventually find you have one or two favourites. Given a little time, I am sure you will also develop your own personal and individual way of using them.

5. *Sketching with Charcoal*

A stick of charcoal is a delightful medium for sketching. Used with intelligence and sensitivity it gives results that have a softness and charm that is difficult to obtain with any other medium. A vast range of tones is available to the artist—all under his control by the smudge of a finger or the flick of a rubber.

Many people fail with charcoal because they think of it as a linear instrument, rather like a pencil. It is not. It is much too soft and crumbly for making a great number of fine and sharp lines. Its outstanding quality is its capacity to cover an area quickly and efficiently without the necessity for any hard lines. Interest is created by subtle merging and changing of these areas, so that eventually the scene appears to grow from the paper. In this respect it is very similar to painting, and many artists make a preparatory sketch in charcoal before committing themselves to their chosen medium. It was for exactly this reason that the charcoal study was recommended in the opening chapters as an admirable introduction to painting.

It is now intended to take the subject a little further so that the work is no longer a preparatory exercise, but is elevated to the status of a thoughtful and effective study, completely acceptable as a serious piece of work. The absence of hard lines and sharp edges can bring a most distinctive quality to this very expressive medium.

Just to remind you, here are the things you will need:

1. Box of Willow Charcoal
2. Putty Rubber
3. Fixative } or fixative in aerosol can
4. Spray Diffuser }
5. Cartridge Paper

To give you a better idea how to proceed, I will try to explain step by step the principles in making an imaginary sketch of an outdoor scene. Having put down an even film of tone, look very carefully at the scene and decide which are the lightest patches and closely observe their shape and position. You can then lift these light areas out with the plastic rubber. If you make a mistake at this stage it is no disaster, as it merely means smudging everything together again and having another try. You have now established two values of tone—middle tone and almost white. Look now for other tones between these two and for the subtle areas that are a little darker than the original film of charcoal. Whilst putting these down also concentrate on improving the shapes (another form of drawing), using the rubber, the charcoal, and your finger for smudging.

Finally, put in corrections and additions. Trees receive their foliage and a few extra branches, and lights and darks are put in to give the feel of bumps and breaks on the ground. Slight changes of tone give shadow and dimension; the scene is complete.

Although a plastic rubber is quite effective, it will not work nearly so well if the paper is constantly being rubbed. It is therefore important, before getting too involved, to carefully 'read' the scene in front of you and decide exactly where the important light areas occur. Remember, too, that the real charm of good charcoal sketches is the careful establishing of the various areas of different tone. Do not draw a line round them first, as this is almost impossible to lose and you will find it quite offensive. Occasionally a very fine stroke is needed, but it is advisable to use a linear stroke only when absolutely necessary. At all costs preserve the delightfully cloudy and evocative understatement which makes the charcoal sketch so deeply satisfying. When you have finished give the sketch a good spraying with fixative and, unless it is treated very violently, you should get it home quite safely.

Although cartridge paper has been recommended because it is eminently satisfactory and easily obtainable, this does not mean that other types of paper with slightly different texture should be excluded. Try them. The only kind I would not suggest are those with an extremely rough surface. Necessity once forced me to use a paper which is produced specially for poster printing. One side is smooth and the other is rough. I found the rough side was ideal for charcoal work, and this shows the value of experimenting or perhaps—to be more accurate—of improvising. However, there are many other papers more easily available which are well worth attention, and it would be wise to see what your art stockist has to offer.

Another interesting way of using charcoal is to work on tinted paper. This can serve two purposes. The first is that it will add a touch of colour to the scene and thereby give your work an added appeal—if a pastel paper such as Ingres is used there is a choice of some thirty or more variations of colour, giving ample scope for selecting one which is sympathetic to your own particular interpretation. The second advantage is that it removes the need for placing a film of middle-toned charcoal over the work as a first stage. The paper itself becomes the middle tone.

As we have noted when we were working with pencil on coloured paper, any very light passages have to be inserted with a good quality white chalk. A type of chalk known as Conté is ideal for this purpose. Should you like this method—one which I find gives very pleasing results—it is better to leave these extra light touches until last. There are two good reasons for this: it prevents them getting smudged whilst the work is in progress, and by placing them into a sketch that is almost finished one can readily see exactly how much emphasis is required. To include them at too early a stage might well make the sketch look overdressed. It is unwise to try placing chalk over an existing charcoal stroke. Much better results are obtained by placing it directly on to the tinted paper even though it may mean erasing some of the charcoal first. Do not forget that it is better to break off a piece of chalk about $\frac{1}{2}$ in. long and use it flat, because you will cover the areas much more evenly and thickly. One can always find a little worn corner for any sharp linear accents.

Should you prefer something a little more colourful, charcoal can be combined quite successfully with water-colours. There are two methods of making charcoal-and-wash sketches. The first is to make a normal charcoal sketch on white paper in exactly the same way as outlined earlier. Blow away any surplus dust and give the work a liberal application of fixative. It will now be ready to accept nice fluid washes, which should be placed over the original drawing in very much the same way as when we tinted the pen-and-ink sketches. A warning must be given not to use the paints 'dry', because you will have to handle the brush so vigorously that it will destroy the thin protective film of fixative, and your charcoal will lift and ruin the sketch. Keep the washes very fluid and the brush strokes gentle, and I am sure the results will delight you.

The second method, which gives very similar results, is to put down the colour washes first and place the charcoal over them when the paint is thoroughly dry. Put in an extremely faint pencil drawing first and then apply colour in a very watery way. Have no qualms about the colours running a little, for you will find the final charcoal work will hold the sketch together quite satisfactorily, and the little accidents where the colours have run often produce very fascinating effects. The next stage requires a little courage, for once the paint is dry a film of charcoal is rubbed all over it. Then comes the exciting part. By lifting out the light areas with a plastic rubber, delightful patches of colour appear and the sketch starts to take on both shape and form. By smudging, erasing and adding, the work now progresses in exactly the same way as a normal black and white charcoal sketch.

Almost everyone finds charcoal-and-wash drawing deeply satisfying. The gentle changes and variations are mellow and subtle, and the softening effect of the charcoal gives the colour a unique quality. Whichever of the two techniques you choose, I am sure you will find that a few studies will very quickly lift your work above and away from the ordinary.

So ends my chapter on charcoal. Often it is a neglected medium due to misunderstandings about its use, or because of the more strident claims of other materials, but I hope that, like me, you will find it a joy to use. Remember never to work on a damp surface and always fix the sketch before packing your gear. With the guiding principles which have been outlined, I think you will spend many happy hours with this simple but most expressive sketching medium.

6. *Conté Crayon*

Conté crayons are very high-grade compressed chalks produced in Paris. Each stick is approximately $\frac{1}{4}$ in. square in section and $2\frac{1}{2}$ in. in length. The colours are black, white, Sanguine (a lovely terracotta red) and Bistre (a rich warm brown). There are three grades. Although much depends on personal preference, I usually find the softest (No. 3) to be the most sympathetic. The best way to use it is to break off a piece about $\frac{1}{2}$ in. long and make firm strokes with the whole of one of the flat surfaces.

At first glance a black-on-white Conté sketch looks rather similar to one made with charcoal, particularly as both media rely very strongly on good tone values and the effects produced by the texture of the paper. However, a closer inspection will soon reveal that the Conté sketch has certain other attributes. The most obvious of these is the rather decisive and rectangular quality of most of the strokes. The sketch of the church porch shown in *Figure 74* was chosen as an example of this. The architectural nature of the subject has obviously helped, but these broad flat patches of tone can even be seen in the sky, as well as being particularly noticeable on the left-hand building and in the foreground shadows.

While charcoal can be smudged and erased, Conté does not respond well to such handling. It is much better used direct and left alone. This means that from the outset the artist must have a definite idea of the effect he wishes to obtain. He must draw accurately, with firm bold strokes, each of which covers a considerable area in one vigorous movement.

Before looking further into the possibilities of this new medium, there is one good hint for me to pass on. Far better results are achieved if the drawing board is covered with about thirty thicknesses of newspaper before the sketching paper is attached. Not only will this give a nice soft pad on which to work, but the spaces between the layers of newsprint will act as a temporary storage for finished sketches.

Having attached an odd piece of cartridge paper to the padded board and broken off a small piece of black crayon, copy the strokes shown in *Figure 75*. This will demonstrate how quickly the padding brings out the texture of the sketching paper. The pad also responds very quickly to any change of pressure, and consequently it is easy to control the degree of blackness of the strokes. Use the flat sides of the crayon for broad areas, and the whole length of one of the corner edges for finer strokes. Change the pressure and vary the angle and all kinds of exciting results ensue. One of the most useful effects is that shown in the three vertical strokes at the top right of *Figure 75*. The first is a simple stroke with the crayon held firmly but perfectly flat, but in the second greater pressure on the right has given a much darker look. Thus in one single stroke we have produced something which looks quite cylindrical. The third stroke shows how, with a little intelligent wobbling, this can be put to good use when drawing trees. A few sheets of trials and experiments will give you quite an interesting selection.

As we are denied the use of a rubber, it could prove most difficult to produce very light lines. We could use white chalk, but this is not always satisfactory because there is a tendency for one colour to sully the other, resulting in a loss of sharpness. One method of overcoming this problem is to score the lines first with something hard but smooth—a fingernail or the pointed end of a paint-brush, for example. This leaves a small indentation in the paper which misses contact with the crayon when it is covering surrounding areas. Beware of over-

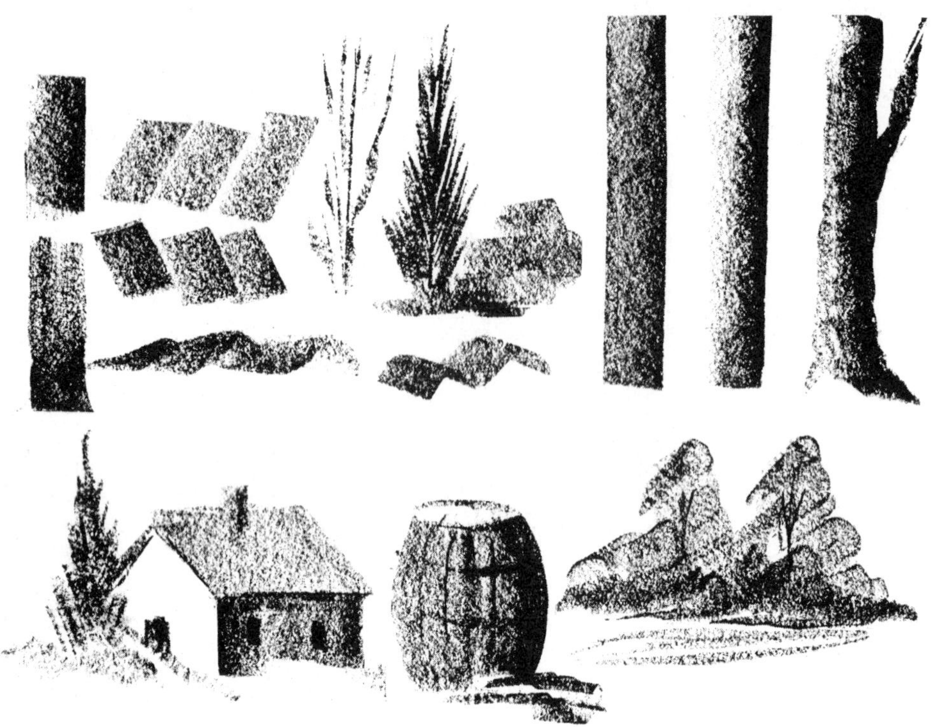

Figure 75. A single piece of Conté crayon held flat but at different angles can produce a variety of effects

working this idea: it is just a hint to help you get the occasional white streak. Remember that Conté is used to better advantage in covering masses, and too much linear emphasis will destroy much of its true quality.

At first I recommend that you keep to black crayon on a white or light-tinted paper, trying various surfaces to see which suits your hand. My own favourites are a slightly textured cartridge and the previously-discussed Ingres pastel paper—but try others. Once you have the feel of things it would be a good idea to take one of your previous sketches—possibly a linear one in pen and ink—and translate it into terms suitable for expression with Conté. You will not be able to copy it exactly because each medium has a different 'language', but it is marvellous practice because it encourages you to think of the behaviour and scope of the material you are using and not just the subject. As when using any medium that is difficult to erase, it is a wise plan to make an extremely faint pencil drawing first. Your completed work should be sprayed with fixative.

The white chalk comes into use when working on tinted and coloured papers. The general principle is the same as when such papers were used for pencil and charcoal. The paper becomes the middle tone. Increasing the pressure on the black crayon will darken the paper, and on the white crayon will make it lighter. *Figure 76* shows the use of black and white Conté on a tinted paper. The scene is in the village of Shaldon in Devon, and the extremely well-defined shapes of the various areas—some of them most conveniently broken up by interesting shadows—make it an ideal subject for this particular medium.

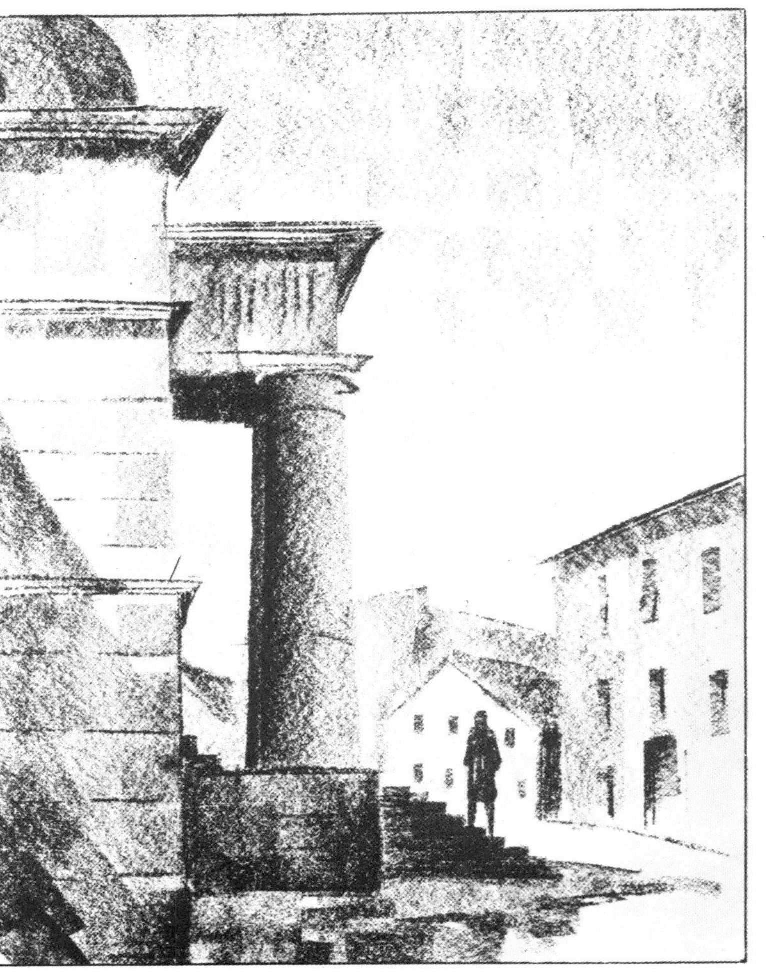

Figure 74. The Church Porch, showing the rectangular nature of the strokes made with Conté crayon

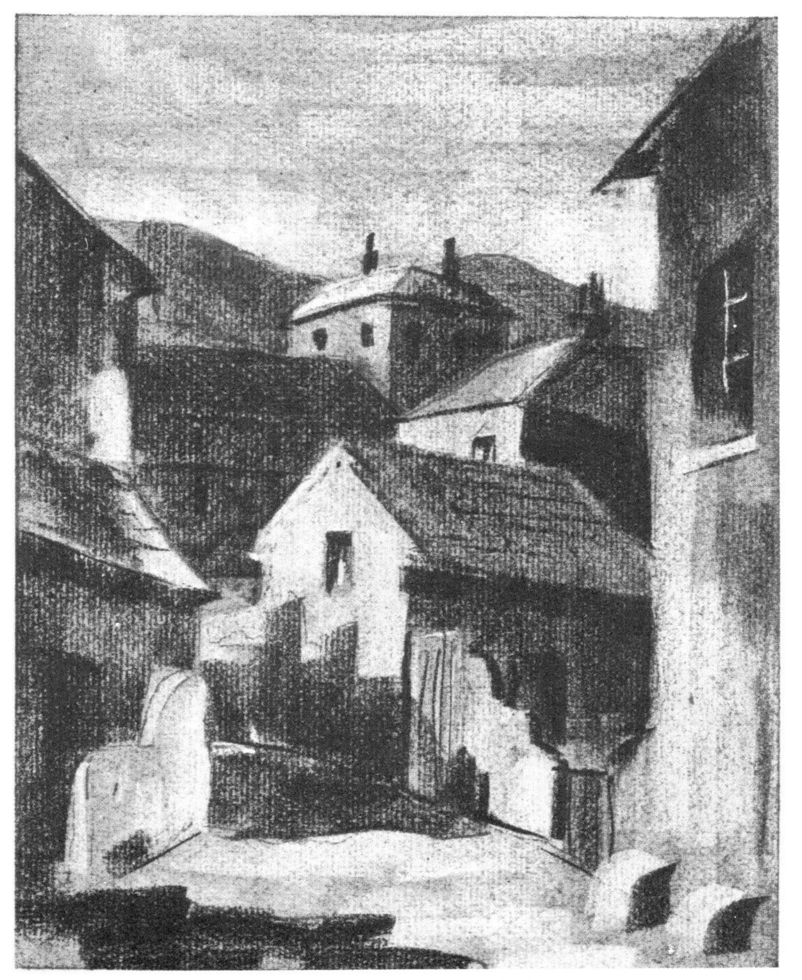

Figure 76. Shaldon, Devonshire. Here black and white Conté has been used on a blue-grey paper

Next let us consider our remaining two crayons—the Bistre and the Sanguine. These are used in exactly the same way as the others, except that careful consideration must be given to how each will look on the chosen paper. The colour of the paper will automatically alter the effect of the coloured crayons. Bistre (brown) will look darker on a cream paper than it would on, say, a navy blue. The simplest and wisest plan is to make a few trial strokes on the paper you are thinking of using, to see whether they are producing the desired effect.

Should you desire something unusual, you can make your own background colour by placing a water-colour wash on to a white or lightly tinted paper. This idea can be taken a stage further. Several suitable washes can be applied first and the Conté crayon can be placed over them in a similar manner to that employed in the charcoal-and-wash technique. Conté crayons are worthy of a place in your sketch-bag. True, they call for a dexterity of touch and an understanding of drawing, but I feel sure you will agree that, when handled with facility and knowledge, they are capable of reaching great heights of artistic expression.

Throughout this part on sketching my aim has been to explain, in a simple way, the delightful results that can be obtained by a sympathetic and understanding use of ordinary materials. Although many recognized media have been dealt with—and in some cases a combination of two within one sketch has been suggested—this certainly does not mean that all possibilities have been explored. Occasionally, a coloured pencil can be used with ordinary pencil work; pen sketches can be made with two or more suitably coloured inks, with or without subsequent washes of colour; with care, there is no reason why a fibre-tipped pen should not join forces with a steel nib; a suggestion of some form of linear work could be included in a Conté sketch—and so on, with many variations. One thing may lead to another. Using Conté may tempt you to try the full range of pastels, or the application of washes may prompt you to take up painting.

By all means experiment; but my earnest plea is that you use a new material, or an unusual combination, only because you feel the result will help you obtain a desired interpretation. Do not use them merely as a stunt or a gimmick. Hopping from one slick trick to another is disillusioning and never leads to true satisfaction. Work at that which pleases you and eventually you will develop an individual style, rich in quality and expression.

Part VI
Mounting, Framing and General Advice

1. *Mounting and Framing*

General Hints on Framing

Just as a good commodity can have a poor reception due to bad presentation and packaging, so can a perfectly good painting be spoilt by an unsuitable and ill-chosen frame. Nearly always, when I am asked to comment on work, the more adverse criticism is not so much of the paintings as of the method of presentation—the frames.

A frame has two functions. One is to blend with the work in a happy, neutral manner, thereby giving the whole thing a nice finishing touch, and the other is to separate the work from its immediate surroundings. Therefore, I implore you, do not just look around the attic for something the right size and casually and haphazardly place it around your painting. Think of all the love and thought that went into your work and surely you must agree it deserves something better than some Victorian monstrosity which at its very best looks like a dark rectangle of highly-varnished cocoa. With a little thought and ingenuity these old frames, if in good repair, can be repainted or renovated in many clever ways, but if you are just not that sort of person, please do not accept them as they are, for what may have suited a large dark print will hardly be fitting to display your own colourful painting.

Unless you are a very skilled woodworker, I would not recommend you to make your own frames. It is a very tricky task to cut eight well-mitred and exact joints and I have seen the most mild-mannered artists reduced to exasperation bordering on fury, when hours of labour have resulted in rather poor results. If, however, you are capable of handling tools with accuracy, there are many other finishes apart from polishing bare wood. Often a little colour is needed, and it is a very good plan to visit some exhibitions and gather ideas on the various finishes that would be suitable for your style of work. By far the best plan is to consult your frame-maker and have two or three made in your favourite size and of a pattern which suits your own personal style of work. Keep your paintings to the size of your frames and you will always be able to ring the changes. You will also be able to hang them as soon as they are finished. This helps you to assess your work and, what is even nicer, it often seems to improve its appearance.

Frames for Oils and Acrylic Paintings

There are always exceptions to every rule, but in the main it will be found that oil paintings and acrylics need a fairly wide and robust frame to enhance and blend with the boldness of the paintings. On the other hand the frame should never be in competition with the work by being over-dominant or discordant. It is interesting to note that a very small painting (about 4 × 6 in.) can happily accept a moulding some $2\frac{1}{2}$ in. wide, but one cannot merely enlarge on this proportionately. That would mean that a picture measuring a mere 8 × 12 in. would be surrounded by a frame about 5 in. wide, which would indeed be far too overpowering. It is difficult to generalize about the correct width of mouldings, but for normal purposes one between 2 and $2\frac{1}{2}$ in. would be suitable for paintings measuring about 16 × 20 in.

In *Figure 77* you can see four frames suitable for oils or acrylics, but there are many variations on each of them. The simplest type, shown as *A*, looks quite pleasant, as the deep recess picks up changes of light, making a nice contrast. It must not be too large, in spite of my previous generalization, and one about $1\frac{1}{2}$ in. wide would be quite suitable for most

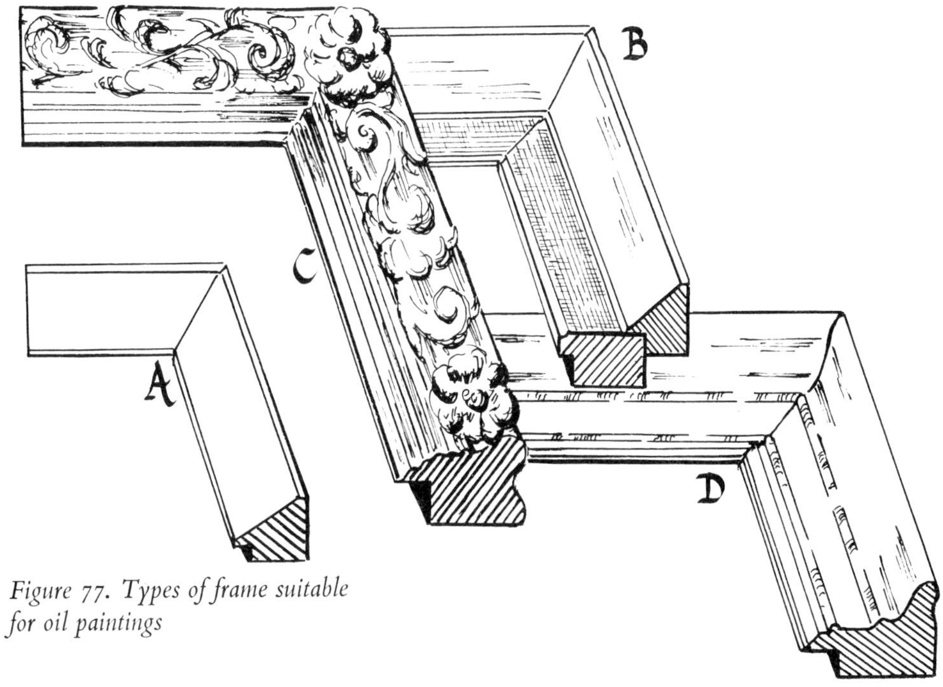

Figure 77. Types of frame suitable for oil paintings

work. Avoid choosing plain wood, for there are a variety of much more interesting finishes. Some have a streaky, ivory-like appearance, with the flat edges in pure white or gold. These are suitable for many styles of painting.

The type shown in *B* is similar but has an addition, known as an inset, of natural canvas with white or white-and-gold edging, which gives the effect of a frame within a frame. Thus from the many insets and numerous mouldings an almost infinite variety of combinations can be made.

A more decorative type of frame is shown in *C*. This is a traditional one, often called a Dutch frame. It has a large embossed decoration at each corner and halfway along each side, with a vine-like decoration between. It is usually quite neutral in colour, often being a warm grey streaked with gold, with a little extra gilt on all raised surfaces: a most suitable frame for the more traditional subjects and often used for flower paintings.

The last of the four sketches, *D*, illustrates a good bold moulding which can almost be said to be all-purpose. It will suit most paintings, for the various planes and ridges can be treated in many ways and there is a wide choice of subtle colourings. Because of this, and because of its strong appearance, such a frame can be used to enclose all kinds and styles of work and still be offensive to none. There are, of course, many variations of mouldings of this kind and I have merely tried to show one that has good general characteristics.

These then are four fairly representative shapes, but there are numerous modifications to all of them, so you should be able to find one which is exactly what is needed to show your work to its greatest advantage. One final point: apart from colour and size, try to have a style which helps the general effect of your work. For example, a picture which has great distance and strong recession would be helped by a moulding similar to *D* which leads the eye *into* the distant areas, almost as if one were looking through a square-shaped funnel. On the other hand, a painting which consists of fairly flat and facing planes would have its general effect improved by a frame which has rather similar characteristics, such as the one shown in *B*.

Mounts and Frames for Water-Colours and Sketches

Even the simplest form of mount is flattering. Take a sketch from your sketch-book: the edges are probably ruffled, the corners dog-eared, there may be trial strokes around the borders and the top edge is probably rough through tearing. But trim the edges directly around the sketch and place it on any plain surface, such as a table top, and its appearance is immediately improved. Greater appreciation is possible when the subject is separated from its surroundings, and that is why sketches and water-colours are so often given a 'mount'. This is merely a piece of thick card with a rectangular aperture cut in it which is slightly smaller than the picture. The card is usually white or pale cream, but may be tinted. It is very much like a large viewfinder, except that the bottom margin is slightly wider than the other three.

Making your own mounts is not too difficult, but if you are unhappy when making accurate measurements and unsure when using a sharp knife, it is a task which can safely be delegated to your frame-maker, who will probably offer many helpful suggestions. It is a wise plan to produce water-colours and sketches in one or two set sizes, and keep a few suitable mounts in reserve. Then you will always have one ready to place around your work and so boost your morale.

If you do decide to make your own mounts, the equipment is quite simple—a pencil, a ruler, a strong knife, and a steel straight-edge. Card for mount-making can be obtained in various thicknesses from good stationers or artists' suppliers and is known as 'mounting board'. The knife must be extremely sharp. I find the type which has interchangeable spare blades, and is used for marquetry and model making, is ideal. You will also need some cardboard or a sheet of thick glass to act as a working surface.

The rectangle which is to be removed should be marked very carefully with a pencil, and it is a good idea to allow these lines to cross at the corners. This avoids confusion when the straight-edge covers part of the area on which you are working. For a nice professional look, use the knife at an angle of about 45 degrees; then the edges of the aperture will have a pleasant chamfer which slopes inwards towards the sketch. It is a mistake to have too narrow margins.

As a guide to relative size, many of the sketches and studies in this book were 8 in. × $5\frac{1}{2}$ in. and for them I used mounts measuring 14 in. × $11\frac{1}{2}$ in. For a water-colour measuring 15 in. × 11 in. a good size would be 21 in. × 18 in., thus giving a 3 in. margin at the top and sides and one of 4 in. at the bottom.

An added refinement is to place lines and bands of colour around the margins. These must first be marked in pencil, very lightly but with great accuracy. As coloured inks are rather dominant in hue, I prefer using small puddles of water-colour paint watered down to a consistency suitable for use with a pen. Subtle and unobtrusive colours can be obtained by this method. The type of nib used for manuscript lettering works extremely well for making lines, and there are various thicknesses to choose from. It is possible to attach a metal 'reservoir' which prevents blotting and uneven distribution of colour. Bands of colour are painted first and a line ruled on either side to camouflage any slight imperfections. When painting these bands it is best to start at one corner and work outwards from it in

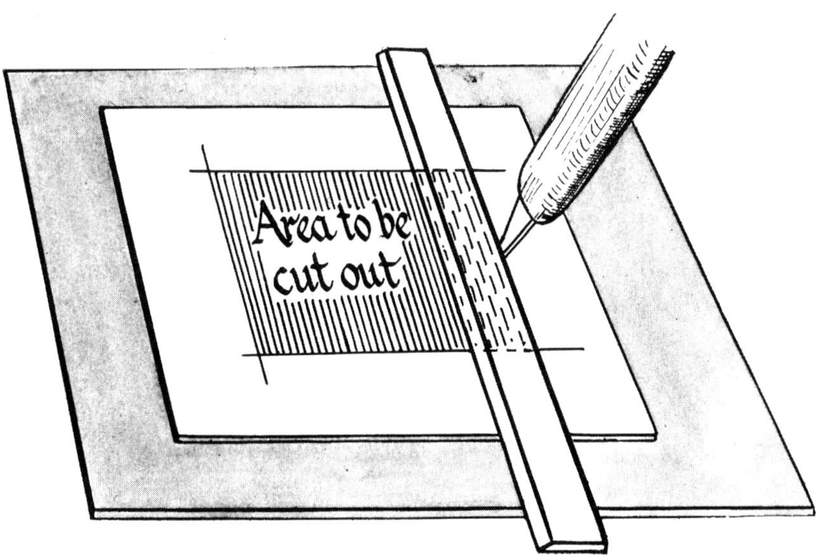

Figure 78. Method of marking out and cutting a mount

both directions, alternating your attention between one side and the other, so that you finish by joining two wet patches. If you proceed in one direction only, you will finish with an unpleasant join where wet paint meets dry.

Having made your mount the next thing is to fit the sketch behind it. This is best done by placing a small piece of gummed paper at each corner of the sketch and allowing enough to protrude for sticking to the back of the mount. Do not place long strips of gummed paper around all the edges, as this encourages buckling due to the varying shrinkage rates of card and paper.

I hope that among your mounted studies there will be several worthy of framing. Because the mount has already done much towards the final presentation, the frames for water-colours and sketches are fairly slender and much more delicate than those used for displaying work done in oils. Once again confer with your frame-maker and purchase two or three of a favourite style and size. Keep your mounted sketches to the size of these frames and you will always have something available in which to hang your work immediately it is finished. This helps you to assess its quality.

Although there are some good general guide-lines for framing, it is difficult to lay down explicit rules. So much depends on the style and qualities of each individual piece of work. Choosing a suitable frame can be very difficult and is a further reason for making use of the services of a competent expert who will do all he can to enhance, and even improve your work. With his help, and the advice given here, it is hoped that your paintings and sketches will always be framed in a manner which does full justice to all the thought and effort expended in their creation.

2. *Random Thoughts*

No book on painting and sketching, however comprehensive, could ever cover every aspect, and this one is no exception. Its purpose has been to help you make a start by suggesting a general direction, and thereby to enable you to steer a course clear of the many hazards which confront the beginner. There were occasions when I was tempted to include all kinds of extra information and detail, but such a plan was rejected for fear I should lose the essential direction. In this last chapter I have written down some of the many things that have been in my mind while writing the book. I offer them now, rather in the nature of a postscript.

One very important point is to keep the work *clean*. In a pure water-colour painting no white paint is used, and lightness and brilliance are obtained by the application of semi-transparent 'washes', or films of colour, which allow the whiteness of the paper to show through the paint. Even in very dark passages this idea of transparency must be kept in mind. The painting should never look opaque or inky and should always give the feeling that the paper beneath is doing a lot of the work by trying to peep through. Such purity can never be obtained if brushes, palette or water are dirty. Use plenty of water and change it often. This is equally true of all other media, for whatever you are using, be it oils, acrylics or water-colour, if your mixtures are muddy and colourless, and if your palette and brushes are messy, you will never produce a good piece of work. Oil painters are well-advised to keep a few clean brushes in reserve, so that the last stages of the work are kept fresh and clean.

A good general plan for the water-colourist is to work from light to dark. By keeping the water clean for the delicate areas and by restraining your enthusiasm, this method will help to retain the essential freshness of the work. Only change this plan if, by so doing, you will capture some particular effect that you wish to register as an essential yardstick of comparison for the rest of the painting.

When out of doors make a habit of continually giving a backward glance, for the best subjects are often behind you. The habit of turning around will often reward you with the presentation of an entirely new viewpoint and may save a lot of fruitless searching.

Cheap materials cannot produce good work. It is always a source of surprise to me when I hear of someone who, on taking up a hobby such as photography, will set off cheerfully and spend a considerable amount on quite expensive materials, but when taking up painting will often use very poor quality stuff. A good artist is a craftsman too, and cannot work well with poor tools. For this reason he buys the best he can afford—and looks after them. Do as he does and keep your materials in good order. Wash and re-shape brushes after use and keep them attached to a strip of stout card with an elastic band to prevent the points from becoming bruised.

Beware of too many gadgets, particularly those which are complicated and have all manner of bits and pieces that are detachable and liable to get lost. Organize your kit as the professional does, so that there is a smooth rhythm in all you do, with the minimum of paraphernalia that can go wrong and cause frustration. For painting, your outlook must be relaxed and untroubled: the screw that will not turn, or the device that will not unfold, can play havoc with your inspiration.

Water-colourists should use good quality papers and experiment with various surfaces.

Heavyweight papers (about 250 g.s.m.) will not require stretching, but below this weight they will wrinkle if unstretched. A good all-purpose paper is a 190 g.s.m. NOT surface.

Extra colours should only be purchased after careful consideration. It may be that you have difficulty in mixing certain colours and wish to try a different approach—Monastral Blue and Raw Sienna give a beautifully rich green, for example—but never rush off and get lots of additional colours just because a certain person always uses them. Make changes gradually and, after experimenting, either accept them as a replacement or, most important, reject them if they do not suit you. Never over-load the paint-box with too many colours, but gradually sort out what is suitable for your particular temperament.

Carry a small sketch-book with you and sketch like mad at every opportunity. Do not try and make finished pictures, but use it as a personal record of things seen and observed. This will not only be extremely good practice but will serve you well as both a physical and mental record, and will slowly build itself into a vast library of information from which you can draw facts and impressions at will.

If you see something which impresses you, but are without materials, quietly absorb it and ask yourself how you would set about painting it. I call this 'painting with your eyes'. It is truly surprising how these scenes and the problems they present can be remembered, and the knowledge used when you are painting something similar.

Never purchase a stool that has little projections on the corners of the seat. The full significance of such a warning can only be fully appreciated by those who have sat on one—and then tried to stand.

Whenever possible go to the best exhibitions and study the works of those artists whose style impresses you. Look for the painting which has successfully mastered problems which you yourself found difficult, and try to understand how such difficulties were overcome. Keep your sights high, but not too high, remembering that the artist whose work you so admire also began at the beginning.

Do not seek cheap praise. It may make you feel good for a time, but ultimately it does nothing to make you stretch your talents and improve your style. On the other hand, do not allow ill-informed criticism to disturb you or cause needless uncertainty. If possible, join an Art Society, where there will be serious talks and criticisms by visiting experts, and where advice will be offered with friendship and sincerity.

When painting out of doors try to find a spot which offers a good view but does not allow the onlooker to come breathing down the back of your neck. With onlookers my advice is: never get into conversation unless you are a very steadfast person. Simply carry on quietly, stopping occasionally for very long searching looks at your subject, and they will soon wander away. Failure to do this may lead to inexpert and infuriating comments, a short history of their early talents, and a dramatized version of how great-uncle really should have been an artist but the family . . . All of which may be interesting, but is guaranteed to spoil your painting.

The best subjects in summer are always to be found where there are thousands of flies, bluebottles and other insects. At least, such has been my experience. Keep a little bottle of insect repellent in your sketch-bag, and you can carry on painting in comfort whilst your friends are only to be seen through a cloud of buzzing and tickling marauders. A further very good tip is to insert a fringe of grass-heads inside your hat so that they point downwards over your forehead and the nape of your neck—it works!

Quietly contemplate those so important shadows. Observe how the material on which the shadow is cast always affects the final colour. You will notice that although shadows are usually cool, most of them contain a *little* warmth. It will also be observed that the warmer the light, the cooler the shadow. Remember, too, to make shadows look transparent by touches of 'broken' colour, for within them there are usually further shadows. A shaded cobbled street is a good example, for although the surface is dark there are even denser darks which will tell us that the street is bumpy.

Meditate on reflections. These will be affected by the colour of the water, its depth, its movement and what is beneath it, but in general you will find that they do not usually have as great a range of tones as the objects being reflected. The image is never *quite* the same colour or tone as the original.

Practise painting with strokes which have a definite and deft technique. An example is a flick-stroke which will give a wonderful sense of movement to represent, say, tall swaying grasses. Any other method would make them look like card cut-outs, rigid and stark, instead of being soft and willowy. It needs courage, but this 'carefully careless' technique should be mastered, for in some cases it is the only way of getting the effect you want.

If your water-colours harden, they can be softened by one or two drops of glycerine. Should this not be available, place a damp folded rag across the paints overnight.

Always pack an extra cardigan or sweater. Sitting still can often be chilly, even on what appears to be quite a mild day, and nobody can work well if he is not relaxed and comfortable. A raincoat is essential too. The type that can be folded up very small is extremely useful. It is compact, will protect you from the odd shower, will act as a windcheater and, what is perhaps most important, can be used to protect the painting from rain spots.

It has often been said that a successful painting is one that you can live with. It is a good plan to prop up your mounted picture in some prominent place in the home. Look at it often. First thoughts are not always best; neither are the second. If after a fortnight a painting still pleases you, it is fairly safe to say your effort is successful.

View your work in a mirror! Often the sudden reversing of the composition will show up faults that had previously not been at all obvious.

Never despair at failures, for they are really stepping-stones. Artists have one thing in common with men who bet—they do not advertise their losses. All artists have their failures too, but without them success would never have been possible.

Remember that the road through the world of landscape-painting never ends, but the route is beautiful and refreshing. Keep your medium clean, your colours fresh, your eyes wide open—and enjoy yourselves.

Throughout this book I have dealt solely with the problems of landscape painting, but I, wish to point out that everything that has been said about tone, colour, form, composition drawing and the effects of air and space is equally true whatever the subject may be. Be it portraiture, interiors, still-life or flower studies, the same basic principles hold good.

With the preceding random thoughts I now end my attempt to start you painting and sketching. I hope it has whetted your appetite and made you keen to continue with a delightful, but by no means easy pastime. At whatever stage we may be as artists, the sincere help and advice of friends and fellow-painters is of inestimable value. If this book has helped you, it will, in an indirect way, be a repayment to many people who have been generous to me with their help and encouragement. What we have achieved together in this book is only a beginning, but if you have decided to make painting your hobby you are, automatically, a member of a powerful guild of friendship whose unwritten law is that each gives freely of his talents to those interested. Thus, as you paint so do you learn, and the world is rich with ever-increasing pleasure.

Index

References in italics refer to illustrations